Dermot F. Reynolds

# Open for Business

## The Complete Textbook for Junior Certificate

### Gill & Macmillan

Published in Ireland by
Gill & Macmillan
with associated companies throughout the world
www.gillmacmillan.ie

© Dermot F. Reynolds 2010

978 0 7171 47182

Design and typesetting by webucation.ie

# Contents

# Part 3: Enterprise

# Part 4: Information Technology

# Preface

*Open for Business* has been written and designed to provide both student and teacher with all the information necessary for the Junior Certificate Business Studies examination.

The learning objectives are displayed at the beginning of each chapter. The use of pictures provides strong visual metaphors and should give a good route to the text. Key terms are highlighted in bold text. The main part of each chapter is shown as a two-page spread and side bars give additional information. The explanations are concise and easy to read.

The activities at the end of each chapter begin with straightforward chapter review questions to enrich the learning process and bring the student up to the required standard. Examination-style questions are included where relevant.

Great effort has been made to assist the teaching of bookkeeping. The use of double-page spreads allows for the clear display of question and solution without the need to turn to another page. The examples are ruled up in a way similar to record books one, two and three.

The accompanying workbook has additional material to supplement the textbook. The workbook also contains the templates for the payslips, budgets and other documents referred to in the textbook questions.

Worked Solutions to this book are available on *www.gillmacmillan.ie*. The solutions are to questions of a numerical nature, e.g. wages, budgets, accounts, etc.

Enjoy.

Dermot F. Reynolds
October 2009

## eTest.ie – what is it?

A revolutionary new website-based testing platform that facilitates a social learning environment for Irish schools. Both students and teachers can use it, either independently or together, to make the whole area of testing easier, more engaging and more productive for all.

## Students – do you want to know how well you are doing? Then take an eTest!

At eTest.ie, you can access tests put together by the author of this textbook. You get instant results, so they're a brilliant way to quickly check just how your study or revision is going.

Since each eTest is based on your textbook, if you don't know an answer, you'll find it in your book.

Register now and you can save all of your eTest results to use as a handy revision aid or to simply compare with your friends' results!

## Teachers – eTest.ie will engage your students and help them with their revision, while making the jobs of reviewing their progress and homework easier and more convenient for all of you.

Register now to avail of these exciting features:

- Create tests easily using our pre-set questions OR you can create your own questions

- Develop your own online learning centre for each class that you teach

- Keep track of your students' performances

eTest.ie has a wide choice of question types for you to choose from, most of which can be graded automatically, like multiple-choice, jumbled-sentence, matching, ordering and gap-fill exercises. This free resource allows you to create class groups, delivering all the functionality of a VLE (Virtual Learning Environment) with the ease of communication that is brought by social networking.

To Eithne, Sarah, David, Orla and Thérèse,
all patient saints

## Acknowledgments

The author acknowledges with thanks the comments and suggestions from the teachers who reviewed this book. Sincere thanks also to the editors and staff at Gill & Macmillan for their support and encouragement: Anthony Murray, Hubert Mahony, Emma Farrell, Aoileann O'Donnell, Tony Hetherington and Jane Rogers.

## Photos

Thanks to the following for saying yes to the photos:
- Karen Moore, Aer Lingus • Caoimhe NiBhradaigh, HMV Swords • Staff at Kylemore Café • Movies@: Colm Roche; Kevin Corrigan; Lynsey Butler; Ramindas; Robert Brown • Eddie Carton, Excellence, Baldoyle Ind Est • Frank Carr, Abbey Woods • Tom McFadden, McMullan Transport • George Cook, Sole Trader • Declan Landon, ESB • Kevin Beatty, A.K. Corporate Cars • Musgrave Market Place: Andy Murray; George Stringer • John Derham, Connolly Station vending machine • Daithi O'Doubhlabhan, Supplier • Jenny McNally, Farmers' Market, Temple Bar • Diarmuid Brerton, Jeweller • Chris, Delivery Driver • Wedding of Nigel Upcott and Catherine McKay, TCD • Rob Nulty, Dublin Fire Brigade, Tara Street • Sina Swschulz, Tourist • Nadin Kwasny, Tourist • Lubos, Delivery Man • Tom King, Painter, Adare, County Limerick • O'Sheas, Killarney • Avoca Handweavers, Caha Mountain Pass • Joseph Ryan, Student • Craig Egan-Kearns, Student

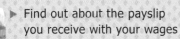
▶ Find out about the payslip
you receive with your wages

▶ Learn how to record cash
coming in and going out
of a household

# Chapter 1

## Understanding *income*

# Different people, different income

Most people have some regular income. You might already get **pocket money** from your parents. This is your income and you can choose to spend it or save it. When you get older you will have a job and then you will receive either **wages** or a **salary**. Traditionally, wages are paid every week and salaries are paid every month.

Some workers are paid in relation to the amount of sales they make and this is called **sales commission**. If you are a good salesperson you can earn a lot of money in this way.

Other people are out of work and they are paid **jobseeker's benefit**. This helps them to survive while they are seeking another job.

People over 65 years of age can retire and get a **pension**. A pension is not usually as much as wages.

Regular income should be enough to keep the family going from week to week but it is always nice if you can get a little extra.

## ADDITIONAL INCOME

Additional income is extra income that a person receives occasionally. Pocket money is regular income but the money you get from your aunts or uncles at Christmas is additional income. You might also get **interest on your savings**. For workers it is similar. Wages are regular income and any **overtime** worked is additional income. Some workers even get a **Christmas bonus** or **summer bonus**.

Every employee is given a payslip showing how much they have earned and the total deductions. The deductions reduce the amount of money taken home by the employee. There are two types of deduction: statutory and non-statutory. Statutory deductions are required by law.

# UNDERSTANDING YOUR PAYSLIP

| Statutory Deductions | | Non-statutory Deductions | | |
|---|---|---|---|---|
| PAYE | PRSI | Union | Health insurance | Pension |

**Statutory Deductions**
Your employer is legally required to take tax (PAYE) and insurance (PRSI) from your wages. These are statutory deductions. Your employer is breaking the law if these deductions are not made from your wages.

**Non-statutory Deductions**
Most employees have other deductions taken from their wages. These are voluntary deductions which the employees have agreed to have taken from their wages, e.g. union dues, health insurance, pension contributions (superannuation).

| **Wages Slip:** EMMA CLEARY | | | | **Week:** 12 |
|---|---|---|---|---|
| **PAY** | **€** | **DEDUCTIONS** | **€** | **NET PAY** |
| Basic | 576.00 | PAYE | 132.00 | |
| Overtime | 72.00 | PRSI | 35.00 | **€466.00** |
| | | Health Insurance | 15.00 | |
| **GROSS PAY** | 648.00 | **TOTAL DEDUCTIONS** | 182.00 | |

**Gross pay**
Your gross income is the total income you have earned before any deductions have been made. It is usually made up of basic pay plus overtime, but it can also include a bonus or commission earned.

**Deductions**
These are the statutory and non-statutory items that are taken away from your gross pay.

**Net pay**
The difference between your gross pay and your total deductions is your net pay. This is your take-home pay.

> **Gross pay** = Basic Pay + Overtime + Commission + Bonus
> **Total Deductions** = Statutory + Non-statutory Deductions
> **Net pay** = Gross pay − Total Deductions

*more about*

# STATUTORY DEDUCTIONS

It is very important that you understand the statutory deductions from wages. As a worker you have no control over these – your employer must deduct them before handing over your wages.

### PAYE – Pay As You Earn

The main deduction from a person's income is tax. This is called the Pay As You Earn (PAYE) system. Under this arrangement, tax deductions are made by your employer before you get any money. Your employer passes this money on to the Revenue Commissioners – a government department. The money is used by the government to run the country, e.g. to build hospitals and schools and to pay the wages of doctors and teachers.

### PRSI – Pay Related Social Insurance

Every employed person aged 16 and over must contribute to Pay Related Social Insurance (PRSI). The amount you earn determines the amount of PRSI you pay. PRSI is **compulsory insurance for employees** and people who pay PRSI for 39 weeks in a year can claim the benefits operated by the Department of Social, Community and Family Affairs, e.g. unemployment benefit, maternity benefit, old-age pension.

## FRINGE BENEFITS

These are additional benefits given by the employer, and are often called **benefits-in-kind** or **perks**. They are given in addition to regular wages as an incentive to an employee to stay with the company. Fringe benefits make the job more attractive.

**Official fringe benefits**
These vary from company to company and depend on the type of work you do. They can include:
● travelling expenses
● luncheon vouchers
● company car
● medical insurance
● social facilities.

**Unofficial fringe benefits**
These are practices that the employer is either unaware of or is prepared to ignore:
● paper and pens taken by staff for personal, unofficial use
● phones used for private calls.

# Cash Account

The cash account can be used to record the income and expenditure of a household. Any money coming into the household is listed on the left (debit) of the account, e.g. wages. Any money going out of the household is listed on the right (credit), e.g. spending on food, car expenses and electricity.

You can use **Record Book 3** to help you lay out your cash account. Alternatively, draw a large 'T' on a page of your copybook. This divides the page into three. Above the line write the account name: Cash Account. Then list income on the left and expenditure on the right.

## Question

Mr and Mrs Campbell keep the following record of their money:

| Sep | | € | |
|---|---|---|---|
| 1 | Cash in house | 90 | Income |
| 2 | Mr O'Neill received his wages | 640 | Income |
| 2 | Paid supermarket | 120 | Expenditure |
| 3 | Mrs O'Neill received her wages | 720 | Income |
| 3 | Paid butcher | 18 | Expenditure |
| 4 | Paid for petrol | 55 | Expenditure |
| 5 | Paid mortgage | 700 | Expenditure |
| 6 | Paid supermarket | 23 | Expenditure |
| 7 | Mrs O'Neill bought new coat | 99 | Expenditure |

## Solution

| Dr | | | Cash Account | | | | Cr |
|---|---|---|---|---|---|---|---|
| Date | Details | F | Total | Date | Details | F | Total |
| Sep | | | € | Sep | | | € |
| 1 | Balance | b/d | 90 | 2 | Supermarket | | 120 |
| 2 | Wages | | 640 | 3 | Butcher | | 18 |
| 3 | Wages | | 720 | 4 | Petrol | | 55 |
| | | | | 5 | Mortgage | | 700 |
| | | | | 6 | Supermarket | | 23 |
| | | | | 7 | Coat | | 99 |
| | | | | 7 | Balance | c/d | 435 |
| | | | 1,450 | | | | 1,450 |
| 8 | Balance | b/d | 435 | | | | |

To balance the account, add up the cash that came in (the items on the debit side). This comes to €1,450. Now subtract the money spent, €1,015 (the items on the credit). The difference, €435, is the balance. This balance becomes the opening balance the following week and is available for spending then.

**Balance** = Total income – Total expenditure

## Activity 1.1 Chapter Review

**1** List five types of regular income.

**2** Explain, giving examples, what is meant by additional income.

**3** Explain the difference between gross and net income.

**4** Name two statutory and two non-statutory deductions from a person's income.

**5** How does a person benefit from paying PRSI?

**6** What does the government do with the PAYE money it collects?

**7** What is another name for take-home pay?

**8** What is another name for fringe benefits?

**9** Name the fringe benefits for:
- an Aer Lingus employee
- an Eason's employee
- a bank official.

**10** Write a brief note about unofficial perks.

## Activity 1.2 Payslips

Complete payslips for each of the following *(templates are provided in the workbook)*:

**1** Shane Tracy, basic pay €160, overtime €20, PAYE €8, PRSI €3, union dues €3.

**2** Linda Tierney, basic pay €330, overtime €50, PAYE €47, PRSI €16, Quinn Healthcare €20.

**3** Kevin O'Neill, basic pay €570, overtime €60, PAYE €97, PRSI €30, pension €50.

**4** Sinead Ryan, basic pay €700, overtime €100, PAYE €131, PRSI €35, union dues €5.

**5** Brendan Doyle, basic pay €200, overtime €80, PAYE €27, PRSI €15, VHI €20.

## Activity 1.3 Cash accounts

Complete cash accounts for each of the following. *(To be completed in Record Book 3.)*

**1** Michael keeps the following record of his money for the first week of July:

Jul 1 Cash on hand, €0.50
2 Bought chocolate, €0.60
3 Received pocket money, €15.00
4 Went to the cinema, €7.00
5 Bought magazine, €5.00
6 Bus fares, €2.80

**2** Brigid keeps the following record of her money for the first week of August:

Aug 1 Cash on hand, €4.30
2 Bought magazine, €4.70
3 Received pocket money, €10.00
4 Went to the cinema, €5.50
5 Bought chocolate, €0.60
5 Bus fares, €2.40
6 Received gift from aunt, €50.00
7 Bought make-up, €25.00
7 Bought music CD single, €4.99

**3** Mrs Higgins keeps the following record of her money for the first week of September:

Sep 1 Cash on hand, €90
2 Received her wages, €780
3 Bought a new coat, €110
4 Paid for supermarket shopping, €80
5 Paid butcher, €25
5 Bought petrol, €54
6 Paid supermarket, €110
7 Paid butcher, €22
7 Bought television licence, €150

**4** Mr and Mrs Troy keep the following record of their money for the first week of October:

Oct 1 Cash on hand, €60
2 Mr Troy received his wages, €890
3 Paid supermarket, €120
4 Paid for petrol, €50
5 Paid for cinema tickets, €18
5 Paid supermarket, €70
6 Paid butcher, €21
7 Paid phone bill, €110

**5** Mr and Mrs Nugent keep the following record of their money for the first week of November:

Nov 1 Cash on hand, €80
2 Mr Nugent received his jobseeker's benefit, €220
3 Paid supermarket, €120
4 Paid butcher, €19
5 Mrs Nugent received her wages, €610
5 Paid gas bill, €160
6 Paid chemist, €80
7 Mr Nugent bought new suit, €230

eTest.ie
Try a test on this topic

# Chapter 2

*Personal expenditure*

# Getting the most from your money

As a young adult your family still pays for most of your clothes. They feed you and give you somewhere to sleep. These are a person's **basic needs** and much of your family's expenditure goes into providing these for you and the other members of the family.

If there is any money left over, your family might be able to give you some pocket money. You do not need to spend this on food, clothing or shelter – these are already provided. Instead you can afford to buy sweets, magazines, DVDs or some of the other **luxuries** of life.

Most family expenses are obvious: the trip to the supermarket has to be paid by cash, cheque or credit card. Other expenses build up less noticeably, e.g. gas bill or electricity bill. Electricity is one of those expenses that you use first and pay for it later. It is known as an **accrual** as the expense accrues before it is paid.

## OPPORTUNITY COST

Most people do not have enough money to do everything they want and they have to make choices about how they will spend their money. For example, Brendan has enough money to go to the cinema or buy a book, but he does not have enough money to do both. If he decides to go to the cinema he must do without the book. This is known as the **opportunity cost**. The opportunity cost of going to the cinema is the book and the opportunity cost of the book is going to the cinema.

**Impulse buying** is the purchase of unplanned items: for example, Emma goes to the shop at the cinema to buy a drink and buys popcorn as well. The popcorn is an impulse purchase. She was in the shop, saw the popcorn and decided to buy it. There was no plan. Shop and supermarket displays are designed to make you buy on impulse with special offers and bargains positioned near the cash register to catch your attention. You can avoid impulse buying by using a shopping list.

# Types of Spending

**1  Fixed Expenditure**

Fixed expenditure is where the timing or the amount is the same each month. The mortgage repayment is normally the same amount each month and is an example of fixed expenditure. Other examples are the repayment of the car loan, weekly milk bill, annual car insurance. It is possible to plan for these items, since it is known when they will occur and how much they will cost.

**2  Irregular Expenditure**

In this case either the timing or the amount changes each month. The electricity bill does not follow a pattern and is said to be irregular. Families tend to use more electricity in winter than in summer. Other examples like this are: phone and Internet costs; car and house expenses; emergency spending such as doctor's fees. With each of these either the amount or the timing of the bill varies, and this makes planning for these bills more difficult.

**3  Discretionary Expenditure**

This is the money you spend on luxuries like going to the cinema, taking a holiday or buying a handbag or make-up. People spend most of their money on necessities, and any money spent after this is discretionary expenditure.

**4  Capital Expenditure**

This is expenditure on goods which will last a long time before they wear out. Spending on consumer durables, such as televisions, CD players and washing machines is called capital expenditure.

**5  Current Expenditure**

Spending on day-to-day items like bread and milk is called current expenditure. For example, Jack buying a car is an example of capital expenditure but buying petrol for the car is current expenditure.

# ELECTRICITY BILL

| | |
|---|---|
| | Your account number     90 123 456 |
| Mr & Mrs Fay<br>Navan | Date of issue     23 May 2010 |

## Your electricity bill

| Meter Readings<br>Present  Previous | Units and<br>Rates (cent) | Description of Charges | Amount €<br>(Cr= Credit) |
|---|---|---|---|
| 14762  13653 | 1109 x 15 | GENERAL DOMESTIC | 166.35 |
| | | STANDING CHARGE | 20.50 |
| | | VAT @ 13.5% ON 186.85 | 25.22 |

| Billing period | Payment due by | Total due € |
|---|---|---|
| FEB - MAR 2010 | 4 JUNE 2010 | €212.07 |

**1**    The new meter reading was 14762

**2**    The old meter reading was 13653

**3**    The difference between the old and the new is 1109 units (14762 − 13653). This is the number of units used in February and March

**4**    The price of one unit of electricity is 15 cent. So the general domestice charge is €166.35 (1109 x 15 cent)

**5**    The fixed expense for the electricity is €20.50. So the total so far is €186.85 (166.35 + 20.50)

**6**    The VAT is €25.22 (186.85 x 13.5%)

**7**    The total amount due is €212.07
(166.35 + 20.50 + 25.22)

---

# PAYING REGULAR BILLS:
## Direct debit vs. Standing order

In most cases, Aoife pays her expenses using cash, cheques or credit card. Some expenses, like her car loan repayments and electricity bills, occur regularly and there is the chance she could forget to pay them. Banks offer two services that can help her:

**Standing order (SO)**
This is where she gives permission to her bank to pay a fixed amount on a fixed date each month. It is an ideal way to pay the car loan repayment.

**Direct debit (DD)**
This is where she gives permission to her bank to pay a bill when it is presented for payment. It is the ideal way to pay bills where the amount is not known in advance, such as the electricity bill.

# Analysed Cash Account

The analysed cash account is used to group expenses together. In the example below the expenses are grouped using the following headings: Household; Light and heat; Car. This gives a household a clearer picture of where the money is being spent.

You can also see that the Campbells took cash from an ATM to pay for some of their shopping and they paid the other expenses by cheque.

## Question

Mr and Mrs Campbell keep the following record of their money. Complete an analysed cash account for their income and expenditure.

| Oct | | € | |
|---|---|---|---|
| 11 | Cash in bank | 60 | |
| 14 | Took cash from ATM to pay the supermarket | 110 | Household |
| 16 | Paid electricity bill by cheque, no. 81 | 130 | Light and heat |
| 17 | Mr Campbell lodged his wages in the bank | 1,200 | |
| 18 | Mrs Campbell lodged her wages in the bank | 1,300 | |
| 20 | Paid for petrol by cheque, no. 82 | 50 | Car |
| 22 | Took cash from ATM to buy birthday cake | 80 | Household |
| 25 | Paid instalment of car loan by standing order | 420 | Car |
| 27 | Paid for meat in butchers by cheque, no. 83 | 25 | Household |
| 28 | Paid for heating oil by cheque, no. 84 | 490 | Light and heat |

## Solution

| Dr | | | | | **Analysed Cash Account** | | | | | Cr |
|---|---|---|---|---|---|---|---|---|---|---|
| Date | Details | F | Total | Date | Details | F | Total | Household | Light and heat | Car |
| Oct | | | € | Oct | | | € | € | € | € |
| 11 | Balance | b/d | 60 | 14 | Supermarket | ATM | 110 | 110 | | |
| 17 | Wages | | 1,200 | 16 | Electricity | 81 | 130 | | 130 | |
| 18 | Wages | | 1,300 | 20 | Petrol | 82 | 50 | | | 50 |
| | | | | 22 | Birthday cake | ATM | 80 | 80 | | |
| | | | | 25 | Car loan | SO | 420 | | | 420 |
| | | | | 27 | Butchers | 83 | 25 | 25 | | |
| | | | | 28 | Heating oil | 84 | 490 | | 490 | |
| | | | | 31 | Balance | c/d | 1,255 | | | |
| | | | 2,560 | | | | 2,560 | 215 | 620 | 470 |
| Nov | | | | | | | | | | |
| 1 | Balance | | 1,255 | | | | | | | |

## Activity 2.1 Chapter Review

**1** Give three examples of your basic needs that your parents provide for you and three examples of luxuries you like to treat yourself to each week.

**2** Sharon spent €1,500 on a new computer instead of taking her family on a holiday which would have cost the same amount. What is the opportunity cost of the computer?

**3** Explain what is meant by the terms:
(a) impulse buying
(b) opportunity cost.

**4** List three examples of:
(a) fixed expenditure
(b) irregular expenditure
(c) discretionary expenditure.

**5** John is very forgetful. How does the bank help John pay each of the following?
(a) Monthly mortgage.
(b) Electricity bill.
(c) Car loan repayment.

**6** Give reasons for paying by:
(a) standing order
(b) direct debit
(c) cash.

**7** In the analysed cash account what is shown:
(a) on the debit side; (b) on the credit side?

**8** What is the difference between:
(a) a standing order and a direct debit?
(b) capital expenditure and current expenditure?

**9** In this chapter, what did the following people buy?
(a) Brendan.
(b) Emma.
(c) Jack.

**10** In this chapter:
(a) how does Aoife pay most of her expenses?
(b) how could the bank help her pay her car loan and her electricity bill?

## Activity 2.2 Analysed cash accounts

Complete analysed cash accounts for each of the following using **Record Book 1**. In each case the expenses are grouped using the following headings:

**Income: Total**

**Expenditure: Total, Household, Light and heat, Car, Other.**

**1** Mr and Mrs Farrelly keep the following record of their money:

| Mar | | € |
|---|---|---|
| 1 | Cash in bank | 90 |
| 2 | Mr Farrelly lodged his wages | 860 |
| 2 | Paid for petrol by cheque, no. 72 | 57 |
| 3 | Paid for medicine by cheque, no. 73 (Other) | 42 |
| 3 | Mrs Farrelly lodged her wages in the bank | 740 |
| 4 | Paid for groceries by cheque, no. 74 | 126 |
| 4 | Paid for birthday cake by cheque, no. 75 | 43 |
| 5 | Paid for heating oil by cheque, no. 76 | 214 |
| 6 | Paid monthly mortgage by standing order (Other) | 521 |
| 7 | Withdrew cash from ATM for entertainment (Other) | 50 |

**2** Mr and Mrs Wallace keep the following record of their money:

| Apr | | € |
|---|---|---|
| 1 | Cash in bank | 94 |
| 2 | Paid for petrol by cheque, no. 801 | 51 |
| 3 | Paid electricity bill by cheque, no. 802 | 116 |
| 3 | Mr Wallace lodged his wages in the bank | 1,200 |
| 4 | Took cash from ATM to pay for entertainment | 100 |
| 4 | Paid for car service by cheque, no. 803 | 98 |
| 5 | Paid monthly mortgage by standing order | 720 |
| 5 | Mrs Wallace lodged her wages in the bank | 1,670 |
| 6 | Paid for meat in butchers by cheque, no. 804 | 28 |
| 7 | Paid for supermarket groceries by cheque, no. 805 | 114 |

**3** Mr and Mrs Kearns keep the following record of their money:

| May | | € |
|---|---|---|
| 1 | Cash in bank | 79 |
| 1 | Took cash from ATM to pay the supermarket | 120 |
| 2 | Paid for petrol by cheque, no. 41 | 53 |
| 2 | Mr Kearns lodged his wages in the bank | 1,430 |
| 2 | Mrs Kearns lodged her wages in the bank | 1,380 |
| 3 | Paid for car service by cheque, no. 42 | 124 |
| 4 | Took cash from ATM to buy birthday cake | 30 |
| 5 | Paid instalment of car loan by standing order | 450 |
| 6 | Paid for rent of apartment by cheque, no. 43 | 850 |
| 7 | Paid for electricity bill by cheque, no. 44 | 97 |

eTest.ie

Try a test on this topic

# Chapter 3

# Household *budget*

## Planning for success

The best way to control your money is to make a plan. This plan should show **estimates** of future income, expenditure and savings. A plan like this is called a **budget**, and making plans into budgets is called budgeting.

Everyone who will be affected by the budget can be involved in its creation. In a household the estimates of income may rest with just one or two people, i.e. those earning a wage or salary. However, everyone can get involved in the estimates of expenditure.

Budgeting your expenditure does not mean being stingy or buying cheap goods. It is more about being careful and trying to get good value for your hard-earned income. This will make your money go further and enable you to buy, or save, more.

## FALSE ECONOMIES

A **false economy** is a purchase that appears to save you money but actually costs you more in the long run. It's all a matter of getting a balance between quality and value for money. For example, you buy a cheap school bag. It's broken by Christmas. You buy another cheap school bag. It's broken by Easter, and so on. Would it have been better value to buy a more expensive, more durable bag that lasts the whole year, or two years? The original school bag could be considered a false economy because you ended up paying more in the long run than if you had bought the expensive bag in the first place.

You will need your calculator when you are preparing the household budget. There are lots of figures to add together and some to subtract from each other.

# HOUSEHOLD BUDGET FOR THE O'NEILL FAMILY

The budget is made up of two sections: the income and the expenditure. The income is totalled to give the row marked A. TOTAL INCOME on the opposite page. The expenditure has three parts: Fixed, Irregular and Discretionary. Each part has a subtotal. The three subtotals are then added to give the row marked B. TOTAL EXPENDITURE.

The last three rows usually cause students the greatest difficulty. To get the net cash row you subtract the total income from the total expenditure. So, for example, in January the total income is €7,900 and the total expenditure is €6,620. The difference is €1,280 and this is the net cash. It is similar for the other months.

You will be told the opening cash. In this question it is €950. Add the €950 to the net cash of €1,280 and you get €2,330. This then becomes the opening cash for February. This is repeated for March and April, but for the total you use the original €950 figure again.

Estimates of income and expenditure

**Estimate of income**
Joe O'Neill earns €3,600 net per month and expects to receive a tax refund of €900 net in February. Tanya O'Neill earns €3,800 net per month and expects to take a full month's leave without pay in April. Child benefit is expected to be €500 per month.

**Estimate of fixed expenditure**
House mortgage of €1,300 per month will increase by €200 per month from 1 March. House insurance premium, €1,200 per year, is payable monthly from 1 January. Repayments on car loan (to be fully paid by the end of March) are €900 per month until then.

**Estimate of irregular expenditure**
Household expenses are €1,800 per month, except in March, when they will be €600 less. Car running costs each month will be €300 for Tanya and €100 for Joe. Light and heat bills are expected to amount to €400 in January and €350 in March, while oil will cost €1,400 in February. The household is charged €60 per month for an Internet connection. Mobile phone 'top-ups' will cost €160 per month.

**Estimate of discretionary expenditure**
Birthday presents will cost €800 in February. Entertainment will cost €900 each month, except in February, when it will be double. The O'Neills have booked a holiday costing €3,000. They must pay the travel agent a deposit of €600 in January, a further instalment of €1,000 in March and the balance in April.

**Surplus or deficit**
In April there is a deficit of €2,220. All the other months have a surplus. The total surplus is €1,420 and this is the estimated savings for the four months.

| O'NEILL HOUSEHOLD | JAN | FEB | MAR | APR | TOTAL |
|---|---|---|---|---|---|
| PLANNED INCOME | € | € | € | € | € |
| Joe O'Neill – Salary | 3,600 | 4,500 | 3,600 | 3,600 | 15,300 |
| Tanya O'Neill – Salary | 3,800 | 3,800 | 3,800 | – | 11,400 |
| Child Benefit | 500 | 500 | 500 | 500 | 2,000 |
| A.  TOTAL INCOME | 7,900 | 8,800 | 7,900 | 4,100 | 28,700 |
| PLANNED EXPENDITURE | | | | | |
| *Fixed* | | | | | |
| House mortgage | 1,300 | 1,300 | 1,500 | 1,500 | 5,600 |
| House insurance | 100 | 100 | 100 | 100 | 400 |
| Car loan | 900 | 900 | 900 | – | 2,700 |
| Subtotal | 2,300 | 2,300 | 2,500 | 1,600 | 8,700 |
| *Irregular* | | | | | |
| Household expenses | 1,800 | 1,800 | 1,200 | 1,800 | 6,600 |
| Car running costs | 400 | 400 | 400 | 400 | 1,600 |
| Light and heat | 400 | 1,400 | 350 | – | 2,150 |
| Internet | 60 | 60 | 60 | 60 | 240 |
| Mobile costs | 160 | 160 | 160 | 160 | 640 |
| Subtotal | 2,820 | 3,820 | 2,170 | 2,420 | 11,230 |
| *Discretionary* | | | | | |
| Birthday presents | – | 800 | – | – | 800 |
| Entertainment costs | 900 | 1,800 | 900 | 900 | 4,500 |
| Holiday | 600 | – | 1,000 | 1,400 | 3,000 |
| Subtotal | 1,500 | 2,600 | 1,900 | 2,300 | 8,300 |
| B.  TOTAL EXPENDITURE | 6,620 | 8,720 | 6,570 | 6,320 | 28,230 |
| Net Cash (A – B) | 1,280 | 80 | 1,330 | (2,220) | 470 |
| Opening Cash | 950 | 2,230 | 2,310 | 3,640 | 950 |
| Closing Cash | 2,230 | 2,310 | 3,640 | 1,420 | 1,420 |

# SURPLUS

The total income and total expenditure are subtracted to see how much is left at the end of the month. Usually there is some money left over – this is called a surplus.

# DEFICIT

Sometimes the expenditure is greater than the income – this is called a deficit. To finance a deficit the family could:

- alter their spending habits
- use some of their savings
- take out a short-term loan (overdraft).

# BREAKEVEN

When the expenditure is equal to the income this is called breakeven.

# OPENING CASH

In January the €950 opening cash is added to the net cash of €1,280 to give the closing cash of €2,230. The €2,230 now becomes the opening cash for February. This continues across the budgeted months, except in the total column, where the €950 is used again.

# COMPARISONS H

By comparing the actual and the budgeted income and expenditure it is possible to spot trends and avoid mistakes in the next budget. Here is a comparison of the budgeted and actual spending for the O'Neills:

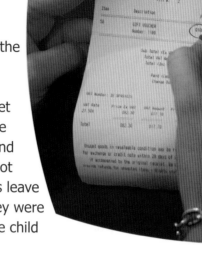

| O'NEILL HOUSEHOLD | BUDGET | ACTUAL | DIFFERENCE |
|---|---|---|---|
| PLANNED INCOME | € | € | € |
| Joe O'Neill – Salary | 15,300 | 14,400 | – 900 |
| Tanya O'Neill – Salary | 11,400 | 15,200 | + 3,800 |
| Child Benefit | 2,000 | 2,000 | 0 |
| **A.  TOTAL INCOME** | 28,700 | 31,600 | + 2,900 |
| PLANNED EXPENDITURE | | | |
| *Fixed* | | | |
| House mortgage | 5,600 | 5,600 | 0 |
| House insurance | 400 | 440 | + 40 |
| Car loan | 2,700 | 3,600 | + 900 |
| Subtotal | 8,700 | 9,640 | + 940 |
| *Irregular* | | | |
| Household expenses | 6,600 | 6,300 | – 300 |
| Car running costs | 1,600 | 2,500 | + 900 |
| Light and heat | 2,150 | 2,850 | + 700 |
| Internet | 240 | 240 | 0 |
| Mobile costs | 640 | 780 | + 140 |
| Subtotal | 11,230 | 12,670 | + 1,440 |
| *Discretionary* | | | |
| Birthday presents | 800 | 1,200 | + 400 |
| Entertainment costs | 4,500 | 4,200 | – 300 |
| Holiday | 3,000 | 3,600 | + 600 |
| Subtotal | 8,300 | 9,000 | + 700 |
| **B.  TOTAL EXPENDITURE** | 28,230 | 31,310 | + 3,080 |
| Net Cash (A – B) | 470 | 290 | – 180 |
| Opening Cash | 950 | 950 | 0 |
| Closing Cash | 1,420 | 1,240 | – 180 |

1. They got the wages wrong. Mr O'Neill did not get the tax refund he was expecting and Mrs O'Neill did not take the month's leave without pay. They were correct about the child benefit.

2. They got the mortgage right. The house insurance was higher than they expected.
They thought the car loan would finish in April but it did not finish until May.

3. The household costs were lower than they expected but the car running costs and the light and heat bills were higher. They got the Internet charge correct but they underestimated the mobile phone costs.

4. The money they spent on birthdays was higher. They spent more on the family holiday than they budgeted for, but their entertainment costs during the six months were lower.

5. They thought they would have €1,420 left over, but they only had €1,240 left at the end of the four months.

## Activity 3.1 Chapter Review

**1** What is a budget?

**2** Explain, giving an example, what a false economy is.

**3** What is the difference between a surplus and a deficit?

**4** For the O'Neill family:
  (a) how do we know they have children?
  (b) how do we know Mr and Mrs O'Neill are working?
  (c) what is their estimated total income for January?
  (d) what is their estimated total income for the four months January to April?
  (e) now can you work out their estimated annual income?
  (f) how do we know they are buying their own house?
  (g) how do we know they had to borrow to buy a car?
  (h) what are their total expenses for January?
  (i) do they have a surplus or deficit in January?
  (j) what are their estimated savings for the four months?

**5** The following figures are shown in the budget for the O'Neill family. Say what each figure represents:
  (a) €4,500
  (b) €500
  (c) €100
  (d) €400
  (e) €160
  (f) €8,800
  (g) €2,500
  (h) €80
  (i) €2,220
  (j) €1,420

## Activity 3.2 Comparisons

**1** How much did the O'Neills estimate they would save during January to April?

**2** How much did they actually save?

**3** Why is it useful to compare the budget with the actual income and expenditure?

**4** The following figures are shown in the comparison for the O'Neills. Say what each figure represents:
  (a) €31,600; (b) €31,310; (c) €950; (d) €5,600; (e) €780

**5** Complete a budget for the Burke household for the first four months of the year, given the following information.

Opening cash in hand was €70.

*Planned income:*
- P. Burke earns €1,150 net per month.
- M. Burke earns €1,450 net per month.
- Child benefit is €160 per month.

*Planned expenditure:*
- House insurance premium is €120 per year, payable monthly from January.
- Annual car insurance of €400 is due for payment in March.
- Annual car tax is €130 and due in February.
- Repayments on car loan will cost €300 per month.
- House rental is €800 per month but will increase by €50 from the beginning of March.
- Car running costs are expected to be €110 per month.
- Household expenses are expected to be €800 per month.
- Electricity bills are expected to be €90 in February and €110 in April.
- Entertainment will cost €500 each month.
- Birthdays will cost €90 in January and €80 in March.

**6** Complete a budget for the Brady household for June, July, August and September, given the following information.

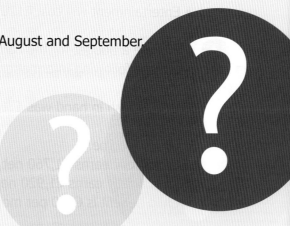

Opening cash in hand was €130.

*Planned income:*
- Mr Brady earns €1,210 net per month.
- Mrs Brady earns €1,670 net per month.
- Child benefit is €160 per month.

*Planned expenditure:*
- Annual car insurance of €460 is due for payment in July.
- Repayments on car loan will cost €350 per month.
- The health insurance premium is €50 per month. This will increase to €60 per month from the beginning of July.
- House mortgage is expected to be €650 per month.
- Electricity bills are expected to be €80 in July and €100 in September.
- Car running costs are expected to be €180 per month.
- Groceries are usually €900 per month.
- The telephone bill is expected to be €120 in July and €140 in September.
- Birthday presents will be €200 in July.
- Entertainment will cost €240 each month.
- The family expects to spend €1,600 on a holiday in July.

*Templates for these questions are provided in the workbook.*

 **1** The following is a budget for the Hughes household for the first four months of the year.

Opening cash in hand was €150.

*Planned income:*
- Aidan Hughes earns €1,025 net per month.
- Fiona Hughes earns €850 net per month.
- Child benefit is €160 per month.

*Planned expenditure:*
- House rental is €600 per month but will increase by €50 per month from the beginning of March.
- House contents insurance premium of €120 per year is payable monthly from January.
- The Hughes family pays health insurance of €55 per month. This will increase to €60 per month from the beginning of March.
- Groceries are usually €350 per month.
- Aidan pays €50 a month and Fiona pays €55 a month on bus and train fares.
- The family expects to spend €600 on clothes in the January sales.
- Electricity bills are expected to be €95 in January and €80 in March.
- A fill of heating oil costing €320 will be needed in February.
- A birthday will cost €100 in February.
- Entertainment will cost €120 each month except March, when it will be €300 extra due to a wedding.
- The Hughes family hope to buy a new television costing €700 in April.

(a) Complete the blank household budget form in the workbook using all the above figures.

(b) Do Aidan and Fiona own the house in which they live?

(c) Will the Hughes family have enough money to pay for the television in April? Give one reason for your answer.

(JCOL, adapted)

**2** (a) In the workbook there is a partially completed personal budget form for the O'Malley family for the year. You are required to complete this form by filling in the figures for the 'Estimates April to December' column and the 'Total January to December' column. The following information should be taken into account.

- Enda O'Malley is due a salary increase of five per cent from 1 July.
- Gráinne O'Malley expects to earn an extra €100 per month in November and December.
- Child benefit will increase by €10 per month from 1 October.
- House mortgage is expected to increase by €50 per month from 1 November.
- House insurance, payable monthly, will continue as for the first three months of the year.
- Household costs per month are expected to remain the same for each month until September and to increase by €40 a month beginning in October.
- Car running costs are expected to remain at €60 a month with an additional car service cost of €70 each in June and December.
- Electricity costs for the twelve months (January to December) are estimated at €460.
- The telephone bill is paid every second month and it is estimated that the cost will remain the same as at the beginning of the year.
- Christmas presents are expected to cost €230 in December.
- Entertainment is estimated at €750 for the twelve months (January to December).
- The family holiday in August is expected to cost €1,000.

(b) Answer the following questions.
  (i) Did the O'Malley family have a surplus, deficit or balanced budget in each of the months January, February and March?
  (ii) How much cash did they save in total from 1 January to 31 March?
  (iii) Give a reason why the house mortgage costs increased.

(JCHL, adapted)

▶ Learn about the descriptions found on goods

▶ Discover how to be more careful when shopping, especially on the Internet

# Chapter 4

# Being a good *consumer*

# How to shop sensibly

In the last few chapters you learned a little about shopping sensibly, e.g. how to avoid false economies and impulse buying. In addition you learned the value of creating a budget and sticking to it. If you are to become a sensible shopper you must also try to get value for money and know your consumer rights. The next few chapters look at your rights as a consumer when you are buying goods and services. It is very important for you to understand your rights and to learn how to complain in a manner which is calm and keeps to the point.

Before you buy anything you should consider the following.
● Can you afford it?
● Do you really need it?
● Is it safe?
● Do you have room for it?
● Are there any hidden extras?

If you take the time to answer these questions, you'll be a more informed consumer and in a better position to make sensible purchases.

## GOODS AND SERVICES

A consumer buys goods and services. When you go to the cinema or catch a bus to town you are a consumer of a service. When you buy flowers for your mother you are a consumer of goods. Another name for goods is products.

It is against the law to make false or misleading descriptions about products and services. Descriptions should be read carefully since they will help you decide if you really are making a good purchase.

# Descriptions on products

## Barcode

The barcode is a series of vertical lines that represent the numbers shown below the lines. In shops the barcode is read by scanners at the checkout. The first two or three digits on the left identify the product's country of origin. Ireland and Britain have the code 50.

| 50 | 11002 | 12516 | 0 |
|----|-------|-------|---|
| Country of origin | Company number | Product number | Check digit |

## Price

This is useful to note so that you can compare the price of similar products or the same product in different shops.

## Origin

Where the product is from, e.g. made in Ireland.

## Name and address

The contact details of the producer, packager or seller.

## Symbols

These give assurances of quality and standards, e.g. Guaranteed Irish, Caighdeán Éireannach (Irish standard), Woolmark (Pure New Wool), Approved Quality Symbol. Other symbols are used to encourage the consumer to recycle the packaging.

## Product name

This is a name to identify the product, e.g. Sprite is a recognised brand name.

## Illustrations

These are optional but must not be misleading.

## Unit price

The unit price is the cost of one unit of the product. It is useful to calculate this when comparison shopping. It makes it possible to compare different sizes of similar products and therefore decide which is better money value. Of course you may have to try both products to see which is better quality. To find the unit price, divide the price by the quantity.

$$\text{Unit price} = \frac{\text{Price}}{\text{Quantity}}$$

$$= \frac{180 \text{ cent}}{180 \text{ tissues}}$$

$$= 1 \text{ cent per tissue}$$

**Weight or quantity**
The net weight or quantity.

**Ingredients**
The ingredients are given in descending order of weight.

**Date**
This will take the form of a use by, best before or expiry date.

**Storage**
How the product should be stored, e.g. refrigerated.

## BARCODES

The barcode is the way information about the product goes into the computer database. It tells the database what the product is. When a product is sold the quantity of the product in the computer database is reduced by one. This is very handy for a shopkeeper who can check the computer to see how much of a product is left. If the actual quantity on the shelves is different, the shopkeeper might suspect that the goods have been stolen.

**Advantages for the shopkeeper**
- It is much faster than keying in the price.
- It is possible to have a computerised stock system.
- The computer can help the shopkeeper decide when to reorder goods.
- It can be easier to change the prices of goods.

**Advantages for the customer**
- Faster at check-outs.
- Mistakes are less likely as the computer 'knows' the price to charge.

In most cases, when you buy goods and services the transaction is easy: you pay your money and you get a magazine (a good) or buy a bus ticket to go into town (a service). Even so there are a few cases to be aware of.

# Buying goods and services

## receipt

When you purchase something you are usually given a **receipt**. It's certainly a good idea to ask for one and most shops will issue them, but the law does not insist on shops providing receipts. However, a receipt may be your only proof of purchase in the event of a complaint at a later stage. Written on the receipt will be:
- the date
- details of the items purchased
- the prices
- the name of the shop.

## guarantee

The receipt is often asked for by a shop when you have a problem that is covered under a guarantee. A **guarantee** may be for one year from the date of purchase, and the receipt shows this date.

Receipts should be kept carefully. In the case of durables, such as DVD players, cameras or computers, keep the receipt for at least the duration of the guarantee. Other receipts should be kept until you have checked them carefully for accuracy, e.g. a hotel bill or a supermarket receipt.

## deposit

Sometimes when you are buying an expensive item you will be asked to give a deposit. A **deposit** is an amount of money equal to a small part of the overall cost of the goods. This is to ensure that you will return to collect the goods and pay the balance of the money due. If in the meantime you change your mind about the goods, you normally lose your deposit. This compensates the trader for the inconvenience you have caused.

## credit note

When you have a problem with a product and complain to the shop, the trader may offer you a credit note. Shops prefer to

issue credit notes because they can keep your money and your custom. However, if you have a strong case you do not have to accept a credit note and you may be able to insist on a cash refund.

A **credit note** entitles you to buy something else in the shop to the value stated on the note. The problem is that the shop may not have anything else you are interested in or the shop may be some distance from where you live. In these cases it is sensible to insist on a complete refund and use the cash elsewhere.

Of course, you are not entitled to buy anything you see on sale. The shopkeeper can refuse to sell you some items even if they are on display in a shop window. Some products, such as alcoholic drinks, are only available to adults. Some medicines are only available to adults if they have a doctor's prescription.

## INTERNET SHOPPING

You have the same rights when you order goods by post, phone or over the Internet as when you buy goods in the shop.

However, you must take great care to ensure the goods you order are the ones you want.

### Before you buy

Before you pay for anything you should:

- compare prices
- check postage and delivery fees
- order early to allow plenty of time for delivery.

Also remember to keep receipts and website printouts.

### Paying for goods

Goods ordered by post, phone or over the Internet will normally be paid by cheque or credit card. Here is some advice.

- Never send cash in the post.
- Cheques sent by post should always be crossed.
- When you pay for goods by credit card on the Internet, make sure you are at a secure server. You will know as there will be a lock symbol on the bottom right of the screen.

## Activity 4.1 Chapter Review

**1** (a) Before you buy anything what questions should you ask yourself?
   (b) How can the unit price help you decide which product to buy?

**2** (a) Explain the difference between goods and services.
   (b) Give three examples of goods and three examples of services.

**3** (a) List ten descriptions found on products, and explain any three of them.
   (b) The ingredients of a product are written as W, X, Y, Z. Which of these ingredients is present in the smallest quantity?
   (c) How does a consumer benefit from descriptions on products?

**4** (a) What are barcodes?
   (b) What are the advantages for the supermarket of using barcodes?
   (c) How do consumers benefit from barcodes?

**5** (a) What are your consumer rights when you order goods over the Internet?
   (b) What advice would you give someone who is thinking of buying goods over the Internet?

**6** (a) Can you insist that a shopkeeper sells you something?
   (b) Give an example of a product that you cannot insist be sold to you.

**7** (a) Explain these terms:
       (i)  deposit
       (ii)  guarantee
       (iii)  receipt
       (iv)  credit note.
   (b) Why should you keep receipts?
   (c) Name three items that are normally written on a receipt.

eTest.ie
Try a test on this topic

## Activity 4.2 Unit prices

Find the unit price for each of the following and indicate which is better money value:
(a) Eighty tea bags for €3.20 or 40 tea bags for €2.
(b) 1.5 litres of cola for €1.20 or 500ml for 70 cent.
(c) An 800g sliced pan for €1.60 or a 300g sliced pan for 70 cent.
(d) Three dozen eggs for €5.40 or half a dozen for €1.20.
(e) A box of 40 matches for 20 cent or a box for €1 containing 250 matches.
(f) A copy book with 50 pages costing 20 cent or one with 80 pages costing 40 cent.
(g) A packet of 10 blank DVDs for €15 or a packet of 20 for €25.
(h) A 500g box of breakfast cereal for €2.50 or a 750g box for €3.
(i) 1.5 kilos of washing powder for €4.50 or 2.5 kilos for €8.
(j) Six apples for €1.80 or 12 apples for €3.36.

▶ Find out about the law in relation to consumers

# Chapter 5

▶ Get what you want by following the steps in complaining

▶ Learn how to write a letter of complaint

# Consumer *rights*

# Let the buyer beware (caveat emptor)

The Sale of Goods and Supply of Services Act 1980 details your legal rights as a consumer. Here is a guide to them:

**1** **Goods should be of merchantable quality.**
This means that the goods should be of reasonable quality, taking into account what they are supposed to do, the price paid and how long they should last, e.g. a pen should write.

**2** **Goods should be fit for their purpose,** e.g. glue used for the purpose of fixing ornaments might not glue wood successfully.

**3** **Goods should be as described,** e.g. a hotel that advertises itself as being 'beside the sea' should not require a 2km car journey to reach the beach.

**4** **Goods should conform to sample,** e.g. the carpet you buy should be the same as the sample shown to you in the shop.

(i) INDESIT
To activate your
FREE 12 month guarantee
call us NOW
**0870 4427661**

## GUARANTEE

A **guarantee** ensures that the product is perfect when it is sold to you and if it is not perfect, you can complain. Normally you return to the shop where you bought the goods. However, you are also entitled to complain to the manufacturer if you are not satisfied with the way you were treated in the shop. You may be happy if you manage to get the product repaired or replaced for free. Sometimes, however, you may want a full refund.

## GETTING A FULL REFUND

Some shops will give a full refund of your money provided you complain promptly. You have no rights if you misuse the goods or if you change your mind about wanting the product. Suppose you buy a television and it breaks, what are you entitled to? If the fault occurs soon after you buy the television and you complain promptly you can insist on a complete refund. If the fault does not occur until after several weeks or months you may only get a replacement or a repair.

# Steps in complaining

## 1

### Stop using the product

If you continue to use the faulty television you may not be entitled to a full refund.

## 2

### Inform the shop

Tell the shopkeeper you are having a problem with the television. You could call into the shop, phone, email or send a letter. It is better to complain in writing as there is a written record of the complaint.

## 3

### Bring the product back

The person you buy the goods from (usually the shopkeeper) is the one you complain to. You must do this soon after you discover the fault. If you delay and continue to use the goods, you may lose your rights. Some faults are easy to prove and you will have no trouble getting a remedy. However, if the fault doesn't appear until a while after you buy the product, the retailer may say the fault is due to normal wear and tear or to misuse.

## 4

### Agreement

Try to reach a sensible agreement. The remedies you may be entitled to are:

- a **refund** (you get your money back)
- a **replacement** (the faulty television is exchanged for a good one)
- a **repair** (the faulty television is taken back and fixed).

### Disagreement

If you cannot come to an agreement with the shop, you will have to consult a **third party**. This is dealt with in the next chapter.

# MAKING A WRITTEN COMPLAINT

**Your address** → Harbour View
Howth
County Dublin

**Today's date** → 23 July 2010

**The shop's address**
(find it in the phone book or on
the Internet) → Home Sound and Vision
Shop Street
Dublin

**Greeting**
(use Sir or Madam if you do not
know who to complain to) → Dear Sir or Madam

**The date you bought the product** → I wish to complain about a television I bought in your shop last Monday, 19 July 2010.

**The problem** → The left speaker is broken.

**The remedy you want** → I would like a complete refund.

**Do not send your evidence!** → I enclose a photocopy of my receipt.

Yours sincerely

**Sign your name here** → *Frank Ryan*

Frank Ryan

# MAKING AN ORAL COMPLAINT

Shopkeeper: How can I help you?
**You: I wish to make a complaint.**
Shopkeeper: What's the problem?
**You: I bought this television here last week and the speaker is not working.**
Shopkeeper: We can take it in and repair it.
**You: No, I want a complete refund.**
Shopkeeper: I'm sorry, we don't give refunds.
**You: You sold me a faulty television and I am entitled to a refund.**
Shopkeeper: I'm sorry, we don't give refunds.
**You: You aren't listening to me, so I'll go now. But I'll get the help of a third party to help me make my case to you.**

## Activity 5.1 Chapter Review

**1** (a) Why must the buyer beware when purchasing goods and services?
   (b) What are the consumer's legal rights?
   (c) State the remedies a consumer may be entitled to if a fault develops in a product they have bought.

**2** (a) What steps should be taken in making a complaint?
   (b) Why is the consumer advised to complain in writing?

**3** (a) What is a guarantee?
   (b) Should you complain to the shop or make a claim under the guarantee?
   (c) Can you insist on a refund or must you accept a repair?

**4** Explain these terms:
   (i) repair; (ii) replacement; (iii) refund.

**5** Explain these terms:
   (i) goods should be of merchantable quality
   (ii) goods should be fit for their purpose
   (iii) goods should be as described
   (iv) goods should conform to sample.

eTest.ie
Try a test on this topic

**6** When you are writing a letter of complaint you should include details about (i) the *date*, (ii) the *problem* and (iii) the *remedy* you want. Explain these terms.

## Activity 5.2 Consumer problems

**1** You go out for a family meal on 12 January to the Steak Restaurant, New Street, Athlone and your parents pay by cheque. When you get home you study the receipt and discover they have overcharged you: they have included three items that you didn't order. Your parents ask you to write a letter of complaint to the restaurant about this.

**2** You buy an expensive new plasma TV on 17 March. A fault develops in the first few days after you take it home. Write a letter of complaint to the Discount Store, Shop Street, Galway, where you bought the TV.

**3** You bought a hair straightener four weeks ago from Power Electric, Main Street, Dundalk but didn't use it until tonight. When you switched it on, smoke started coming from the cable. You find the guarantee and it says that there is a one year guarantee. Write a letter of complaint to the shop about this.

**4** You buy a new games console and one of the buttons becomes loose within a few days. However, you continue to use it and only today, three months later, do you decide to complain to the shop. Write a letter of complaint to ComGames, High Street, Sligo about this.

# Chapter 6

# Consumer protection

## Claims and descriptions

Traders or manufacturers make claims to influence you to buy their goods and services. These claims must be true, otherwise you may be entitled to compensation.

In 1978 the government passed the **Consumer Information Act**. This act is designed to protect consumers from false and misleading descriptions or advertisements about goods, services and prices. This means that advertisements in the media, catalogues and pictures on packets must not contain any claims or descriptions that might mislead the consumer.

Typical **claims about goods** are: pure new wool; Irish made; waterproof; no artificial additives.

Typical **claims about services** are: one hour photo; Bord Fáilte approved; direct flights.

## PRICES

It is an offence to mislead the consumer about the:

- **actual price,** e.g. it would be wrong to quote €180 for a bike and then charge another €50 for the saddle. In this case the consumer expects the saddle to be included in the price quoted.
- **previous price,** e.g. during a sale the previous price is often shown. For this to be legal the product must have been on sale at this higher price for at least four consecutive weeks in the previous three months.
- **recommended retail price,** e.g. it is an offence for a shop to artificially inflate the maker's recommended price.

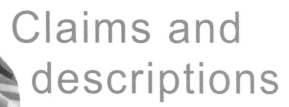

*Chapter 6 Consumer Protection*

If you aren't happy with the way the shop has handled your complaint you will have to consult a third party. This is someone who will act on your behalf to reach a settlement with the shop. In some cases your parents may act as a third party for you. In other cases you may have to use some of the third parties listed below.

# GETTING THE HELP OF A THIRD PARTY

### The Office of the Director of Consumer Affairs

This office was set up under the Consumer Information Act 1978. It publishes pamphlets to inform you about your rights as a consumer. The office is run by the Director of Consumer Affairs. They are concerned about the truth of advertisements and the descriptions of goods and services.

### Trade Associations

There are many trade associations in Ireland that may be able to deal with your complaint in relation to one of their members. Many travel agencies, for example, are members of the Irish Travel Agents' Association (ITAA). Local shops could be members of the Retail Grocery, Dairy and Allied Trades Association (RGDATA). An electrician might be a member of the Association of Electrical Contractors.

### The Ombudsman

The Ombudsman is appointed by the government to investigate complaints by the public relating to state agencies. For example, if you have a problem with An Post, the health boards or a government department and you aren't happy with the way they deal with your complaint, you can ask the Ombudsman to investigate and see if you have been treated fairly.

### Small Claims Court

If you're looking for a remedy of €2,000 or less from a trader, you can use the small claims procedure in the District Court. It is popular because it doesn't involve the expense of a solicitor and is very informal. Claims can be made for bad workmanship and faulty goods. The fee for making a small claim is €15.

### Consumers' Association of Ireland

This association publishes the monthly information magazine *Consumer Choice*. The magazine is distributed to members of the association and is not available in shops. It has articles about consumer issues, e.g. insurance costs compared, electrical goods compared. It will represent members who have a complaint against a government department or a private company.

## Activity 6.1 Chapter Review

1. (a) How does the Consumer Information Act protect consumers?
   (b) Give three examples of claims about goods.
   (c) Give three examples of claims about services.

2. (a) How can the price of a product or service be misleading?
   (b) In a sale, how can information about the previous price be illegal?

3. (a) What is a third party?
   (b) What does the Director of Consumer Affairs do?
   (c) How can the Ombudsman help?

Try a test on this topic

4. (a) Describe how the small claims procedure works.
   (b) Why is it popular?

5. (a) Which consumer organisation publishes the magazine *Consumer Choice*?
   (b) How would you get a copy of this magazine?
   (c) How often is it published?

## Activity 6.2 Consumer problems

1. You are just back from a holiday in Greece that you booked through Inter-Travel. The brochure described your hotel as 'quiet and beside the beach', when in fact it was beside a noisy building site and three miles from the beach! You have complained to Inter-Travel but they say they can't help you.
   (a) What principle of consumer law has been broken in this situation?
   (b) Do you feel you are entitled to a full or a partial refund? Give one reason to support your answer.
   (c) How could the Irish Travel Agents' Association help you?

2. Your laptop computer won't play movies and you bring it to a local shop for repair. You choose this shop because a sign in the window says it guarantees all repairs and that it is a member of the Association of Electrical Contractors. The repair costs you €40. Two days later the computer won't play movies again. When you return to the shop they insist that the repair will cost another €40.
   (a) What is the legal basis for your complaint? Explain it briefly.
   (b) Are you entitled to a complete refund? Give a reason for your answer.
   (c) What third party could you ask to help in this situation?

3. Your family takes a short break in a Bord Fáilte-approved guesthouse in Kerry. The brochure stated that the price was €200 per night for a family, but your parents end up paying €250 per night. When you get home, your parents decide to complain to the guesthouse.
   (a) What is the legal basis for the complaint? Explain it briefly.
   (b) Are your parents entitled to a complete refund? Give a reason for your answer.
   (c) What third party could your parents ask to help in this situation?

## Activity 6.3 State Exam Practice

**1**   (a)   Peter Cooney of 16 Castle Street, Ennis bought a new Roller bicycle, Model RB 25, from Frank Clarke, manager of the Bike Shop Ltd of Nenagh Road, Limerick on 11 April. He paid €179 by cheque. After a few days' use, the bicycle started to give trouble. It made a lot of noise when he was cycling and the chain seemed to slip every time he went up a hill. After a week he had to get off and walk up every hill with it. He was very disappointed. You, as Peter Cooney, are asked to write a suitable letter of complaint to the Bike Shop Ltd.

      (b)   If the Bike Shop Ltd does not satisfy him, suggest two steps that Peter Cooney could take.

(JCOL, adapted)

**2**   Mary Noonan bought a new jacket in Angel's Boutique on a recent holiday. She paid €85 for it. On her return home she noticed that the stitching on one sleeve was ripped and also that one shoulder was larger than the other. She was very disappointed. As the boutique is over 70 kilometres from where she lives, she has decided to write to them about it and return the jacket. She isn't sure whether or not she should return the receipt. She wants a full refund.

      (a)   Using your knowledge of consumer legislation, answer the following questions.

          (i)   What is the legal basis for Mary's complaint? Explain it briefly.

          (ii)   Do you think Mary is entitled to a full refund? Give a reason for your answer.

          (iii)   If the boutique owner offered Mary a credit note for the full amount should she accept it? Explain your answer.

          (iv)   What advice would you give Mary on whether or not she should include the receipt with her letter?

      (b)   Assume you are Mary Noonan. Write the letter of complaint to the manager of Angel's Boutique. (You may choose any address, date, etc. that are required for yourself.)

**3**   Your friends went shopping recently and asked you to advise them with their consumer problems.

      (a)   David bought a tin of paint in a sale for half the normal price. When his mother saw the paint she said it was a very inferior brand and its purchase was a *false economy* and a typical example of David's *impulse buying*. David wishes to return the tin of paint to the shop with the receipt.

          (i)   Is David entitled to a full refund of his money? Give a reason for your answer.

          (ii)   Explain the italicised terms above.

      (b)   Aisling bought a dress in a shop from a stand that displayed a sign stating that the goods were shop-soiled. When Aisling fitted on the dress at home she noticed that the collar was faded. Aisling decided to return the dress to the shop. The shop assistant refused to take it back even though Aisling had proof of purchase.

          (i)   Was the shop assistant correct? Explain your answer.

          (ii)   The manager of the shop knew that Aisling was a regular customer and offered her a credit note, which she accepted. Why did the manager do this?

          (iii)   Give two reasons why it is important to get a receipt when you buy goods.

      (c)   A customer is considering the purchase of a new household electrical item. List three factors to take into account when choosing one brand or model over another.

(JCHL, adapted)

▶ Read about the different places to save your money

▶ Learn how to write a cheque and make it safe

# Chapter 7

# Money and *banking*

## Keeping your money safe

So far you have been learning about getting money and managing your own money so that you get the best value from it. In the next few chapters you will learn about professional services that are available to help you manage your finances. You will learn the value of insuring yourself and your property. You will also learn how to borrow sensibly.

But first we look at money and banking to see what services there are to help make your financial life easier.

Many of these services were once exclusive to one type of financial institution but are now available in other financial institutions. For example, at one time if you wanted a mortgage you could only apply to a building society. Nowadays, however, you can also get a mortgage at a bank.

## AUTOMATED TELLER MACHINE

**Automated Teller Machines (ATMs)** or cash dispensers are a handy way to use many of the banks' services. Customers who wish to use ATMs are given a cash card and a **personal identification number (PIN)**. After keying in the PIN at the ATM the customer may then lodge money or withdraw money and pay bills such as gas, electricity or telephone.

# FORMS OF MONEY

Money is anything that people are prepared to accept as payment for goods and services. Cattle, gold and silver were all used as money at one time or another. A good form of money is: divisible (can be broken down into smaller values); portable (can be carried easily); and durable (will withstand normal wear and tear). When people lose confidence in money they often revert to an old form of trade called **barter**. This simply means swapping goods.

There are five main forms of money used in Ireland today:

### Cash
The notes and coins in daily use. These are **legal tender**, i.e. they must be accepted as payment for goods and services.

### Cheques
A person who has a current account is able to write cheques to pay for goods and services.

### Laser card
You can use a laser card to pay for shopping and also get cash while at the checkout. It is also known as a debit card and is cheaper than writing a cheque.

### Credit card
A credit card allows a person to buy goods and services now and pay for them later, e.g. MasterCard, Visa. You get a statement each month and you can pay the full amount due or make a partial payment. However, you will pay high interest on the outstanding balance.

### Charge card
This is like a credit card except you must pay the amount due when you receive your statement each month, e.g. Diners Club, American Express.

# GOOD PLACES TO

### post office
This is a good place to start saving as there may be a branch near you and you get a high rate of interest on your savings. All savings in the post office are state guaranteed so your money will be safe. The following are not subject to DIRT (Deposit Interest Retention Tax):

### Savings Certificates
Invest from €50 to €80,000 and earn 16% after five years and six months on deposit.

### Savings Bonds
Invest from €100 to €80,000 and earn eight per cent after three years on deposit.

### Instalment Savings
Invest from €25 to €50 each month for a year and then earn 15% after five years on deposit.

### building society
The main reason for saving in a building society is to get a mortgage loan to buy a house. Most people begin by opening a savings account. This is a deposit account in which you save money by buying shares in the society.

# SAVE YOUR MONEY

## credit union

Credit unions are located all over the country and it's likely there is one in your local area. It is well worth saving in a credit union as you will be entitled to get a personal loan at a low interest rate. They offer two main accounts.

### Savings accounts
You can save your money in a savings account and get interest in the form of a dividend each year. The dividend paid is related to the amount of cash available to the credit union and the amount you have saved.

### Deposit accounts
Alternatively you can lodge your money in a deposit account and get interest on your savings at a higher rate than in the bank.

## commercial bank

The main commercial banks are Bank of Ireland, Allied Irish Banks, National Irish Bank, Ulster Bank and Permanent TSB Bank. They offer two main accounts.

### Deposit accounts
This is where you save money and earn interest on your deposits.

### Current accounts
Holders of current accounts get a cheque book. This is not a good account to use to save money as there is no interest paid and it's too easy to take out money.

# CHOOSING SOMEWHERE TO SAVE YOUR MONEY

Saving is a good habit and the earlier you begin, the better. You could save your money at home, but it's safer if you deposit your money in a financial institution. There are several to choose from and here are some questions to ask yourself before you decide on one.

## Will my savings be safe?
Keeping cash at home is not a safe place to save. It could be stolen and is too easy to 'dip into'. Soon your savings will be gone. It is much wiser to use a financial institution.

## What am I saving for?
Good savers have a target – something they want to buy that they can't afford yet, e.g. a bike, an apartment or a house. At that time it would make sense to have been saving in the institution you intend asking for a mortgage.

## Is it easy to withdraw my savings?
You can withdraw your money easily from a financial institution. Withdrawing large sums may require written notice.

## Will my savings earn interest?
You will get interest on your savings but you will have to shop around to get the best rates. The rates quoted will show the Annual Equivalent Rate (**AER**). This is where the interest earned is combined with the original balance and the next interest earned will be based on a higher account balance. An interest rate of four per cent AER means you get €4 on every €100 you save for a year.

## Will I have to pay tax?
In most cases you have to pay Deposit Interest Retention Tax (**DIRT**). You don't have to pay DIRT on some schemes operated by An Post.

Money lodged in a current account doesn't earn interest. However, the account is popular as there are several easy ways to take money out of it, e.g. cheques, standing orders and direct debits.

# CURRENT ACCOUNT

Writing a cheque for €120 is the same as going to the bank and taking €120 out of your account except you don't have to go to the bank, fill in a form and wait in a queue. It is therefore a convenient way to pay bills while you are shopping.

To get a cheque book you need to open a current account in a bank. You will be asked to fill in a form giving details about your name, address, occupation and annual income. In addition, you must give a specimen signature. You will be issued with an account number, cheque book and cheque card. You may then lodge money into the account and write cheques.

You may also pay regular bills like car loan or electricity by standing order and direct debit. These were explained in Chapter 2.

**Counterfoil**
The counterfoil (stub) lets you keep a record of the cheques you write. As a minimum you should write the date, the amount and the payee's name.

**Payee**
The name of the person or company receiving the cheque.

**Date**
A cheque must have a date. Normally this is the same as the day of issue.

**Drawee**
The name of the bank that has issued the cheque book. The customer has a current account in this bank.

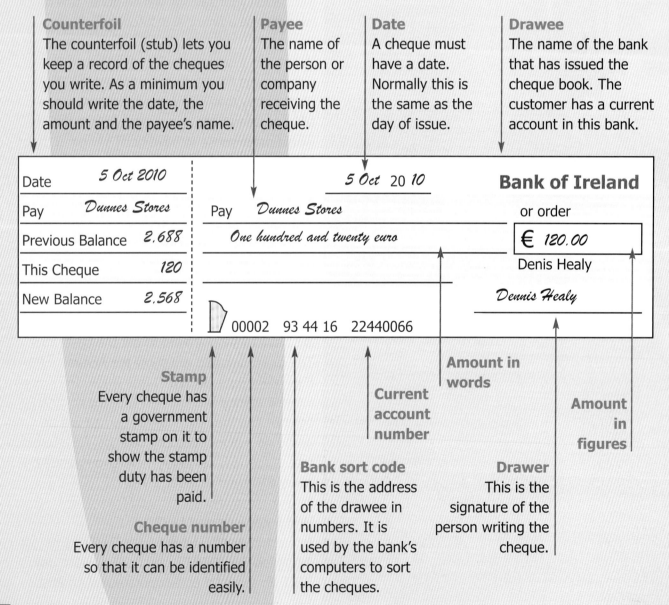

| Date | 5 Oct 2010 |
| Pay | Dunnes Stores |
| Previous Balance | 2,688 |
| This Cheque | 120 |
| New Balance | 2,568 |

5 Oct 20 10

Pay Dunnes Stores

One hundred and twenty euro

00002   93 44 16   22440066

**Bank of Ireland**

or order

€ 120.00

Denis Healy

Dennis Healy

**Stamp**
Every cheque has a government stamp on it to show the stamp duty has been paid.

**Cheque number**
Every cheque has a number so that it can be identified easily.

**Current account number**

**Bank sort code**
This is the address of the drawee in numbers. It is used by the bank's computers to sort the cheques.

**Amount in words**

**Drawer**
This is the signature of the person writing the cheque.

**Amount in figures**

## *making cheques* SAFER

Cheques can be lost or stolen and attempts may be made to forge the drawer's signature. Crossing a cheque makes it safer, and most shopkeepers will want to see a cheque card.

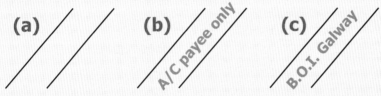

**(a)**  **(b)** A/C payee only  **(c)** B.O.I. Galway

### Crossed cheques

Crossing a cheque makes it safer, as it must be paid into another bank account and not simply cashed.

**(a)** This is the most commonly used crossing: two parallel lines are drawn on the face of the cheque.
**(b)** This cheque must be paid into the payee's account.
**(c)** This cheque must be presented at the Bank of Ireland, Galway.

### Cheque card

Most people and firms will accept a cheque instead of cash, especially if the cheque is supported by a cheque card. This is a guarantee by the financial institution issuing it to pay cash to the person receiving the cheque. A cheque card is about the size of a credit card. The shopkeeper compares the signature on the cheque card with the signature on the cheque and makes sure the card is not out of date. Then the card number is written on the back of the cheque.

## TYPES OF CHEQUE

**Dishonoured cheques**
A dishonoured cheque is a cheque that the bank will not pay. It is also known as a 'bounced cheque'. It is marked RD (refer to drawer). This can happen if:
- the cheque is more than six months old (stale)
- the amount in words doesn't match the figure
- the cheque isn't signed
- the signature doesn't match the sample signature
- there isn't enough money in the drawee's account.

**Endorsed cheques**
A cheque may be passed on to someone else as payment of a debt. To do this the payee signs or endorses the back of the cheque.

**Other cheques**
A **blank cheque** lacks the date, the amount of money and/or the payee's name. An **open cheque** is a cheque with no crossing on it. A **postdated cheque** has some future date on it and may not be cashed before that date. An **antedated cheque** has a previous date as the date of issue.

# Overdraft

If you write cheques for a value greater than the amount of money you have in your current account you will overdraw your account. Interest is charged on overdrafts and you may have the embarrassment of your cheques 'bouncing'. To avoid overdrawing your account you should keep a record of cheques paid out and lodgments made to your account. A simple bank account like the one below is the handiest way of recording these transactions. If it looks familiar it is because it is very similar to the cash account you learned about in Chapter 1.

**Paypath**

This is a system that allows an employer to pay staff wages directly into their bank accounts. It is very handy for the employer as the wages are paid electronically. The employee just has to go to an ATM machine to withdraw their wages.

## Question

Mr and Mrs Healy keep the following record of their money:

| Oct | | € | |
|---|---|---|---|
| 1 | Debit balance in bank account | 1,700 | Income |
| 2 | Mr Healy received his wages by Paypath | 510 | Income |
| 3 | Mrs Healy received her wages by Paypath | 520 | Income |
| 4 | Paid for petrol by cheque no. 1 | 42 | Expenditure |
| 5 | Paid for groceries by cheque no. 2 | 120 | Expenditure |
| 6 | Withdrew cash from ATM to pay for car service | 200 | Expenditure |
| 7 | Paid mortgage by standing order | 2,000 | Expenditure |

## Solution

The folio (F) column is where you place the cheque number.

| Dr | | | | Bank Account | | | Cr |
|---|---|---|---|---|---|---|---|
| Date | Details | F | Total | Date | Details | F | Total |
| Oct | | | € | Oct | | | € |
| 1 | Balance | b/d | 1,700 | 4 | Petrol | 1 | 42 |
| 2 | Wages | | 510 | 5 | Groceries | 2 | 120 |
| 3 | Wages | | 520 | 6 | Car service | ATM | 200 |
| | | | | 7 | Mortgage | SO | 2,000 |
| | | | | 7 | Balance | c/d | 368 |
| | | | 2,730 | | | | 2,730 |
| 8 | Balance | b/d | 368 | | | | |

Income ↑      Expenditure ↑

To balance the account, add up the money that came in (the items on the debit). This comes to €2,730. Now subtract the money spent, €2,362 (the items on the credit). The difference, €368, is the balance.

# Bank Reconciliation Statement

A bank statement is a letter from the bank giving details about your current account.
It lists the flow of money into and out of the account.

| Bank Statement | | | | |
|---|---|---|---|---|
| Date | Particulars | Debit | Credit | Balance |
| Oct | | € | € | € |
| 1 | Balance forward | | | 1,700 |
| 2 | Lodgment | | 510 | 2,210 |
| 6 | Cheque no. 1 | 42 | | 2,168 |
| 6 | ATM Mullingar | 200 | | 1,968 |
| 7 | Credit transfer | | 280 | 2,248 |
| 7 | Standing order | 2,000 | | 248 |
| 8 | Bank charges | 15 | | 233 |

**Expenditure ↑    Income ↑**

The balance column of the statement shows a running balance. This decreases when payments are made (debit) and increases when there are lodgments (credit). The final figure (€233) is the amount of money the bank considers the Healy family has in their account. This is their actual spending money.

## Adjusted bank account

| Dr | Bank Account | | | | | | | Cr |
|---|---|---|---|---|---|---|---|---|
| Date | Details | F | Total | Date | Details | F | Total | |
| Oct | | | € | Oct | | | € | |
| 8 | Balance | b/d | 368 | | Bank charges | | 15 | |
| | Credit transfer | | 280 | | Balance | c/d | 633 | |
| | | | 648 | | | | 648 | |
| 8 | Balance | b/d | 633 | | | | | |

You will also notice that the Healys did not know about the bank charges and the credit transfer. When these are entered into their bank account you get a new balance of €633, which is the same as the final figure in the bank reconciliation statement. This is the true bank balance and it represents the money the Healys have available to spend.

## Bank reconciliation statement

| Bank Reconciliation Statement | | | |
|---|---|---|---|
| Balance per statement | | | 233 |
| Lodgment not yet credited | | | + 520 |
| | | | 753 |
| Cheque not yet presented | | | - 120 |
| Balance per bank account | | | 633 |

By comparing the bank statement with the bank account on the previous page you will notice that there are some figures missing from the statement that the bank does not know about yet: the lodgment of €520 and the cheque for €120. When these are shown you get a new bank figure of €633.

## Activity 7.1 Chapter Review

**1** (a) What is bartering?
 (b) What forms of money are used in Ireland?
 (c) Why wouldn't sand be a good form of money?

**2** (a) Why do people save money?
 (b) What factors will influence where you save your money?
 (c) List four institutions where you could save your money and name the savings schemes offered by one of those you mention.

**3** (a) Why are cash dispensers so popular?
 (b) What services are available at a cash dispenser?
 (c) Name two bank services not available at a cash dispenser.

**4** (a) What do the letters ATM stand for?
 (b) What is a PIN used for at the ATM?
 (c) Why do people prefer to use the ATM rather than go into the bank?

**5** (a) What are the differences between a current and a deposit account?
 (b) Give two reasons why a current account is not a good place to save.

**6** (a) Explain what the following terms mean:
  (i) stale cheque
  (ii) blank cheque.
 (b) What does each of the following do to a cheque?
  (i) drawer
  (ii) drawee
  (iii) payee.
 (c) Why might a bank refuse to cash a cheque?

**7** Write the following amounts in words:
 (a) €45
 (b) €51
 (c) €89
 (d) €819
 (e) €3,413
 (f) €294
 (g) €756
 (h) €1,279
 (i) €5,826
 (j) €4,338.

**8** Write the following amounts in numerals:
 (a) Seventeen euro
 (b) Eighty-five euro
 (c) One thousand and four euro
 (d) Two hundred and seventy-five euro
 (e) Four hundred and sixteen euro
 (f) Fourteen euro
 (g) Sixty-four euro
 (h) Three thousand and seventy euro
 (i) Five hundred and twenty-six euro
 (j) Two hundred and eleven euro.

# Activity 7.2 Bank accounts

**1** (a) Prepare the bank account for Conor Ryan given the following information and balance the account:

    Jun 1  He had €210 debit balance in his bank account.

        5  He lodged his wages, €317, in the bank.

     10  He sent a cheque for €56 by letter to Hugh O'Neill.

     18  He paid a telephone bill of €106.

     23  He received a bonus of €70 and lodged it in the bank.

     26  He paid for petrol by cheque, €60.

  (b) What is an overdraft?

**2** (a) Prepare the bank account for Edward O'Grady given the following information and balance the account:

    Jul 1  He had €545 debit balance in his bank account.

        7  He sent a cheque for €98 by letter to Rory O'Connor.

     13  He lodged his wages, €923, in the bank.

     19  He paid his golf club membership by cheque, €300.

     27  He received a bonus of €30 and lodged it in the bank.

     31  He paid for petrol by cheque, €60.

  (b) Why is a current account not a suitable place to save money?

**3** (a) Prepare the bank account for Mary Melody given the following information and balance the account:

    Aug 1  She had €153 debit balance in her bank account.

        3  She received a cheque for €679 from Eileen Keane and lodged it in the bank.

     12  She bought a computer from Comsupp Ltd for €1,359 and paid by cheque.

     15  She paid a credit card bill of €254 by cheque.

     24  She paid for theatre tickets by cheque, €38.

     31  She paid for airline tickets by cheque, €260.

  (b) How much should she lodge to her current account to clear her overdraft?

**4** (a) Prepare the bank account for Aidan Doyle given the following information and balance the account:

    Sep 1  He had €23 credit balance in his bank account (overdrawn).

        9  He lodged his wages, €1,864, in the bank.

     12  He paid the mortgage by cheque, €450.

     17  He paid Quinn Direct for car insurance by cheque, €465.

     29  He received a cheque for €310 from Con Colbert and lodged it in the bank.

     30  He paid for groceries by cheque, €72.

  (b) What does '€23 credit balance' mean?

## Activity 7.3 Bank reconciliation statements

**1** On the right is Amy Smith's bank account and below it is the statement for February that arrives from the bank. Prepare a bank reconciliation statement and bring the bank account up to date.

| Dr | Bank Account | | | Cr | | | |
|---|---|---|---|---|---|---|---|
| Date | Details | F | Total | Date | Details | F | Total |
| Feb | | | € | Feb | | | € |
| 1 | Balance | b/d | 451 | 3 | Cash | ATM | 231 |
| 11 | Wages-lodged | | 616 | 14 | Telephone | 986 | 174 |
| 21 | Wages-lodged | | 642 | 19 | Electricity | 987 | 741 |
| | | | | 27 | Mattys Garage | 988 | 178 |
| | | | | 28 | Balance | c/d | 385 |
| | | | 1,709 | | | | 1,709 |
| 28 | Balance | b/d | 385 | | | | |

| | Bank Statement | | | |
|---|---|---|---|---|
| Date | Particulars | Debit | Credit | Balance |
| Feb | | € | € | € |
| 1 | Balance forward | | | 451 |
| 3 | ATM | 231 | | 220 |
| 11 | Lodgment | | 616 | 836 |
| 15 | Bank charges | 3 | | 833 |
| 18 | Car loan DD | 14 | | 819 |
| 21 | Cheque 987 | 741 | | 78 |
| 25 | Credit transfer | | 73 | 151 |

**2** On the right is Joe Burke's bank account and below it is the statement for March that arrives from the bank. Prepare a bank reconciliation statement and bring the bank account up to date.

| Dr | Bank Account | | | Cr | | | |
|---|---|---|---|---|---|---|---|
| Date | Details | F | Total | Date | Details | F | Total |
| Mar | | | € | Mar | | | € |
| 1 | Balance | b/d | 340 | 2 | Supermarket | 916 | 114 |
| 12 | Wages-lodged | | 2,100 | 9 | Telephone | 917 | 70 |
| 29 | Bonus-lodged | | 100 | 16 | Cash | ATM | 90 |
| | | | | 26 | Doctor | 918 | 55 |
| | | | | 30 | Balance | c/d | 2,211 |
| | | | 2,540 | | | | 2,540 |
| 30 | Balance | b/d | 2,211 | | | | |

| | Bank Statement | | | |
|---|---|---|---|---|
| Date | Particulars | Debit | Credit | Balance |
| Mar | | € | € | € |
| 1 | Balance forward | | | 340 |
| 4 | Cheque 916 | 114 | | 226 |
| 10 | Bank charges | 20 | | 206 |
| 12 | Lodgment | | 2,100 | 2,306 |
| 18 | Interest | 10 | | 2,296 |
| 21 | Cash ATM | 90 | | 2,206 |

**1** Linda Jones received the following bank statement through the post.

## AIB Bank, Ennis, Co. Clare

ACCOUNT: Linda Jones      Account No: 71429533
12 Shannon Street       Date: 31 May
Ennis

| Date | Particulars | Debit | Credit | Balance |
|------|-------------|-------|--------|---------|
| May | | € | € | € |
| 1 | Balance forward | | | 125 |
| 4 | Lodgment | | 250 | 375 |
| 10 | ATM Limerick | 60 | | 315 |
| 15 | Cheque no. 113 | 120 | | 195 |
| 26 | Bank charges | 10 | | 185 |

(a) In what bank and branch does Linda have her account?
(b) Is it a current account or a deposit account?
(c) Explain what happened on May 10.

Linda's own bank account in her record book looked like this on the same date.

| Dr | | | | | | Bank Account | | Cr |
|----|---------|-----|-------|------|----------|-----|-------|
| Date | Details | F | Total | Date | Details | F | Total |
| May | | | € | May | | | € |
| 1 | Balance | b/d | 125 | 10 | Cash | ATM | 60 |
| 4 | Lodgment | | 250 | 12 | Rent | 113 | 120 |
| | | | | 29 | Groceries | 114 | 40 |
| | | | | 31 | Balance | c/d | 155 |
| | | | 375 | | | | 375 |
| 31 | Balance | b/d | 155 | | | | |

Linda noticed that one of the items on the bank statement had not yet been entered in her bank account.
(d) Bring Linda's bank account up to date and show her adjusted balance.
(e) Make out a bank reconciliation statement for Linda.

(JCOL, adapted)

**2** Bríd O'Mara has a current account with Ulster Bank. She received this statement on 31 March.

### Ulster Bank Limited

| ACCOUNT: | Bríd O'Mara | | Account No: | 473815 |
|---|---|---|---|---|
| | Oak Lawn | | Account type: | Current |
| | Celbridge | | Statement No: | 73 |

| Date | Particulars | Debit | Credit | Balance |
|---|---|---|---|---|
| Mar | | € | € | € |
| 1 | Balance forward | | | 157 DR |
| 9 | Cheque 454 | 84 | | 241 DR |
| 10 | Lodgment | | 879 | 638 |
| 11 | ATM | 59 | | 579 |
| 13 | Cheque 452 | 124 | | 455 |
| 16 | SO Car loan | 118 | | 337 |
| 18 | Credit transfer | | 93 | 430 |
| 22 | DD Telephone | 57 | | 373 |
| 25 | Cheque 455 | 88 | | 285 |
| 31 | Current a/c fees | 8 | | 277 |
| 31 | Interest | 6 | | 271 |

Study this statement and answer the following questions:

(a) Explain what is meant by DR on 1 March.

(b) Explain the appearance of interest on the bank statement on 31 March.

(c) Name one use for an ATM card and a cheque card.

(d) Bríd O'Mara's employer has offered to pay her salary using Paypath. Explain what this means and state one advantage of it to her.

(e) The following is Bríd's own account of her bank transactions. Compare this bank account with the bank statement she received from the bank and answer these questions.

   (i) Make whatever adjustments are necessary to Bríd's own records to update her bank account.

   (ii) Prepare a bank reconciliation statement as on 31 March.

(JCHL, adapted)

| Dr | | | | | Bank Account | | | Cr |
|---|---|---|---|---|---|---|---|---|
| Date | Details | F | Total | Date | Details | F | Total | |
| Mar | | | € | Mar | | | € | |
| 7 | Salary | | 879 | 1 | Balance | b/d | 157 | |
| 31 | Sale of bicycle | | 45 | 6 | T. Nolan | 452 | 124 | |
| | | | | 7 | Hardware | 453 | 87 | |
| | | | | 8 | Car repairs | 454 | 84 | |
| | | | | 11 | Groceries | ATM | 59 | |
| | | | | 16 | Car loan | SO | 118 | |
| | | | | 21 | Insurance | 455 | 88 | |
| | | | | 31 | Balance | c/d | 207 | |
| | | | 924 | | | | 924 | |
| 31 | Balance | b/d | 207 | | | | | |

eTest.ie
Try a test on this topic

▶ Find out how to get a loan

▶ Read about the different ways to borrow money

▶ Learn how to calculate the cost of repayments on a loan

# Chapter 8

# Borrowing money

# Buy now, pay later

Credit involves buying something now and paying for it later. It may seem simple enough but there are many ways to borrow and the cost can vary greatly. The wise borrower will shop around and get the best deal.

Borrowing is so complicated that the rights of the borrower are protected by several laws, including the **Hire Purchase Acts 1946** and **1960** and the **Sale of Goods and Supply of Services Act 1980**. The main objective of these laws is to safeguard the borrower by making the lender disclose:

● the cash price of the goods
● the interest being paid.

**BUY NOW, PAY LATER**

MONTHS BUY NOW, PAY LATER PLAN     available ➤     WHEN YOU SPE €275 OR MO

# 22.99% APR fixed

No Deposit. Settle the loan in full by repaying the credit amount of €275 within 6 mo is not settled with 6 months of the date of the agreement, then pay 48 monthly in Total amount payable €452.16. Written quotations available on request. Finance years of age or over and resident in Ireland. Credit provided by Creation Consum Royston House, 34 Upper Queen Street, Belfast BT1 6FD. Terms and conditions

R BUY NOW PAY LA
Y TILL

## GIVING SECURITY FOR A LOAN

**Security** is your way of proving to the lender that you will repay the loan. There are two main forms of security: a guarantor and collateral. A **guarantor** is a friend or relative who signs a document agreeing to pay the interest and loan if you do not. For example, if you have no regular income or are under 18 years of age you may be required to get a guarantor, e.g. your mother or father.

**Collateral** is something valuable that can be sold if you fail to pay back the loan. For example, if you are looking for a loan to buy a house, the deeds of the house are given as collateral to the building society. This means that if you fail to pay the money due, the house can be sold and the debt cleared.

To get a loan you must first fill out a **loan application form** giving your name, address, occupation, earnings, other loans you may have and the purpose of the loan. You may have to get a guarantor or provide some collateral. Of course, you also have to prove that you will be able to pay the interest on the loan. A loan will normally be granted when:

- you can show you will be able to repay the loan and interest
- you can give suitable collateral
- you have a good savings record
- you were able to repay previous loans.

# CREDIT UNION

Credit unions offer loans at very low interest rates. The loans can be repaid as quickly as you like without penalty. Members take out loans for a variety of reasons, e.g. to buy a car, build a house extension or take a holiday. Every loan is insured by the credit union at no cost to the member. In the event of the member's death during the term of the loan, the loan is cleared by the insurance – this avoids any extra hardship on the family.

# Sources of finance ←

## short-term

Short-term loans must be repaid in less than a year, e.g. credit cards and bank overdrafts.

### Credit cards

Credit cards can be used for short-term borrowing to pay for holidays or to buy goods in many shops. The credit card company only requires you to pay a certain minimum amount each month, but they charge high interest rates on the outstanding balance.

### Bank overdraft

This is a short-term loan available to people with a current account. With the bank's permission you can write cheques even though you don't have enough money in your account and the bank will honour these cheques up to your overdraft limit.

## medium-term

Medium-term loans must be paid back over a period of one to five years, e.g. personal loans and hire purchase (HP).

### Personal loans

Personal loans are available from credit unions, banks and building societies. They are called personal loans because they are given to individuals and not to businesses.

### Hire purchase (HP)

HP is mainly used for the purchase of cars and expensive household goods. It is costly but popular because no security is necessary, the repayments are small and you get the goods at once. With HP you pay a deposit and then you make regular payments for a few years. The longer the period of time, the lower the

monthly repayments but the higher the total cost of the goods. You do not own the goods until the last repayment has been made and the cost is always greater than the cash price.

## long-term

Long-term loans must be paid back over a period of five to thirty years, e.g. a mortgage.

### Mortgage

A mortgage is a long-term home loan used to buy a house. You usually have to save with the bank or building society in order to get this loan.

## INTEREST

In most cases credit is expensive to buy. The price paid for credit is called interest.

### Rates of interest

The level of interest charged is called the interest rate. For example, an interest rate of 5% per annum means a person is charged €5 each year on every €100 borrowed. This is the cost of the loan, and different finance companies will charge different interest rates.

### Compound annual rate (CAR)

The CAR is the rate where the interest is added to the principal. The next year, if no loan repayment has been made the interest is based on a higher account balance.

### Annual percentage rate (APR)

The APR is the real cost of a loan when interest and additional charges related to the loan are taken into account. If you want to find the cheapest loan, compare the APR of the loans available to you. In the example below, the interest rate on a loan is the same in each of the banks. However, Bank A is the cheapest loan as the APR is 4.6%. The percentage difference may appear small, but on large sums borrowed this difference can amount to hundreds of euro each month.

| Loan | Interest Rate | APR |
|---|---|---|
| Bank A | 4% | 4.6% |
| Bank B | 4% | 5.1% |
| Bank C | 4% | 4.8% |

## GOING BANKRUPT

If a person cannot pay part or all of debts owed, certain assets given as collateral may be sold or the guarantor may be required to pay the balance due. If this is not enough to pay the debt, the person may be declared **bankrupt** or **insolvent**.

# Worked Examples

## Question

On 1 February 2010 Renita Keogh bought a mountain bike on hire purchase. She paid a deposit of €20 and agreed to pay 12 monthly instalments of €15 beginning on 1 March 2010.

(a) What is the total cost of the bike for Renita?

(b) When will Renita own the bike?

## Solution

**(a)**

| | € |
|---|---|
| Deposit | 99 |
| Repayments (12 x €150) | 435 |
| **TOTAL COST** | **1,450** |

**(b)** There are 12 monthly repayments and Renita will own the bike after the repayment on 1 February 2011.

## Question

Jean Sebastian got the following details about a €2,000 home cinema system.

Hire purchase: Deposit of €300 plus €160 per month for one year.

Rental: €50 per week.

(a) What is the total cost by hire purchase?

(b) What is the total rent for a year?

## Solution

**(a)**

| | € |
|---|---|
| Deposit | 300 |
| Repayments (12 x €160) | 1,920 |
| **TOTAL COST** | **2,220** |

**(b)**

| | € |
|---|---|
| TOTAL RENT (52 x €50) | 2,600 |

## Question

Philip got the following details about a €400 guitar.

Hire purchase: Deposit of €100 plus €14 per month for two years.

Personal loan: A €400 loan costs €5 each month per €100 borrowed for two years.

(a) What is the total cost by hire purchase?

(b) What is the total cost by personal loan?

## Solution

**(a)**

| | € |
|---|---|
| Deposit | 100 |
| Repayments (24 x €14) | 336 |
| **TOTAL COST** | **436** |

**(b)**

| | € |
|---|---|
| TOTAL COST (24 x €20) | 480 |

## Activity 8.1 Chapter Review

1. (a) What is credit?
   (b) Under the law, what must the lender disclose about a loan?
   (c) Why is it necessary to have collateral when you are getting a loan?

2. What is the difference between:
   (a) a guarantor and a guarantee?
   (b) a personal loan and a home loan?
   (c) income and interest?
   (d) a credit card and a cheque card?

3. (a) What services are offered by banks to facilitate short-term borrowing?
   (b) Explain how any one of these services works.

4. (a) Why is HP so popular?
   (b) Under HP, when do you own the goods?
   (c) Name two items that will be included in a HP agreement.

5. (a) Other than your name and address, name three items you must include on a loan application form.
   (b) What services are offered by credit unions to borrowers?

## Activity 8.2 Repayments

1. Calculate the cost of borrowing in each of these cases.
   (a) €700 borrowed for 18 months if it costs €7 per €100 per month.
   (b) €1,500 borrowed for 12 months if it costs €10 per €100 per month.
   (c) €1,500 borrowed for 18 months if it costs €6 per €100 per month.
   (d) €2,000 borrowed for 24 months if it costs €5 per €100 per month.
   (e) €3,000 borrowed for 36 months if it costs €4 per €100 per month.

2. A fridge-freezer costs €650 cash or €15 per week over one year with no deposit.
   (a) What is the HP price?
   (b) By how much is the HP price greater than the cash price?

3. A car may be bought for €14,000 cash or for a €2,000 deposit and €400 each month for three years.
   (a) What is the HP price?
   (b) By how much is the HP price greater than the cash price?

4. A friend of your family is buying a cooker and has asked your advice about HP. Which of these is a better HP arrangement?
   (a) A cooker for €600 cash or €200 deposit and repayments of €10 weekly for one year.
   (b) Another cooker for €600 cash or €100 deposit and repayments of €50 monthly for one year.

**1** On 1 December 2009 Gary McCarthy bought a Sonar music system on hire purchase. He paid a deposit of €50 and agreed to pay 12 monthly instalments of €40 beginning on 1 January 2010. The hire purchase company's name is High Finance Ltd, 25 Main Street, Limerick.

(a) What was the total cost of the music system for Gary?

(b) When would Gary become the owner of the music system?

Gary lost his job on 5 May 2010. He was made redundant because the firm for which he worked went bankrupt. On 10 May he wrote to the manager of the hire purchase company telling him about this. He also wrote that because he had lost his job he was unable to keep paying the instalments on the music system. He told the manager that he wished to end the hire purchase agreement and asked him to send someone to take away the music system.

(c) Write the letter that Gary sent to the hire purchase company. Gary's address is 12 Strand Road, Tralee, Co. Kerry.

(JCOL, adapted)

**2** Na Fianna Sports Club, Clonkeen, Co. Kerry, is considering the purchase of a new grass mower which has a retail price of €7,000. They have discovered the following alternatives:

**Option 1: Bank Loan**
Borrow €7,000 for three years on which interest is charged at a flat rate of 11% per annum. The loan and interest would be repaid in six equal half-yearly instalments.

**Option 2: Hire Purchase**
Pay a deposit of €500 plus 36 monthly instalments of €270 each.

**Option 3: Rental Purchase**
Pay a monthly rental of €190 each month for four years plus a final payment of €99 at the end of the lease to acquire ownership of the mower.

Calculate the total cost of each option.

(JCHL, adapted)

Try a test on this topic

# Personal *insurance*

# Covering your risks

The insurance business began 600 years ago. It came about largely because of the dangers of the sea, e.g. storms, pirates and scurvy. These dangers interfered with the lucrative business of trading European wool and cloth for Eastern silks and spices. Insurers or underwriters, as they are also called, agreed to compensate sailors and merchants who lost their cargoes and ships at sea, which encouraged trade.

Insurance, therefore, is concerned with risks, and most risks can be insured against. Examples of **insurable risks** are:
● house insurance
● holiday insurance
● car insurance.

There are also **noninsurable risks.** For example, you can't insure against the risk of failing an exam as it would be very difficult to quantify the risk involved and therefore the premium can't be calculated. In general, risks of a gambling nature can't be insured against.

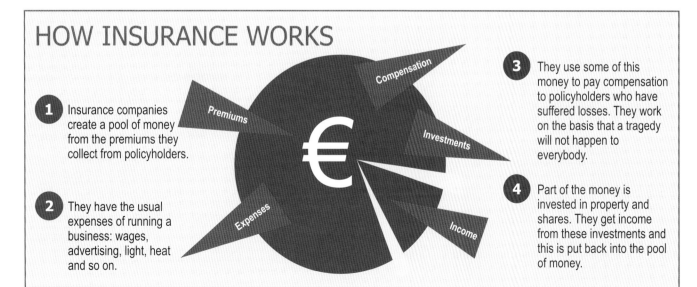

## HOW INSURANCE WORKS

**1** Insurance companies create a pool of money from the premiums they collect from policyholders.

**2** They have the usual expenses of running a business: wages, advertising, light, heat and so on.

Compensation
Premiums
€
Investments
Expenses
Income

**3** They use some of this money to pay compensation to policyholders who have suffered losses. They work on the basis that a tragedy will not happen to everybody.

**4** Part of the money is invested in property and shares. They get income from these investments and this is put back into the pool of money.

# TYPES OF INSURANCE ←

Risks that inevitably *will* happen, such as death or retirement, are covered under **life assurance** policies. Rsks that *may* happen, for example damage to a house or car, are covered under **general insurance**. The price paid for insurance is called the **premium**. In general, the greater the risk, the higher the premium.

## 1 Life assurance

Life assurance is not compulsory, though many people take it out. It covers death, retirement, school fees and investment schemes. It is concerned with risks that will occur. There are two types of policy offered:

### Whole life assurance

In this case the life of the person is insured. On the death of the insured person a lump sum is paid to a relative or close friend. A husband may insure the life of his wife and she may insure his life. Payment is made to the remaining spouse on the death of the other.

### Endowment assurance

This is a type of savings scheme designed to give you a lump sum of money after a number of years. Most are taken out for ten years, and during that time the insured pays monthly contributions. The benefits are:

- If the insured dies during this time, money is paid to a relative or friend.
- Most schemes allow the insured to **encash** the policy. This means that the insured stops the policy and gets cash before the term is finished. The money received is the **surrender value** of the policy.
- It is a useful way of saving and at the same time insuring your life.

## 2 House insurance

You don't have to, but most householders insure their house and its contents. The house is the actual bricks and mortar of the buildings. The contents are the furniture, clothes, wallpaper, carpet and even your bicycle if you have one. The risks covered are fire, flood and burglary. A few special cases are worth mentioning:

### All risks

Certain valuables, such as jewellery, golf clubs or laptop computers, may be specified in the policy for a special cover called 'all risks'. These items are then covered in the event of loss or accident and are even insured while they are outside the house.

### Loadings

There is a loading if the house is located in a risky area, e.g. somewhere prone to flooding.

### Discounts and deductions

There may be a discount if the house has an alarm.

### Average clause

If a house has a market value of €500,000 but is only insured for €250,000, the insured can claim only €250,000 if the house is completely destroyed. In the case of partial damage the average clause takes effect. So, for example, if a carpet valued at €800 is damaged, only €400 will be paid in compensation.

# Worked Examples

## Motor insurance

**3** Motor insurance is compulsory. It is a legal requirement for every car owner to have insurance on their vehicle.

### Third party, fire and theft
This is the minimum insurance that a driver must have on a car. The policy doesn't cover the driver or any damage to the vehicle. It only covers damage to a third party, i.e. someone you crash into or injure in some way.

### Fully comprehensive
This policy covers third parties as well as the driver and his or her vehicle. Although this type of motor insurance is not compulsory and is more expensive, most drivers prefer it.

### No-claims bonus
A no-claims bonus is a reduction on the premium because the insured person hasn't made a claim for one, or more, years.

### Loading
This is an extra amount added onto the premium because of additional risks. For example, there is a loading if the driver is under 30 years of age, the car is over ten years old or if the driver lives in an urban area.

### Discounts and deductions
A non-drinker may be given a discount on the premium.

## Question
Clara is quoted a basic life assurance premium of €650. There is a loading of 20% of the basic premium as she is an enthusiastic scuba diver. However, she gets a discount of 10% of the basic premium because she is a non-smoker. Calculate her premium.

## Solution

|  | € |
|---|---|
| Basic premium | 650 |
| + loading for scuba diving | |
| (650 x 20%) | 130 |
|  | 780 |
| – discount for non-smoker | |
| (650 x 10%) | 65 |
| **TOTAL PREMIUM** | **715** |

## Question
A house is valued at €400,000 and the contents at €50,000. Insurance for the house costs €3 per €1,000 value, and contents insurance costs €5 per €1,000 value. The owners decide to get the contents insured for the full value but only get the house insured for €200,000.

(a) Calculate the total premium.

(b) In the event of fire damage to the house of €50,000, how much compensation will be paid out?

## Solution

**(a)**

House
$$\frac{€200,000}{€1,000} \times €3 = €600$$

Contents
$$\frac{€50,000}{€1,000} \times €5 = €250$$

**(b)**

Average clause applies
$$\frac{€20,000}{€400,000} \times €50,000$$
$$= €25,000$$

## Question
A family has two cars. The €14,000 car has third party, fire and theft insurance costing €40 per €1,000 insured. The €18,000 car has fully comprehensive insurance costing €60 per €1,000 insured. Calculate the total premium for each car.

## Solution

**Car A**
$$\frac{€14,000}{€1,000} \times €40 = €560$$

**Car B**
$$\frac{€18,000}{€1,000} \times €60 = €1,080$$

# INSURANCE PEOPLE

## Actuary

The actuary is employed by the insurance company to determine the risk involved in something. Actuaries make extensive use of statistics to calculate risks and the premiums that should be charged.

## Insurance brokers

If you require insurance you may go directly to an insurance company or to a broker. The broker has information about the different policies offered by different insurance companies. Here you will get advice on which policy will best suit your needs. A small commission, called **brokerage**, is charged for this service.

## Loss adjuster

The loss adjuster is hired by the insurance company to determine whether the amount of the claim is fair. The loss adjuster studies the claim and may inspect the damage. A decision is then made on a fair settlement.

## Assessor

The person making a claim may also hire someone to determine the amount of the compensation. In this case the person is known as an assessor.

# DOCUMENTS

**Alpha Insurance Company Ltd**

PROPOSAL

| | |
|---|---|
| Name of proposer | *Stephen Collins* |
| Address | *4 Quay Street, Galway* |
| Occupation | *Journalist* |

| | |
|---|---|
| Estimated value of buildings | *700,000* |
| Estimated value of contents | *300,000* |
| All risks on jewellery | *5,000* |
| All risks on computer | *3,000* |
| Have you any other insurance on the above property? | *No* |
| Have you made a claim in the last five years? | *No* |

I declare that the above details are correct:

*Stephen Collins*

## Proposal form

This is the form you fill in when you are looking for insurance. It is like an application letter where you must tell the truth and reveal all the facts. Two important **principles of insurance** are relevant when applying for insurance.

- **Utmost good faith.** All facts must be revealed. If some details are withheld, the insurance company may refuse to pay out a claim.
- **Insurable interest.** The insured must suffer a loss in the event of the item insured being damaged.

## Cover note

There is usually a delay of a few days while the insurance company decides whether to insure you or not. In the meantime a temporary insurance, known as a **cover note**, may be issued.

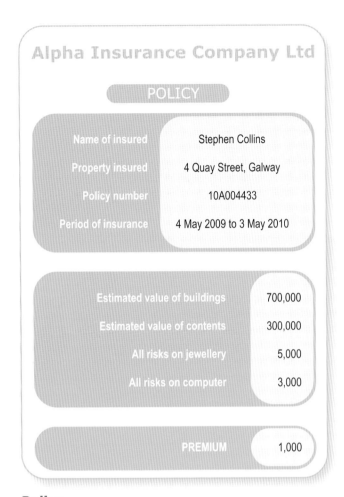

**Alpha Insurance Company Ltd**

**POLICY**

| | |
|---|---|
| Name of insured | Stephen Collins |
| Property insured | 4 Quay Street, Galway |
| Policy number | 10A004433 |
| Period of insurance | 4 May 2009 to 3 May 2010 |

| | |
|---|---|
| Estimated value of buildings | 700,000 |
| Estimated value of contents | 300,000 |
| All risks on jewellery | 5,000 |
| All risks on computer | 3,000 |

| | |
|---|---|
| PREMIUM | 1,000 |

**Alpha Insurance Company Ltd**

**CLAIM FORM**

| | |
|---|---|
| Name of insured | Stephen Collins |
| Address | 4 Quay Street, Galway |
| Policy number | 10A004433 |
| Details of loss | House burglary |

| Description | Date of purchase | Cost price | Wear and tear | Amount claimed |
|---|---|---|---|---|
| Computer | May 2009 | 1,200 | | 1,200 |
| Printer | May 2009 | 200 | | 200 |
| Camera | July 2008 | 800 | 200 | 600 |
| | | | TOTAL >>> | 2,000 |

I declare that the above details are correct:

*Stephen Collins*

## Policy

This is the contract between the insurance company and the insured. It gives details of the risks covered and any conditions attached to the policy. It is prepared by the insurance company.

## Claim form

In order to make a claim for compensation it's necessary to complete a claim form. You may be required to support this claim with estimates or quotations for the cost of repairing the damage or replacing the loss.

## Compensation

This is the money paid out by an insurance company as a result of a claim for damages or loss. The amount paid will depend on the damage caused. The insurance company will apply three insurance principles when a claim is made.

- **Contribution.** Suppose your family car is insured with two different companies. In the event of a claim each company will only pay a portion towards the loss.
- **Indemnity.** When an accident occurs, the insured person is entitled to compensation. However, he or she cannot make a profit out of the loss.
- **Subrogation.** When an insurance company pays you compensation it can then take over your rights against the person causing the loss.

## Activity 9.1 Chapter Review

**1**
(a) What are insurable risks? Give examples.
(b) What are noninsurable risks? Give examples.
(c) Briefly explain how insurance works.

**2**
What is the difference between:
(a) insurance and assurance?
(b) whole life assurance and endowment assurance?
(c) loadings and discounts?

**3**
(a) Give examples of general insurance.
(b) What would happen if someone were to encash a policy?
(c) What is the surrender value of a policy?
(d) How does the average clause work?

**4**
(a) What is the insurance premium?
(b) When do you get compensation?
(c) Explain what 'all risks' means.

**5**
What does each of these terms used in motor insurance mean?
(a) Third party, fire and theft.
(b) Fully comprehensive.
(c) No-claims bonus.

**6**
Briefly describe the work of each of these insurance people.
(a) Actuary.
(b) Insurance broker.
(c) Loss adjuster.
(d) Assessor.

**7**
Give the meanings of the following principles of insurance:
(a) utmost good faith
(b) insurable interest
(c) contribution
(d) indemnity
(e) subrogation.

**8**
When is each of these used?
(a) Proposal form.
(b) Policy.
(c) Claim form.
(d) Cover note.

eTest.ie
Try a test on this topic

## Activity 9.2 State Exam Practice

**1** David Egan, 13 River Road, Athlone has his house and contents insured with Delta Insurance Co. Ltd for a premium of €200 per year.

On 24 April he received a letter from Delta Insurance Co. Ltd stating that his premium was being increased to €600 a year because he lives in an area that is often flooded.

The next day, 25 April, he wrote to the insurance company stating that he was upset and disappointed over this huge increase in his annual premium. He stated that although he lives near a river, his house is build on high ground and has never been flooded. He would not mind paying a small increase but if Delta Ltd insisted on a premium of €600, he would have to transfer his business to another insurance company.

(a) Explain what a premium is.

(b) Name one type of insurance that it is necessary for a person to take out.

(c) Assume you are David Egan. Write the letter that he wrote to Delta Insurance Co. Ltd on 25 April.

(JCOL, adapted)

**2** (a) State one reason why people who own houses need to take out an insurance policy.

(b) When dealing with insurance, there are many terms involved, such as **proposal form, policy, risk, claim, compensation** and **average clause**.

Explain three of the terms underlined above.

(c) **Utmost good faith** is necessary in insurance. Explain what it means and state one reason why it is important.

(d) The Brogan family wish to insure their house for €250,000 and its contents for €90,000. They receive a quotation from an insurance company for €8 per €1,000 for the house and €15 per €1,000 for the contents.

Calculate the total cost of the premium they would have to pay.

(JCOL, adapted)

**3** (a) Explain the difference between insurable and noninsurable risks.

(b) Before taking out insurance, a person must complete a proposal form. State three pieces of information that must be answered in the proposal form for house insurance.

(c) What do insurance companies mean by the term 'insurable interest'? Explain briefly.

(d) John and Mary O'Brien live in their own house, have a family car and are both employed in full-time jobs.
  (i) What insurance cover, if any, are they required to have by law?
  (ii) State two other insurance/assurance policies that you would recommend to them.

(JCHL, adapted)

**4** (a) A female driver has fully comprehensive insurance on her car, which covers the contents being stolen. She also has her €3,000 computer covered under an all risks house insurance policy. She brings the computer in her car one day and it is stolen from the car.
  (i) Can she claim €3,000 under each insurance policy? Explain your answer.
  (ii) What is the maximum compensation she can receive?
  (iii) Which insurance company will compensate her?

(b) Under the average clause, how much compensation is likely to be paid out in the following cases?
  (i) A motorbike is crashed and completely destroyed. It was insured for €1,800, but the insurance company estimates that its true value before the accident was €2,600.
  (ii) A house fire ruins a carpet valued at €750. The house contents were insured for €3,000. However, the insurance company estimates that the true value of the contents before the fire was €6,000.
  (iii) A car insured for €5,000 is stolen and €1,600 worth of damage is caused by the thieves. The insurance company claims that the car was underinsured and that its true value before the robbery was €8,000.

(c) Calculate the premium payable on each of these properties.
  (i) An apartment valued at €350,000, rate of premium 50 cent per €1,000 insured.
  (ii) A bungalow valued at €460,000, rate of premium 40 cent per €1,000 insured.
  (iii) A terraced house valued at €230,000, rate of premium 30 cent per €1,000 insured.
  (iv) A detatched house valued at €500,000, rate of premium 40 cent per €1,000 insured.
  (v) An apartment valued at €290,000, rate of premium 30 cent per €1,000 insured.

(d) (i) A family car is valued at €14,500. The rate of premium is 40 cent per €1,000. Calculate the premium payable if there is a 40% no-claims bonus allowed.
  (ii) A 19-year-old is quoted a basic premium of €900 for car insurance, to which must be added €400 for underage loading. If a 15% beginner's discount is allowed, what premium is payable?

(JCHL, adapted)

# Chapter 10

# What is *economics?*

## Scarcity and choice

Economics looks at wealth – what it is and what causes it. By using the economic resources in Ireland we are able to create wealth, but because these resources are scarce we have to make choices to determine how to use them.

In economic terms, everything is **scarce**. Scarcity exists because the economic resources available to satisfy people's needs and wants are limited.

Our **needs** are food, clothing and shelter. Our **wants** are luxury items like motor cars and holidays. When we don't have enough money we usually have to make choices between our needs and our wants.

## CHOICE

The process of making choices is known as **economising**. Economising ensures you make the best use of the resources available to you. For example, your parents might want to go on a foreign holiday but they know that you need new clothes and they have to pay the mortgage. Faced with a limited amount of money they know they must economise and they may have to postpone the holiday. Similarly, if the government chooses to spend money creating new motorways less money may be available for housing, health and education.

There are four factors of production: land, labour, capital and enterprise. Our society has to decide how to use these in order to get the highest possible standard of living for the largest possible number of people.

# FACTORS OF PRODUCTION

### Land
This refers to natural resources, such as land, forests, rivers and the sea. From these we are able to get meat, cereals, wood, fish and other materials that can be used directly or processed in factories. People with land are paid **rent** for the use of the land.

### Labour
These are the people available to do the work on the land, in factories and in other businesses. They are paid **wages** for the work they do.

### Capital
This is the money needed to run businesses. This money is used to build factories and get the equipment needed to produce new products from raw materials. The money comes from people's savings and they are paid **interest** for the use of their money.

**Enterprise**
All resources need someone with a business idea and the courage to take a risk and start a business. This person is called an entrepreneur (a risk taker), and he or she gets **profit** as a reward for the risk involved in running a business.

# INFLATION

You might have heard or read news reports about rates of inflation. They usually say something like 'the inflation rate is 2%' or 'inflation has risen to 3% this year'. The rate of inflation is expressed as a percentage. An inflation rate of 1% or 2% is not so bad for a country but some countries have inflation rates of 70% or greater.

Inflation means rising prices. Rising wages sometimes follow rising prices but people aren't really any better off as the wages are used to buy goods which now cost more. Inflation makes it difficult for a family to budget because it's hard to guess what the prices of some goods will be. Inflation is also bad for savers and retired people since the money saved isn't worth as much. An inflation rate of 10% a year means that something which cost €200 last year will now cost €220.

### Consumer Price Index
The official measure of inflation in Ireland is called the Consumer Price Index (CPI). The CPI gets the price of a 'basket' of goods and services each month. These prices are then compared with the prices of the same goods and services from the previous month. The change in prices is then combined to give a single index measuring the overall level of prices.

### Causes of Inflation
The main reason for inflation in Ireland is increases in wages, which pushes up prices. High inflation can have both **positive and negative effects**.

- People who borrow money from banks benefit because the real rate of interest is reduced as prices rise.
- Irish exporters suffer because their goods become less competitive as prices rise.
- People who keep their savings in cash suffer as the purchasing power of cash is reduced, and as prices rise their money buys less.

# LOW INTEREST RATES

Interest rates can go up as well as down. When interest rates decrease there are advantages and disadvantages.

Advantages of low interest rates:
- cheaper loans
- more people are willing to invest in businesses.

Disadvantages of low interest rates:
- there is no incentive to save
- people may borrow more than they need and if interest rates rise again they may not be able to afford the repayments.

# ECONOMIC GROWTH

Economic growth occurs when during one year more goods and services are produced than in the previous year. For example, if a factory worker makes four chairs in one week and five in the next week, then his productivity has increased by 25%. In other words, he is producing more in the same time by making better use of the resources available to him.

The official measure of economic growth in a country is called the **gross national product** (GNP). The economic consequences resulting from growth in the economy are:
- a rise in the standard of living
- a rise in the number of people employed.

# RECESSION

Recession occurs when production in the economy decreases. Fewer goods are produced and therefore, fewer workers are needed.

The economic consequences resulting from recession in the economy are:
- a fall in the standard of living
- a rise in the number of people unemployed.

*Open for Business*

## Activity 10.1 Chapter Review

1. In economic terms, why is everything scarce?

2. Some products are scarce at certain times of the year, e.g. strawberries in winter. List five other products like this and say when they are scarce.

3. What is economising?

4. Name the economic resource associated with each of the following: rent, wages, interest, profit.

5. What is the economic term for rising prices?

6. What are the advantages and disadvantages of low interest rates?

7. What causes economic growth?

8. What is the effect of economic growth on the economy?

9. What do the letters GNP stand for?

10. If a carpenter makes 50 tables a month, what will the output be if he increases productivity by 10%?

11. What is a recession? What are the economic consequences of a recession?

## Activity 10.2 Inflation

1. What is meant by inflation?

2. What is the price of the following goods now?

   | Price last year | Annual inflation rate |
   | --- | --- |
   | €120 | 10% |
   | €80 | 5% |
   | €500 | 3% |

3. What is the inflation rate in each of these instances?

   | Price last year | Price this year |
   | --- | --- |
   | €100 | €115 |
   | €50 | €53 |
   | €20 | €30 |

4. What do the letters CPI stand for?

5. What are the causes of inflation?

## Activity 10.3 State Exam Practice

(a)    The bar graph below refers to the inflation rate of a country called Sombia.

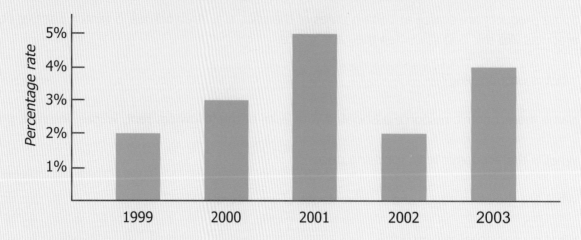

(i)    Explain what is meant by the term *inflation.*
(ii)   Calculate the average rate of inflation for the 5 years shown in the graph above.
(iii)  What change occurred in the rate of inflation in 2002 compared to 2001?
(iv)   Give *one* economic benefit to Ireland of having its inflation rate lower than that of its main trading competitors.

(b)    (i)    Land and capital are two factors of production. Explain what each of these means.
(ii)   There are two other factors of production. What are they?
(iii)  What is the purpose of the factors of production?

(c)    (i)    What are the disadvantages of high interest rates?
(ii)   What are the economic effects of a slow down in economic growth?

(JCHL, adapted)

Try a test on this topic

# Chapter 11

- ▶ Find out about the different types of government income and expenditure

- ▶ Read about what happens when the government sells a state company

- ▶ Learn how to prepare a national budget

# National *budget*

# Balancing the state books

The government spends billions of euro each year on our towns and cities. It also allocates money to local authorities, county councils and health boards that then provide services such as refuse collection, fire service, ambulance service, library service and much more. On your way to school every morning you see many examples of government spending on roads, buses, parks and even street lighting. The money for all this expenditure has to come from somewhere. So each year the government makes a budget. It is like the household budget we studied in Chapter 3 except this one is for the country: the national budget.

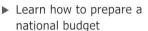

## THE NATIONAL BUDGET

The national budget is a forecast of government income and expenditure for the next calendar year (1 January to 31 December). It is prepared by the Department of Finance and is used to control what will happen to the economy in those months.

**Budget Day** is usually in December each year. For weeks before this the various government departments send in their estimates of expenditure to the Minister for Finance. In general the spending by the departments will take the form of either capital expenditure or current expenditure.

The total of the capital and current expenditure usually comes to millions of euro. The Department of Finance must get money to pay for this level of expenditure. They do this in two ways. They use capital income to pay for capital expenditure and current income to pay for current expenditure.

# Government income and expenditure

---

**capital expenditure**

This is the money the government plans to spend on long-term investments, such as:
- development of harbours and airports
- building new roads, transport, refuse collection
- building electricity power stations, hospitals, schools
- buying privately owned companies and turning them into state companies (**nationalisation**).

---

**current expenditure**

This is money they plan to spend on day-to-day items, for example the wages of medical staff, soldiers and Gardaí. It also includes social welfare expenditure, which is by far the biggest item in the budget. Building a new school is capital expenditure but paying the teachers' salaries is current expenditure.

---

**capital income**

This is also known as **nontax revenue**, which takes the form of money the state gets from the sale of state companies (**privatisation**) or borrowing from banks and from the EU. The money the government borrows is called the **national debt**. Paying back the money borrowed and paying interest is known as **servicing the national debt**. Capital income is used on long-term capital expenditure projects such as new roads, schools and hospitals. The state also gets nontax revenue from the National Lottery and from state company profits.

---

**current income**

The main source of current income for the government is tax. You pay tax when you buy clothes or a bar of chocolate (**VAT**), buy a banana (**customs duty**) or smoke a cigarette (**excise duty**). You also pay tax on your savings (**DIRT**). Businesses pay tax on their profits (**corporation tax**). The current income is then used to pay for the current expenditure during the year, such as teachers' salaries, nurses' salaries, unemployment benefit, old-age pensions, gardaí's salaries and children's allowance.

---

# PRIVATISATION

Privatisation is the sale of a state company to the public. In 1999 the government received €3.8 billion from the sale of Telecom Éireann (now called Eircom), and in 2006 Aer Lingus was privatised. The opposite of privatisation is **nationalisation**, where the state buys a company. In 2009 the government stepped in to nationalise Anglo Irish Bank to prevent the bank collapsing completely.

The advantages of privatisation are:
- more competition is introduced into the service, which can increase efficiency and reduce prices for the consumer
- the government receives money from the sale of the state company.

The disadvantages of privatisation are:
- the privatised company often reduces the number of employees in order to be more efficient and maximise profits
- the privatised company might not provide a service into an unprofitable area, e.g. if the postal service were privatised the new company might not deliver to remote areas.

## Effects on the National Budget

Different events will have different effects on the national budget. Consider the following.

What will be the effect on the national budget of more children being born in Ireland?
- There will be more expenditure on children's allowance.
- There will be more expenditure on maternity benefit.

What will be the effect on the national budget of an increase in unemployment in Ireland?
- There will be more expenditure on social welfare.
- There will be less tax revenue from income tax.

What will be the effect on the national budget of a wage increase for workers in Ireland?
- There will be more VAT revenue as the workers will have a higher standard of living and spend more.
- There will be more tax revenue from income tax.

The national budget lists the expenditure and income for the coming year. The difference between the total income and total expenditure is either a deficit or a surplus.

**Deficit budget**

When expenditure is greater than income there is a deficit. A government needs to borrow money in order to finance a budget deficit. This is called the **national debt**.

**Surplus budget**

When the income is greater than the expenditure there is a surplus. There are a few options open to the government:

- The surplus could be invested
- The surplus could be used to pay off loans
- Taxes could be reduced.

# Worked Example

## Question

**(a)** Draft a national budget from the following information.
Income: VAT €2,000 million; customs and excise €1,500 million; income tax €3,000 million; corporation tax €400 million; other income €80 million.
Expenditure: education €1,200 million; health €1,500 million; security €700 million; social welfare €2,500 million; agriculture €300 million; debt service €2,000 million; other expenditure €50 million.

**(b)** What is (i) the amount of the difference between the income and expenditure and (ii) the economic term used to describe this difference?

## Solution

**(a)**

| National Budget | | | |
|---|---|---|---|
| **Current Income** | | | € million |
| VAT | | | 2,000 |
| Customs and excise | | | 1,500 |
| Income tax | | | 3,000 |
| Corporation tax | | | 400 |
| Other | | | 80 |
| **Total Income** | | | **6,980** |
| **Current Expenditure** | | | € million |
| Education | | | 1,200 |
| Health | | | 1,500 |
| Security | | | 700 |
| Social welfare | | | 2,500 |
| Agriculture | | | 300 |
| Debt service | | | 2,000 |
| Other | | | 50 |
| **Total Expenditure** | | | **8,250** |
| **Difference (Deficit)** | | | **1,270** |

**(b)** (i) €1,270 million.
(ii) This is a deficit budget. The expenditure is greater than the income so there is a deficit. The government needs to borrow €1,270 million to finance this deficit. About half of this will be borrowed in Ireland and the rest abroad.

## Activity 11.1 Chapter Review

**1** (a) What does the government spend its money on?
(b) What is the national budget?
(c) Who prepares the national budget?
(d) When is Budget Day?

**2** What is the difference between:
(a) capital and current expenditure?
(b) capital and current income?
(c) surplus and a deficit?

**3** What do the following stand for?
(a) VAT
(b) DIRT.

**4** Explain each of the following:
(a) privatisation
(b) customs duty
(c) excise duty.

Try a test on this topic

**5** (a) What will be the effect on the national budget of more children being born in Ireland?
(b) What will be the effect on the national budget of an increase in unemployment in Ireland?

## Activity 11.2 Prepare national budgets

For each of the following questions: (a) draft a simple budget to show the sources of income and expenditure; and (b) estimate and identify whether there is a deficit or a surplus.

**1** INCOME: Income tax €2,500m; VAT €1,600m; Customs and excise €1,483m.
EXPENDITURE: Security €700m; Social welfare €2,498m; Education €1,015m; Health €2,100; Agriculture €400m; Interest payments €1,990m.

**2** INCOME: Corporation tax €1,527m; Customs and excise €897m; Income tax €2,950m; VAT €2,310.
EXPENDITURE: Health €2,300m; Security €600m; Education €980m; Interest payments €1,670m; Social welfare €2,127m.

**3** INCOME: EU receipts €70m; Corporation tax €245m; Customs and excise €1,254m; Income tax €3,500m; VAT €2,780m.
EXPENDITURE: Health €2,090m; Defence €236m; Garda €265m; Primary education €402m; Post-primary education €426m; Interest payments €1,173m; Social welfare €2,186m; Agriculture €168m; Fishing €120m; Roads €124m; Housing grants €215m.

**1** (a) Explain what **nationalisation** means.

(b) What is a **deficit budget**? What does the government need to do when there is a deficit budget?

(c) The following figures were presented by the Frostland Government on Budget Day.

| Main Items of Income and Expenditure | € Millions |
|---|---|
| Income from PAYE | 3,750 |
| Income from VAT | 2,940 |
| Health Services Expenditure | 2,350 |
| Social Welfare Expenditure | 2,120 |
| Education and Science Expenditure | 2,480 |

(i) Draft the National Budget of the Frostland Government from the above information.

(ii) Indicate whether it is a 'surplus' or a 'deficit' budget.

(JCOL, adapted)

**2** (a) (i) Explain the term '**National Budget**'.

(ii) State **two** advantages of privatisation.

(b) The following table shows the rate of inflation in a country over the past five years:

| Year: | 2000 | 2001 | 2002 | 2003 | 2004 |
|---|---|---|---|---|---|
| Rate: | 8% | 4% | 6% | 5% | 2% |

(i) Draw a line graph **or** bar chart to show the above information.

(ii) If the workers in the above country were granted a wage increase of 3% in 2003, explain the effects of this increase on their standard of living.

(iii) State **two** benefits to the consumer of the low inflation rate in 2004.

(c) The following figures were produced by a Minister for Finance on Budget Day:

| Main items of Revenue and Expenditure | € Millions |
|---|---|
| Debt Servicing | 190 |
| PAYE | 2,550 |
| VAT | 1,470 |
| Health Services | 1,720 |
| Social Welfare | 1,230 |
| Education and Science | 1,340 |
| Corporation Tax | 260 |
| Customs Duties | 235 |

(i) Draft the National Budget from the above information. State whether it is a surplus or a deficit budget.

(ii) Explain **two** effects of an increase in employment on the above National Budget.

(iii) Explain the following terms: debt servicing; corporation tax; customs duty.

(JCHL, adapted)

# Chapter 12

# Foreign *trade*

## Giving you a better choice

Goods purchased from other countries and brought into Ireland are called **imports**. Goods sold to foreign countries are **exports**. This exchange of goods is known as foreign trade. By trading with other countries Ireland is able to get a better choice of consumer goods, raw materials and producer goods.

Many of the goods we import are not made in Ireland, e.g. TVs, cars and some fruit and vegetables.

These **consumer goods** give Irish people a higher standard of living.

We also import **producer goods**. These are machines and equipment that are used to make other products.

Most of the goods we import are **raw materials** used in the manufacture of other products. For example, oil is imported from the Middle East and used in the production of plastics, paper is imported from Norway and used in the production of books.

## EXPORTS

Exports help Ireland earn foreign currency. Most of our exports are industrial products such as clothes, computers and chemicals. We also export agricultural, forestry and fishing produce. These exports are essential so that we can earn foreign currency to pay for the goods we wish to import.

However, there are **difficulties when exporting** and many firms find exporting is complicated and risky. For example, the goods have to be transported by ship or plane and could be stolen or damaged en route. It can also be hard to communicate or get payment when the customer speaks a foreign language.

*Chapter 12 Foreign Trade* 75

The import and export of goods such as cars, food and computers is called **visible trade**. **Invisible trade** deals with the import and export of services, e.g. tourism, banking, insurance and transport. Remember, when we export something money comes into Ireland. So when tourists come to Ireland it is recorded as an export because money comes into Ireland. However, when you take a foreign holiday it is recorded as an import since money leaves Ireland. When trying to decide if something is an import or export, always follow the money.

# Visible and invisible trade

| **balance of trade** | The difference between visible imports and exports is called the balance of trade. This difference is either a **trade surplus** (exports are greater than imports) or a **trade deficit** (imports are greater than exports). |

| **balance of payments** | When invisible trade is added to the balance of trade we get the balance of payments. If there is a deficit in the balance of payments we must pay for it by borrowing foreign currency. When it is a surplus we can increase our foreign currency reserves or invest more money abroad. |

| Visible and Invisible Trade | | | |
|---|---|---|---|
| **Visible Trade** | | € billion | € billion |
| Visible Exports | | 45 | |
| Less Visible Imports | | 30 | |
| **Balance of Trade — Surplus** | | | 15 |
| **Invisible Trade** | | | |
| Invisible Exports | | 13 | |
| Less Invisible Imports | | 25 | |
| **Invisible Balance — Deficit** | | | (12) |
| **Balance of Payments — Surplus** | | | 3 |

# OUR TRADING PARTNERS

Ireland trades with over one hundred countries around the world. However, the bulk of our trade is with European Union (EU) countries, the United States and Japan. Traditionally Britain has been the main source of our imports and destination for our exports.

## MEMBER STATES OF THE EU

| | | |
|---|---|---|
| Austria | Germany | Netherlands |
| Belgium | Greece | Poland |
| Bulgaria | Hungary | Portugal |
| Cyprus | Ireland | Romania |
| Czech Republic | Italy | Slovakia |
| Denmark | Latvia | Slovenia |
| Estonia | Lithuania | Spain |
| Finland | Luxembourg | Sweden |
| France | Malta | United Kingdom |

## EUROZONE

The Eurozone is a currency union of 16 European Union (EU) states which have adopted the euro as their sole legal tender. It currently consists of Austria, Belgium, Cyprus, Finland, France, Germany, Greece, Ireland, Italy, Luxembourg, Malta, the Netherlands, Portugal, Slovakia, Slovenia and Spain.

### The European Union (EU)

The EU is a market of 430 million consumers in 27 countries. The member states can trade freely with each other. Many of the members now use the euro currency and citizens in the member states may move to and work in any EU state.

The main benefits to Ireland of EU membership are:
- Ireland has received many grants to assist farmers and industry and to improve roads.
- We have also benefited by access to a wider market.
- Since Ireland joined the EU in 1973, hundreds of overseas companies have set up here, providing employment and exporting most of their produce.

# FOREIGN EXCHANGE

Foreign currency may be bought and sold at a bureau de change. Many banks, building societies and department stores offer this service. These institutions have two rates: the 'sell at' rate and the 'buy at' rate.

**1** When you are converting from the euro, the bank is selling you a foreign currency. In this case, multiply by the 'bank sells' rate.

**2** When you have foreign currency that you wish to change into euro, divide by the 'bank buys' rate.

# Worked Examples

## Question

Draft the balance of trade and the balance of payments from the following information. Say if there is a surplus or deficit.

Visible Exports, €8 billion
Invisible Exports, €15
Visible Imports, €12
Invisible Imports, €5

## Solution

| Balance of Trade and Balance of Payments | | | |
|---|---|---|---|
| **Visible Trade** | | € billion | € billion |
| Exports | | 8 | |
| Less Imports | | 12 | |
| **Balance of Trade — Deficit** | | | (4) |
| **Invisible Trade** | | | |
| Exports | | 15 | |
| Less Imports | | 5 | |
| **Invisible Balance — Surplus** | | | 10 |
| **Balance of Payments — Surplus** | | | 6 |

| Bureau de Change | | | |
|---|---|---|---|
| COUNTRY | CURRENCY | BANK SELLS | BANK BUYS |
| Britain | Pound (£) | 0.68 | 0.72 |
| Norway | Kroner (Kr) | 7.27 | 7.70 |
| USA | Dollar ($) | 1.11 | 1.16 |
| Japan | Yen (¥) | 1.32 | 1.41 |

## Question

Convert €200 to pounds sterling.

## Solution

€200 x 0.68 = £136

## Question

Convert $150 to euro.

## Solution

$150 ÷ 1.16 = €129.31

## Activity 12.1 Chapter Review

1. (a) Why does Ireland export goods?
   (b) Explain why importing is important to Ireland.
   (c) Why does Ireland export goods?
   (d) List five exports from Ireland.

2. List two difficulties firms might experience when exporting.

3. Explain the difference between:
   (a) importing and exporting
   (b) consumer goods and producer goods
   (c) visible and invisible trade
   (d) a trade surplus and a trade deficit.

4. (a) List three counties we import from.
   (b) List three countries we export to.

5. List three benefits to Ireland of being a member of the EU.

## Activity 12.2 Balance of trade and balance of payments

From the following details prepare a balance of trade and a balance of payments and indicate if there is a surplus or a deficit.

1. Visible imports €15 billion, visible exports €17 billion, invisible imports €6 billion, invisible exports €9 billion.

2. Visible imports €9 billion, visible exports €12 billion, invisible imports €5 billion, invisible exports €4 billion.

3. Visible imports €14 billion, visible exports €15 billion, invisible imports €5 billion, invisible exports €2 billion.

## Activity 12.3 Convert currencies

Using the rates on the opposite page, answer the following.
(a) Convert €36 to pounds sterling.
(b) Convert €50 to Norwegian kroner.
(c) Convert €80 to US dollars.
(d) Convert €95 to Japanese yen.
(e) Convert €45 to pounds sterling.
(f) Convert 30,000 yen to euro.
(g) Convert 5,000 US dollars to euro.
(h) Convert 3,000 Norwegian kroner to euro.
(i) Convert 3,000 yen to euro.
(j) Convert 4,000 pounds sterling to euro.

## Activity 12.4 State Exam Practice

(a)  (i) With which country does Ireland do most of its trade?
  (ii) Give **one** benefit of imports to the Irish consumer.
  (iii) State **one** reason why exporting is very important for the success of the Irish economy?
  (iv) State **one** difficulty which an Irish firm would experience when exporting goods.

(b) Give **two** examples of Ireland's invisible imports.

(c) The following data relates to the international trade of a country called Agola for the year 2009.

| | € |
|---|---|
| Visible Exports | 9 Billion |
| Invisible Exports | 18 Billion |
| Visible Imports | 13 Billion |
| Invisible Imports | 6 Billion |

Calculate the following trade figures in relation to Agola and state whether they are a surplus or a deficit.
  (i) Balance of trade.
  (ii) Balance of payments.

(d) An Irish importer was quoted stg£18,600 for a new car by an English garage. Your local bank had the following information on a display board in the bank.

| | Bank sells | Bank buys |
|---|---|---|
| Sterling | 79.71 | 80.34 |

  (i) Calculate the cost of the car in euro.
  (ii) State one suitable way for the Irish importer to pay the English garage.

(JCHL, adapted)

eTest.ie
Try a test on this topic

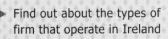

# Chapter 13

# Forms of *business*

## Public and private sector

Ireland has a **mixed economy** with two broad areas of business activity: the private sector and the public sector. Businesses in the private sector are owned by individuals or shareholders and aim to make a profit by getting as large a share of the market as possible. These businesses range in size from small local shops selling a small range of goods to large companies selling in Ireland and overseas.

Companies in the public sector are owned by the state and aim to provide essential services, ensure national security and protect jobs. They include RTÉ, the Gardaí, Coras Iompar Éireann (CIE), An Post, Electricity Supply Board (ESB) and Bord Gáis Éireann.

## COMPARING

Exam questions often require you to compare different forms of business, so when studying this chapter think in terms of the following.

- How is the business set up? (E.g. sole traders are easy to set up but limited companies take time, money and paperwork.)
- Who owns the business? (One individual, several shareholders or the state?)
- How is the business financed? (Does one person put up all the money to start the business or are there shareholders?)
- Who gets the profits? (Does one person get all the profit or is it divided between the shareholders?)
- Does the business have limited liability? (Explained in this chapter.)
- Is it a big or a small business? (Does it have many employees?)

# Private sector

There are four main types of business in the private sector: sole trader, franchise, co-operative and private limited company.

## sole trader

There are thousands of sole traders in Ireland, e.g. the local butcher, newsagent, hairdresser, barber, farmer, builder, taxi driver and solicitor. This is the most common form of business ownership because it is so easy to set up. There are no legal requirements and the only procedure is to register for VAT.

The sole trader has complete control over the running of he business and is his or her own boss. All decision, plans and ideas belong to and are implemented by the owner.

Since there is no one else involved the sole trader must finance the business and provide all the capital by using savings and any loans available. However, the advantage is that the sole trader gets to keep all the profit.

The main drawback is that the sole trader has **unlimited liability**. This means that the sole trader takes all the risks and is personally liable for any debts of the business, even to the extent that his or her own personal possessions may be sold to pay business debts, e.g. a private house and car may be sold to pay off business debts.

## franchise

This is the most modern type of business ownership. The best known franchise is McDonald's; other examples are Abrakebabra and Benetton. Franchises are popular because they have a winning formula. They are based on successful companies and run under licence. The franchiser owns the licence and the franchisee pays for the right to use the franchiser's business name and reputation.

Banks love franchises because they can see similar businesses that have been successful. They are usually happy to give them loans. The franchise has limited liability but the risk associated with this type of business is smaller as there is a proven success rate.

The main drawback is that the franchisee pays rent to the franchiser and also has to pay a share of the profits each year. Another disadvantage is that the franchiser controls the product, packaging and any slogans used.

## co-operative

A co-operative is a business that is run for the benefit of its members. In Ireland the main co-operative you may be aware of is the local credit union. The credit union is a co-op that is run by the members to provide a place for its members to save and to give them loans. Farmers' markets are another type of co-op that has become more common recently. These are locally run co-ops providing the members with fresh farm produce.

Co-ops are financed by the members themselves who buy shares in the co-op. Each member has one **vote** regardless of the number of shares held. The profit is distributed in relation to the amount of work a member does.

The members have limited liability. So if the co-op fails they only stand to lose the amount they have invested by buying shares in the co-op. However, most co-ops are successful as the members themselves are the main market for the product or service provided.

## private limited company

A private limited company usually has the letters Ltd (limited) or Teo (teoranta) after its name, e.g. Brookwood Motors Ltd. It is financed by a group of friends or family members. Each person becomes a shareholder and each share has a vote. So the more shares you own the more votes you have when it comes to making decisions.

The big advantage is that the shareholders have **limited liability**. They only stand to lose the amount they have invested by buying shares in the business. Any profits are divided out at the end of the year between the shareholders. This is known as a dividend. The more shares you own, the bigger the dividend you will receive.

The shareholders own the company but they elect a board of directors each year to run the company. This election takes place at the annual general meeting (AGM). Each share has one vote, so a shareholder with 1,000 shares has 1,000 votes.

Creating a private limited company is complex and is dealt with in the next chapter.

# Public sector

The state gets involved in running businesses for a number of reasons. To begin with, the state must take control of national defence and security, so the army, navy and An Garda Síochána are all run by the state. These are all essential services that cannot be left to private enterprise.

The state is also involved in businesses which require a large amount of capital to start up, e.g. Bord Gáis, DART, ESB and RTÉ. The government provides the capital to run these very large businesses and acts as a guarantor for loans taken out.

Any losses sustained by the business are financed by getting additional loans or extra funding from the state.

Each state company is responsible to a government minister. The minister appoints a board of directors to run the company. The board decides the firm's policy and appoints executives to carry out their policies on a day-to-day basis.

Any profits not retained by the companies are given to the government in the form of a dividend.

## Activity 13.1 Chapter Review

1. What is the difference between the private sector and the public sector?

2. What is a sole trader?

3. What is a franchise?

4. Why do banks like lending to franchises?

5. Give three examples of franchise businesses.

6. What is a co-operative?

7. How many votes does each member of a co-op have?

8. What is a private limited company?

9. How many votes does each shareholder in a private limited company have?

10. What is limited liability?

11. Give four examples of state bodies.

12. Why does the state get involved in transport?

## Activity 13.2 Sole traders

1. List three advantages of being a sole trader.

2. List three disadvantages of being a sole trader.

3. Write down whether each of the following is a sole trader, franchise, co-operative, private limited company or state-owned company:
   - (i) Bord na Mona
   - (ii) Peter Smith, Butcher
   - (iii) Kenmare Credit Union
   - (iv) Music Wholesalers Ltd
   - (v) RTÉ.

4. Describe two differences between a sole trader and a private limited company.

**1** James mixed up the answers in his Business Studies test. He had all the correct explanations but put them in the wrong sentences. This is what he wrote.

    (i) A sole trader is *a safeguard that shareholders can only lose what they invested in a business.*

    (ii) A board of directors is *a business owned and run by its members.*

    (iii) Limited liability is *a business owned and controlled by the government.*

    (iv) A co-operative is *appointed by shareholders to run a company.*

    (v) A state-owned company is *a chance that all money invested could be lost if a business fails.*

    (vi) Unlimited liability is *a business owned and run by one person.*

Compete, in full, each sentence showing the more appropriate explanation in **each** case.

(JCOL, adapted)

**2** The following information, on forms of business ownership in a country, was obtained from a survey.

| Forms of business ownership | State-owned | Co-operatives | Sole Traders | Private Limited Companies |
|---|---|---|---|---|
| Number | 4 | 2 | 28 | 16 |

(a) Illustrate this information on a bar chart.

(b)   (i) List **four** examples of state-owned businesses.
     (ii) Explain **two** reasons why state-owned business exist in Ireland.

(c) Compare sole traders and private limited companies under the following headings:
    (i) ownership
    (ii) formation procedures
    (iii) profits
    (iv) liability.

(JCHL, adapted)

eTest.ie
Try a test on this topic

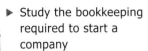

# Chapter 14

▶ Read about the people and money behind companies

▶ Find out about the documents necessary to start a company

▶ Study the bookkeeping required to start a company

# Private limited company

# Forming a company

A private limited company is owned by 2–50 **shareholders**. These shareholders contribute the capital by buying shares in the company. This is the money used by the firm, together with any loans the company can negotiate.

Usually a group of business people will get together because they have an idea for a business. They will select a company name and get stationery designed, e.g. invoices and order forms. They will then complete (a) the memorandum of association, (b) the articles of association and (c) sign a declaration of compliance stating that they agree to follow the rules of company law. They send these to the Companies Registration Office in Parnell Square, Dublin. If all is in order the Companies Office will send them back a Certificate of Incorporation.

## CAPITAL

Capital is the money used to finance the running of the company. There are two types you need to know about.

- **Authorised share capital** is the maximum amount of ordinary share capital a company may issue. This is also called the **nominal share capital**.
- **Issued share capital** is the actual amount of ordinary shares the company has sold. It is the money invested in the company by the shareholders (the owners). For example, a company may have an authorised share capital of €500,000 but only have an issued share capital of €300,000. This means they could issue a further €200,000 if necessary.

## CERTIFICATE OF INCORPORATION

The Registrar in the Companies Registration Office gives a **Certificate of Incorporation** to companies that comply with the Companies Acts. The business can put 'Ltd' in the company name and the shareholders have **limited liability**. This means that if the business fails they only stand to lose the amount they have invested in the company by way of buying shares. Their private resources cannot be sold to pay company debts.

# Company documents

## Memorandum of Association

| | |
|---|---|
| Company name: | **PJs Ltd** |
| Address: | **Castle Ave, Kilkenny** |
| Objectives: | **To manufacture clothes** |
| Authorised share capital: | **50,000 €1 ordinary shares** |

| Shareholders | Shares |
|---|---|
| Pat McCarthy: Castle Ave, Kilkenny | 15,000 |
| Jill McCarthy: Castle Ave, Kilkenny | 15,000 |
| **Total shares issued** | **30,000** |

**Signed:** *Pat McCarthy*
*Jill McCarthy*

**Date:** 1 October

## Articles of Association

The AGM will be held on 15 January each year. Directors will be elected at the AGM for three years. Each share will have one vote.

| Directors' names and addresses |
|---|
| Pat McCarthy: Castle Ave, Kilkenny |
| Jill McCarthy: Castle Ave, Kilkenny |

**Signed:** *Pat McCarthy*
*Jill McCarthy*

**Date:** 1 October

The **memorandum of association** shows the relationship between the company and the shareholders, i.e. the internal rules. It should contain:
- the name of the company
- the company's address
- the company's objectives, e.g. whether it will be a factory making computers, a shop selling clothes and so on.

The **articles of association** shows the relationship between the company and the outside world, i.e. the external rules. It must be signed by at least two people and should contain:
- the frequency of meetings for shareholders. A company must hold at least one meeting each year for the shareholders – the **annual general meeting** (AGM)
- the election procedures and the voting rights of shares. Normally each share has one vote.

# Worked Example

A firm gets money from the owners. This is called the **capital**. A firm uses this money to buy resources, e.g. premises, vans, stock. These resources are the firm's **assets**. The capital is a **liability** of the firm. In its simplest form, this can be recorded as

## ASSETS = LIABILITIES

## Question

On 1 October Alan and Barbara form a limited company called AB Ltd. The company has an authorised share capital of 200,000 €1 ordinary shares. Alan and Barbara each buy 30,000 €1 shares in the company. The money received from the sale of the shares is lodged to the company bank account.

(a) Show the entries in the bank account and the ordinary share capital account.

(b) Prepare a balance sheet for the new company.

## Solution

(a)

| Dr | Bank Account | | | | | | Cr |
|---|---|---|---|---|---|---|---|
| Date | Details | F | Total | Date | Details | F | Total |
| Oct | | | € | Oct | | | € |
| 1 | OSC | | 60,000 | | | | |

| Ordinary Share Capital Account | | | | | | | |
|---|---|---|---|---|---|---|---|
| Oct | | | € | Oct | | | € |
| | | | | 1 | Bank | | 60,000 |

(b)

| Balance Sheet as at 1 October | | | |
|---|---|---|---|
| | | | € |
| **Assets** | | | |
| Bank | | | 60,000 |
| | | | 60,000 |
| **Financed by** | | | |
| Ordinary Share Capital | | | 60,000 |
| | | | 60,000 |

## TIPS ON ANSWERING THIS QUESTION

When you are answering this question you need to keep the following in mind.

**Ledger Accounts**
A ledger account is created for the bank. The €60,000 is entered on the debit (Dr) of the bank account as money is coming into the business. Now we must enter it a second time. The other account we use is the ordinary share capital (OSC) account. It is entered on the credit (Cr) of the OSC account, i.e. the opposite side to the entry in the bank account. This is known as double-entry bookkeeping.

**Balance Sheet**
The balance sheet is used to record the assets and liabilities of a firm. The assets are the things the company owns, i.e. the money it has and the things it spends its money on. The liabilities are the things it owes and that finance the business. The total of the assets must equal the total of the liabilities. In our example we only have one asset: bank, €60,000; and we only have one liability: OSC, €60,000.

## Activity 14.1 Chapter Review

**1** (a) Who are the owners of a private limited company?
   (b) Name **two** documents which must be completed when setting up a private limited company.
   (c) Where are these documents sent?

**2** (a) What is capital?
   (b) What is the authorised share capital of a company?
   (c) What is the issued share capital of a company?
   (d) Suppose a company has an authorised share capital of €500,000 and an issued share capital of €300,000. How many other shares could this company issue?

**3** (a) What is the certificate of incorporation?
   (b) What is limited liability?
   (c) Does a private limited company have limited liability?

**4** (a) What is the AGM?
   (b) How often is the AGM held?
   (c) Who attends the AGM of a private limited company?

**5** (a) Name **three** items contained in the memorandum of association.
   (b) Name **three** items contained in the articles of association.
   (c) Which of these documents contains information about the AGM?

**6** (a) Where does a private limited company get money to start the business?
   (b) What does the company do with this money?
   (c) What are assets?
   (d) Name a liability of a company.

**7** (a) What is recorded in the balance sheet?
   (b) What do you call things the company owns?
   (c) What do you call things the company owes?
   (d) What are assets always equal to?

eTest.ie
Try a test on this topic

## Activity 14.2 Ledger accounts and balance sheet

**1** On 1 March last year Carl and Rita form a limited company called Cari Ltd. The company has an authorised share capital of 300,000 €1 ordinary shares. Carl and Rita each buy 50,000 €1 shares in the company. The money received from the sale of the shares is lodged to the company bank account.
(a) Show the entries in the bank account and the ordinary share capital account.
(b) Prepare a balance sheet for the new company.

**2** On 1 April last year Sylvia and Bill form a limited company called Sybil Ltd. The company has an authorised share capital of 100,000 €1 ordinary shares. Sylvia and Bill each buy 25,000 €1 shares in the company. The money received from the sale of the shares is lodged to the company bank account.
(a) Show the entries in the bank account and the ordinary share capital account.
(b) Prepare a balance sheet for the new company.

**3** On 1 May last year Harry and Maria form a limited company called Hama Ltd. The company has an authorised share capital of 200,000 €1 ordinary shares. Harry and Maria each buy 50,000 €1 shares in the company. The money received from the sale of the shares is lodged to the company bank account.
(a) Show the entries in the bank account and the ordinary share capital account.
(b) Prepare a balance sheet for the new company.

## Activity 14.3 State Exam Practice

**1** On 1 June last year, John Regan of 22 Moy Road, Ballina, Co. Mayo and Nuala Murray of 31 Straide Road, Castlebar, Co. Mayo formed a private limited company called Castina Ltd. The objective of the company is to create websites for customers. The authorised share capital of the company is 100,000 ordinary shares of €1 each. John purchased 20,000 shares and Nuala purchased 10,000.
From the above details, complete a memorandum of association *(there is one supplied in the workbook).*
(JCOL, adapted)

**2** The majority of small businesses in Ireland are owned by sole traders.
(a) State **two** advantages of being a sole trader.
(b) State **two** disadvantages of being a sole trader.

A private limited company is also a common form of business in Ireland.
(c) What do you call the owners of a private limited company?
(d) Name **one** of the legal documents which must be completed when setting up a private company.
(e) State **two** advantages of a private limited company.
(f) State **two** differences between a sole trader and a private limited company.
(JCOL, adapted)

**3** (a) Explain **two** of the following forms of ownership: (i) sole trader; (ii) co-operative; (iii) state ownership.

(b) On 1 May last year Nora Martin, 5 Marino Close, Bray, Co. Wicklow and Joseph O'Connor, 14 Strand Road, Bray, Co. Wicklow formed a private limited company called Educu Books Ltd. They prepared a Memorandum of Association and sent it with all the necessary documents to the Registrar of Companies.

The objectives of the company are to publish and sell educational books. The authorised share capital of Educu Books Ltd is 100,000 €1 ordinary shares.

On 12 May Nora Martin and Joseph O'Connor purchased 25,000 €1 ordinary shares each. The money received from the issue of the shares was lodged to the company bank account.

You are required to:
  (i)  complete the Memorandum of Association *(there is one supplied in the workbook).*
  (ii)  record the issue of shares on 12 May in the ordinary share capital and bank accounts.
  (iii) prepare the opening balance sheet of the company on 12 May.

(JCHL, adapted)

**4** On 1 May last year Maria Burke of 4 Bridge Street, Athlone, Co. Westmeath and Mike Mitchell of 10 Shannon View, Athlone, Co. Westmeath formed a private limited company called At Your Service Ltd. They prepared a Memorandum of Association and sent it and all the other necessary documents to the Registrar of Companies. A Certificate of Incorporation was then issued.

The objective of the company is to provide computer and secretarial services.
The authorised share capital of At Your Service Ltd is 80,000 €1 ordinary shares.

On 10 May Maria Burke purchased 20,000 shares and Mike Mitchell purchased 15,000 shares. The money received from the issue of these shares was lodged to the company bank account.

You are required to:

(a) Complete the Memorandum of Association *(there is one supplied in the workbook).*

(b) Explain **two** advantages of forming a private limited company.

(c) Name **two** other documents which should be sent to the Registrar of Companies when forming a private limited company.

(d)  (i)  Record the issue of shares on 10 May in the ordinary share capital and bank accounts.
     (ii) Prepare the opening balance sheet of the company on 10 May.

(JCHL, adapted)

# Preparing a business plan

## Knowing where you're going

Before a business applies for a loan it may be necessary to make out a **business plan** showing how the business will develop over the next few months. This plan will help you to:

- focus on what is really important in order to be successful
- sound more convincing when you apply for a bank loan

- describe the strengths of your business and the opportunities you are planning to exploit
- identify the weaknesses and threats facing your business.

A very important part of your business plan will be a cash flow forecast. This is very like the household budget you studied in Chapter 3. There is a list of receipts (income) and a list of payments (expenditure).

## ESTIMATES

When preparing a cash flow statement it is necessary to estimate how much cash will be received and paid out over the coming months. Planning ahead like this will help identify times when cash may be scarce. Estimates are really guesses at what is likely to happen. For example, guessing what the sales will be. Or guessing how much the wages, phone and electricity bills will be. When a businessperson has years of experience their guesses can be quite accurate. The whole idea is to try and identify when there may be a cash shortage, and then make a plan to deal with this.

One important short-term source of finance is the **bank overdraft**. This is a loan from the bank which can get a company out of a temporary shortage of cash. When a company runs short of money it is said to be **cash starved**. This is one of the main reasons for business failure. To plan for cash shortages and to minimise them, firms need to monitor the flow of money in and out of the business. This is known as the cash flow.

# PREPARING THE CASH FLOW FORECAST

Consider the following situation that Peter Ryan, an electrician, finds himself in. He has been asked if he would like the job of wiring houses on a new estate. The work will take five weeks to carry out and he will get paid €10,000 when the job is completed. He has €1,000 cash at the moment and he estimates he will have many expenses over the four weeks as shown below:

**Materials**
- sockets (€40 each week)
- wire (€90 in weeks 2, 3 and 4)
- fittings (€40 in week 5).

**Wages**
- for himself (€300 each week)
- for an assistant (€100 in weeks 2, 3 and 4).

**Other expenses**
- petrol (€50 each week)
- telephone (€10 each week)
- postage and stationery (€10 in weeks 2, 3 and 4).

## Estimates of receipts and payments

**Estimate of receipts**
Peter's only income is €10,000 from sales and he will not receive a cent of this money until week 5.

**Estimate of payments**
Peter has to pay for materials, e.g. sockets, wire and fittings. He also has to pay wages to himself and an assistant. He has other expenses such as petrol, telephone and postage and stationery.

**Surplus, deficit**
Peter has a deficit in weeks three and four.

When we summarise the receipts and payments we can see that it will be a profitable job. However, when we study the cash flow forecast we can see that Peter will run out of cash in the third and fourth weeks. If he doesn't plan for this shortage he will go out of business (**go bankrupt**) and never get to see his profit.

| CASH FLOW FORECAST | WEEK 1 | WEEK 2 | WEEK 3 | WEEK 4 | WEEK 5 | TOTAL |
|---|---|---|---|---|---|---|
| RECEIPTS | € | € | € | € | € | € |
| Sales | 0 | 0 | 0 | 0 | 5,000 | 5,000 |
| A.  TOTAL RECEIPTS | 0 | 0 | 0 | 0 | 5,000 | 5,000 |
| PAYMENTS | | | | | | |
| Sockets | 40 | 40 | 40 | 40 | 40 | 200 |
| Wire | 0 | 90 | 90 | 90 | 0 | 270 |
| Fittings | 0 | 0 | 0 | 0 | 40 | 40 |
| Wages for himself | 300 | 300 | 300 | 300 | 300 | 1,500 |
| Wages for assistant | 0 | 100 | 100 | 100 | 0 | 300 |
| Petrol | 50 | 50 | 50 | 50 | 50 | 250 |
| Telephone | 10 | 10 | 10 | 10 | 10 | 50 |
| Postage and stationery | 0 | 10 | 10 | 10 | 0 | 30 |
| B.  TOTAL PAYMENTS | 400 | 600 | 600 | 600 | 440 | 2,640 |
| Net Cash (A – B) | (400) | (600) | (600) | (600) | 4,500 | 2,360 |
| Opening Cash | 1,000 | 600 | 0 | (600) | (1,200) | 1,000 |
| Closing Cash | 600 | 0 | (600) | (1,200) | 3,360 | 3,360 |

Now that he knows when the **cash problems** are likely to occur, he can plan to meet them. He could:

- ask for payment in instalments
- try to buy materials on credit from his suppliers
- negotiate an overdraft with his bank manager.

If he solves the problem of the cash shortages in the third and fourth weeks, he stands to make a sizeable profit. Otherwise, if he goes ahead with the work he will go bankrupt in the third week.

# BUSINESS PLAN

The four elements of a business plan are as follows:

## Product

This part should include:
- product description
- details about the premises
- equipment needs
- labour requirements.

## Market Research

This section describes the market:
- size of target market
- type of market
- selling price of the product
- main competitors.

## Sales Promotion

This should show:
- the methods that will be used to advertise, e.g. advertisements on the radio or in newspapers
- any other ways of promoting the business, e.g. leaflets, sponsorship of local sports teams.

## Finance

An estimate of long-term and short-term finance needed for the business must be given. This should show:
- the total amount required
- the finance available
- the loan required.

# Worked Example

## Question

Hazel Smith and Zoe Kelly decided to set up a hairdressing business. The name of their company is Hazo Ltd, located at 52 High Street, Gorey, Co. Wexford. Hazel Smith is managing director. Their market research has provided the following information.

- There are 3,000 potential customers.
- There are five other hairdresser businesses in the area.
- They estimate that they can deal with 25 customers per day at an average charge of €40 each.

They estimate their costs as follows: equipment €6,500; delivery van €10,000; lease of premises €15,000; working capital €8,500.

They have savings of €15,000 to invest in the business and can obtain a grant of €10,000 if they produce a business plan. They seek your help in preparing this plan.

(a) Calculate the amount of money they would need to borrow in order to set up this business.

(b) Complete a business plan using today's date.

## Solution

(a)

| Estimated costs | € |
|---|---|
| Equipment | 6,500 |
| Delivery van | 10,000 |
| Lease of premises | 15,000 |
| Working capital | 8,500 |
| **Total costs** | **40,000** |

| Sources of funds | € |
|---|---|
| Savings | 15,000 |
| Grant | 10,000 |
| **Total funds** | **25,000** |

| Finance | € |
|---|---|
| Total costs | 40,000 |
| Total funds | 25,000 |
| **Loan required** | **15,000** |

(b)

### Business Plan

**COMPANY DETAILS**

| | |
|---|---|
| Name of company | Hazo Ltd |
| Address of company | 52 High Street, Gorey |
| Shareholders | Hazel Smith, Zoe Kelly |
| Managing Director | Hazel Smith |

**PRODUCT/SERVICE**

| | |
|---|---|
| Description | Hairdressing |

**MARKET RESEARCH**

| | |
|---|---|
| Size of market | 3,000 |
| Competitors | 5 |
| Price per unit | €40 |

**SALES PROMOTION**

| | |
|---|---|
| Methods | Leaflets and local radio advertisements |

**FINANCE**

| | |
|---|---|
| Total required | €40,000 |
| Amount available | €25,000 |
| Loan required | €15,000 |

SIGNED *Hazel Smith*
*Zoe Kelly*

DATE 15 March

## Activity 15.1 Chapter Review

**1** (a) What will a business have to prepare before applying for a bank loan?
   (b) What is a cash flow forecast?
   (c) What is a bank overdraft?

**2** (a) What are the estimates of receipts?
   (b) What are the estimates of payments?
   (c) What is a surplus?
   (d) What does it mean to go bankrupt?
   (e) What can a firm do if it has cash problems?

**3** (a) List **four** elements of a business plan.
   (c) Describe **two** ways to advertise and promote a business.

## Activity 15.2 Cash flow

*Templates for these questions are provided in the workbook.*

**1** Tom and Mary are going to start an electrical shop. Prepare a cash flow forecast for the first four months of the year given the following information:

- Opening cash in hand is €1,000.

*Planned income:*
- Sales of electrical goods are expected to be €3,000 per month.
- Receipts from repairs are expected to be €500 per month.

*Planned expenditure:*
- Repayments on van loan will cost €250 per month.
- Shop insurance premium amounts to €150 per year payable in January.
- Electricity bills are expected to be €200 in February and €300 in April.
- Rent will cost €300 per month.
- The telephone bill is expected to be €130 in February and €140 in April.
- Wages are expected to be €2,000 per month.

**2** Patrick is a lobster exporter. He has advance orders (sales) from European customers for the next four months as follows: May €2,000, June €3,400, July €5,700, August €7,200. He estimates that his expenses over the next few months will be as follows:
- Wages are expected to be €1,500 each month.
- Rent will be €250 per month.
- Electricity bills are expected to be €140 in June and €110 in August.
- The telephone bill is expected to be €150 in June and €170 in August.
- Factory insurance premium is estimated at €240 per year, payable monthly.
- He has opening cash in hand of €750.
   (a) Make out a cash flow forecast for this business for May, June, July and August.
   (b) In which months is there a cash shortage?
   (c) Suggest how he might improve his cash flow.

*A template for this question is provided in the workbook.*

Mary Burke and John Smyth decided to set up a sandwich making and delivery business. The name of their company is SAMBOS Ltd, located at 25 Low Street, Kells, Co. Meath. They have an account in the Bank of Ireland, Kells.

Mary Burke is managing director and John Smyth is the production manager.

Their market research has provided the following information:
- there are 2,000 potential customers
- there are four businesses in the area supplying sandwiches but none of them offers a delivery service
- they estimate that they can sell 500 sandwiches per day at €2.65 each.

They estimate their costs as follows: equipment €5,500; delivery van €12,000; lease of premises €14,000; working capital €7,500.

They have savings of €5,500 to invest in the business and can obtain a grant of €10,000 if they produce a business plan. They seek your help in preparing this plan.

(a) Calculate the amount of money they would need to borrow to set up this business.
(b) Outline **three** suitable methods of advertising and promoting their sandwiches.
(c) Complete a business plan using today's date.

(JCHL, adapted)

Try a test on this topic

Chapter 16

## Company *finance*

## Finding suitable finance

A business needs three types of finance:

- **Long-term finance** is used to buy premises and heavy equipment that will last for more than five years.
- **Medium-term finance** is used to purchase vehicles and equipment. These assets will last for one to five years.
- **Short-term finance** is used for day-to-day expenditure, e.g. paying wages.

Spending on premises, equipment and vehicles is called **capital expenditure**. This expenditure only happens every few years and is financed with long-term or medium-term finance.

**Revenue expenditure** is quite different. It is the day-to-day spending of the business, such as the payment of wages, electricity and insurance. Buying a delivery van is capital expenditure but buying diesel for the van is revenue expenditure.

In general, a firm will use long-term money to finance the purchase of long-term assets and short-term money to finance day-to-day spending.

| SOURCES OF FINANCE | | | |
|---|---|---|---|
| **INTERNAL** | **EXTERNAL** | | |
| Own funds or capital<br>Retained profits | Grants<br>Long-term loan<br>Sale and leaseback | Medium-term loan<br>Hire purchase<br>Leasing | Creditors<br>Unpaid expenses<br>Overdraft |
| **Long-term**<br>(over five years)<br>Used to buy premises, heavy machinery and equipment | | **Medium-term**<br>(one to five years)<br>Used to buy vehicles, computers and light equipment | **Short-term**<br>(less than one year)<br>Used to buy stock and pay wages, telephone, electricity and other bills |

When an entrepreneur starts a business he or she will use savings to finance some of the expenditure. This internal source of finance is rarely enough money to run the business and the entrepreneur will usually have to tap into external sources as well.

# All the places you can get money

## Capital

Capital is the money put into the firm by the owners. In a small firm the capital may come from the owners' savings, redundancy money or a personal loan. Larger firms get capital by issuing shares. The capital is used to buy the premises, machinery and other long-term assets the business needs.

## Retained profit

A successful company will use its capital to make a profit. The part of the profit that is retained by the business (not given out as a dividend) becomes another source of money for the firm.

Using internal sources of finance means that there are no repayments and no interest charges. This money is used to buy premises, machinery and other long-term assets.

## Grants

Some grants are available to small businesses from Enterprise Ireland or the County Enterprise Boards. A grant will rarely exceed 30% of the total finance required by a business. The grant is usually used for capital expenditure on assets such as premises and machinery.

## Long-term loans

Long-term loans from a bank can be expensive. However, sometimes it's the only way to get the extra money needed. These loans are used to pay for premises, machinery and equipment. A company will have up to 20 years to repay the loan and they will have to give collateral (security) for the loan – usually the deeds to the property are given as security.

## Sale and leaseback

This is a special type of leasing where a firm sells an asset and leases it back from the buyer. For example, a firm may be able to sell its premises and then lease the premises back from the leasing company. The benefit to the firm is that it gets a cash injection, but it no longer owns its premises.

## Medium-term loans

These are loans from a bank that take from one to five years to repay. The interest rate is higher than for an overdraft. These loans are used to buy delivery vans and light equipment.

## Hire purchase

This is a popular way for a business to acquire vehicles, office furniture and computers. Under this arrangement:

- the firm pays regular instalments from one to five years
- the firm won't own the goods until the last instalment has been paid.

## Leasing

This is like renting, and while the firm gets the use of the asset they will never own it. With leasing:

- the finance company buys the goods and leases them to the business
- the firm pays monthly rent
- the finance company continues to own the goods.

External sources are used when the firm cannot supply all its own cash needs. A wide variety of finance is available but the cost of getting this outside money can be very high.

## Creditors

The purchase of raw materials can be quite costly. If stock can be bought on credit, then the suppliers who give the stock are helping to finance your firm. Creditors (the suppliers) are therefore a source of short-term money. The cost to the firm of using this source of money is the discount that may be lost from the creditors.

## Unpaid expenses

The money saved by not paying bills is a further source of finance for a business. For example, by not paying electricity, tax or telephone charges the company may save hundreds of euro, and this money can be used elsewhere in the business. However, this is a most unsuitable source of funds, as the service provider may disconnect the service to the firm. Paying bills late or not at all is a sure sign of a company in financial difficulties.

## Overdraft

This is a short-term loan that permits the business to write cheques even though there is no money in the firm's current account. Interest is only paid on the amount overdrawn. This should only be used to finance day-to-day expenses and lodgments should be made as soon as possible to reduce the overdraft.

## TIPS ON ANSWERING THIS QUESTION

When you are answering this question you need to keep the following in mind.

**Term loan**
When you borrow for three years that is the same as 36 months. Now you must multiply this by 14 (as the loan is for €14,000). Finally, multiply this by €30 (the rate per month).

**Type of loan needed**
Always look to see how long the loan is needed for. In this case the loan is for three years so the type of loan has to be medium term.

**Ledger accounts**
A ledger account is created for the bank. The €14,000 is entered on the debit (Dr) of the bank account as money is coming into the business. Now we must enter it a second time. The other account we use is the Quick Finance Ltd account. It is entered on the credit (Cr) of the Quick Finance Ltd account, i.e. the opposite side to the entry in the bank account. This is known as double-entry bookkeeping.

# Worked Examples

## Question
Murray's Bakery got the following details about a €14,000 delivery van.

**Term loan from Quick Finance Ltd:** €30 per month per €1,000 borrowed for three years.

**Leasing:** €125 per week.

(a) What is the total cost of the term loan?
(b) How much would it cost to lease the van for three years?
(c) Which type of term loan would Murray's need?
(d) If they decide to get the term loan on 7 October, how would this be recorded in their ledger accounts?

## Solution

(a) Loan cost: 36 x 14 x €30 = €15,120

(b) Leasing cost: 52 x 3 x €125 = €19,500

(c) A medium-term loan.

(d) The ledger accounts are shown below:

| Dr | | | Bank Account | | | | Cr |
|---|---|---|---|---|---|---|---|
| Date | Details | F | Total | Date | Details | F | Total |
| Oct | | | € | Oct | | | € |
| 7 | Quick Finance | | 14,000 | | | | |

| | | | Quick Finance Ltd Account | | | | |
|---|---|---|---|---|---|---|---|
| Oct | | | € | Oct | | | € |
| | | | | 7 | Bank | | 14,000 |

## Activity 16.1 Chapter Review

**1** Write a short note about each of the following:
   (a) long-term finance
   (b) medium-term finance
   (c) short-term finance.

**2** What is the difference between:
   (a) long-term and short-term finance?
   (b) capital and revenue expenditure?
   (c) internal and external finance?

**3** Write a note about each of the following long-term sources of finance:
   (a) capital
   (b) retained profit
   (c) grants
   (d) long-term loan
   (e) sale and leaseback.

**4** Explain, giving examples, how the following medium-term sources of finance are used:
   (a) medium-term loan
   (b) hire purchase
   (c) leasing.

**5** (a) How are creditors a source of finance?
   (b) What is an overdraft?

## Activity 16.2 Repayments

**1** Calculate (i) the cost of each of these loans and (ii) the amount of the monthly repayment on each loan:
   (a) A €2,000 loan for three years if it costs €30 per €1,000 per month.
   (b) A €1,500 loan for two years if it costs €50 per €1,000 per month.
   (c) A €5,000 loan for four years if it costs €175 per €1,000 per month.
   (d) A €3,000 loan for three years if it costs €40 per €1,000 per month.
   (e) A €4,500 loan for two years if it costs €70 per €1,000 per month.

**2** Calculate which is cheaper for a €4,000 loan.
   (a) A term loan if the repayments are €45 per month per €1,000 borrowed over three years.
   (b) A hire purchase arrangement for two years if the repayments are €200 per month.

**3** Which of these is cheaper for a €7,000 loan?
   (a) A term loan if the repayments are €25 per month per €1,000 borrowed over four years.
   (b) A hire purchase arrangement for three years if the repayments are €160 per month.

## Activity 16.3 State Exam Practice

**1** Hogan's Hardware Store got the following details about a €20,000 delivery van.

**Term loan from Easy Finance Ltd:** €30 per month per €1,000 borrowed for three years.

**Leasing:** €140 per week.

(a) What is the total cost of the term loan?
(b) How much would it cost to lease the van for three years?
(c) Which type of term loan would Hogan's need?
(d) If they decide to get the term loan on 1 November, how would this be recorded in their ledger accounts?

**2** Fagan's Furniture Factory got the following details about a €15,000 finishing machine.

**Term loan from No Fuss Finance Ltd:** €25 per month per €1,000 borrowed for four years.

**Leasing:** €150 per week.

(a) What is the total cost of the term loan?
(b) How much would it cost to lease the van for three years?
(c) Which type of term loan would Fagan's need?
(d) If they decide to get the term loan on 1 December, how would this be recorded in their ledger accounts?

eTest.ie
Try a test on this topic

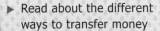
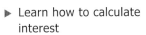

# Chapter 17

## Commercial banks

# Catering for business needs

For most people, starting a small business remains little more than a dream. One of the biggest obstacles is deciding how to approach a bank for a loan. It's worth remembering, however, that banks are accustomed to dealing with the needs of businesses.

Banking is so competitive that many banks have joined up with other financial institutions to offer several **specialist services**. They can now facilitate customers who wish to take out insurance or get a mortgage. They will also give tax advice and arrange pensions.

In this chapter you will learn how banks assist businesses by the variety of services they offer, ranging from giving basic business advice to granting loans.

## OPENING A CURRENT ACCOUNT

When a company opens a current account it must provide the bank with the certificate of incorporation and memorandum of association for the business. The firm must also supply specimen signatures of those entitled to sign cheques.

Before getting a loan the firm will have to:
- state the purpose of the loan
- show it has the ability to repay the loan
- show it has the ability to pay interest
- provide suitable security for the loan.

Banks have many customers and a lot of these will be business people. So banks get to see what is going on in business: what the challenges are and where the opportunities lie. An account manager is allocated to each company with an account in the bank. This manager will talk to the businessperson, suggesting different accounts and arranging loans. A sensible businessperson will build a good relationship with his or her account manager.

# Services provided by banks for business

| **deposit accounts** | Money lodged into a bank deposit account earns interest for the business. Higher rates of interest are paid on large sums of money left for long periods of time. The interest is subject to DIRT. |
| --- | --- |
| **current accounts** | No interest is paid on money lodged into current accounts. However, firms with a current account are given a cheque book and can usually negotiate an overdraft limit. This is an essential service for firms to help them with their cash flow. |
| **loans** | Banks supply much of the capital required by businesses. This can take the form of overdrafts or medium- to long-term loans. They ensure that businesses have access to money at the best possible interest rates. |
| **night safe** | These are used by shopkeepers and traders who wish to make lodgments outside normal banking hours. The customer deposits a special marked bag in the safe. The next day he or she goes to the bank, gets the bag and makes a lodgment in the usual way. |
| **foreign exchange** | The banks buy and sell foreign currency. Firms trading with the USA, Britain, Japan or other countries not in the euro zone may need this service. |

# MONEY TRANSFER FACILITIES

**Paypath:** Many employers pay wages and salaries directly into their employees' bank accounts. The employee can then go to an ATM and withdraw their wages. It is a safe and convenient way to pay wages.

**Standing order:** A standing order (SO) is an agreement between a bank and a customer to pay a stated amount of money at a specific date every month into a third party's bank account. It is used where the payment is the same each month. For example, repayment of a loan on a delivery van could be paid this way.

**Direct debit:** When the amount of the payment is variable, a direct debit (DD) is often used. For example, payment of an electricity bill may be made using a direct debit.

**Bank draft:** This is a cheque written by a bank official using one of the bank's own cheques. There is a small charge for this service. Bank drafts are used when:
- a customer does not have a current account and therefore cannot write cheques
- a customer is paying a firm that insists on a bank draft because the customer is not known to them, the money is to be sent through the post or guaranteed payment is required.

## Bank giro

A customer who knows the bank account numbers of his or her suppliers can make payments to them using the giro system. Credit transfers (CT) like this mean that bills can be paid without writing cheques.

| CREDIT TRANSFER | | | Bank Giro CREDIT TRANSFER |
|---|---|---|---|
| | Destination Branch Code | 90 - 15 - 36 | |

| To Bank *A.I.B.* | To Bank *A.I.B.* | Date *5 Oct* 20 *10* | |
|---|---|---|---|
| Branch *Athlone* | Branch *Athlone* | | Notes *300* |
| A/C *Doris Ltd* | Credit Account *Doris Ltd* | | Coin |
| 6 8 0 7 4 1 5 2 | Paid in by *Fiona Burke* | | Total Cash *300* |
| € *500* | Address *Wexford* | | Cheques *200* |
| | Cashier's Stamp and Initials | Customer's Account Number 6 8 0 7 4 1 5 2 | Total *500* |

When you are answering
this question you need to
keep the following in mind:

**Capital repayment**
Divide the loan (€16,000)
by the number of years
(4). This gives the €4,000
capital repayment.

**Term loan**
The term loan is reduced by
€4,000 each year and
interest is only charged on
the reduced value of the
loan.

# Worked Example

## Question

Enda Mooney, 2 Seaview, Dundalk, has a current account, no. 12147908, in AIB, Dundalk branch. He received a four-year loan of €16,000 from his bank to re-equip his shop. Terms of the loan agreement were:

- capital repayments of €4,000 each year
- interest 12% APR.

**(a)** Calculate the total interest payable over the four years.
**(b)** On 10 May he lodged to his account a cheque for €500 and €600 in notes. Complete the lodgment form.
**(c)** On 16 May he withdrew €300 from his account. Complete the withdrawal form.

## Solution

**(a)**

| | | |
|---|---|---:|
| Year 1 | 16,000 x 12% interest = | 1,920 |
| Year 2 | 12,000 x 12% interest = | 1,440 |
| Year 3 | 8,000 x 12% interest = | 960 |
| Year 4 | 4,000 x 12% interest = | 480 |
| **Interest payable over the four years** | | **4,800** |

**(b)**

LODGMENT RECORD

Name(s) *Enda Mooney*

| 1 | 2 | 1 | 4 | 7 | 9 | 0 | 8 |
|---|---|---|---|---|---|---|---|

€ *1,100*

Please specify account
Current ☐  Savings ☐
Other ☐

**Lodgment**
Please specify account: Current ☐  Savings ☐  Other ☐

Name(s) *Enda Mooney*
Address *2 Seaview, Dundalk*

Date *10 May* 20 *10*

Paid in by *Steve Burke*

Cashier's Stamp and Initials

Customer's Account Number

| 1 | 2 | 1 | 4 | 7 | 9 | 0 | 8 |
|---|---|---|---|---|---|---|---|

| | |
|---|---:|
| Notes | 600 |
| Coin | |
| Total Cash | 600 |
| Cheques | 500 |
| Total | 1,100 |

**(c)**

**Withdrawal**

Branch Number

Account Number

| 1 | 2 | 1 | 4 | 7 | 9 | 0 | 8 |
|---|---|---|---|---|---|---|---|

Current  Deposit  Cashsave

Brand/Initials

Branch *Dundalk*
Received the sum of *Three hundred euro*

Signed *Enda Mooney*
Address *2 Seaview, Dundalk*
Narrative

€ *300*

**For joint Savings Accounts**
I certify that all parties in the account are alive on this date

Date

Signed

## Activity 17.1 Chapter Review

1. (a) List four specialist services banks offer to cater for business needs.
   (b) When opening a current account, what information must a business provide the bank?
   (c) Before getting a loan, what does a firm have to do?

2. Write a note about each of the following bank services:
   (a) deposit accounts
   (b) current accounts
   (c) loans
   (d) night safe
   (e) foreign exchange.

3. Explain, giving examples, how the following money transfer facilities are used:
   (a) standing order
   (b) direct debit
   (c) Paypath
   (d) bank draft
   (e) bank giro (credit transfers).

4. Suggest a suitable money transfer facility to use to pay the following:
   (a) repayment of a car loan
   (b) paying staff wages
   (c) paying a telephone bill
   (d) paying suppliers.

## Activity 17.2 Capital repayments and interest

1. Calculate the total interest payable for each of these loans.
   (a) A €20,000 loan for four years if the capital repayments are €5,000 each year and the interest is 12% APR.
   (b) A €30,000 loan for five years if the capital repayments are €6,000 each year and the interest is 11% APR.
   (c) A €40,000 loan for four years if the capital repayments are €10,000 each year and the interest is 14% APR.

2. Aztec Ltd receive a three-year loan of €21,000. Capital repayments are distributed evenly over the period of the loan and interest is 12% APR. Calculate the total interest payable over the three years.

3. Razzle Ltd receive a four-year loan of €24,000. Capital repayments are distributed evenly over the period of the loan and interest is 9% APR. Calculate the total interest payable over the three years.

**1** (a) Study the following advertisement for a loan and answer the question below.

> **Let M & M Finance Ltd Lend You A Financial Hand**
>
> Loans available on the following conditions:
> Capital repayments are distributed evenly over the period of the loan;
> Interest 9% APR.

Murphy Ltd obtained a three-year loan of €12,000 from M & M Finance Ltd.
Calculate the total interest payable.

(b) S & R Concrete Ltd is a manufacturer of concrete products operating from Quarry Lane, Sligo. It has two directors, Maura Stone and Paddy Rock. S & R Concrete Ltd owns quarries worth €2,000,000 and machinery and trucks valued at €250,000.
It has monthly income of €60,000 and it forecasts that this will increase by 20% if it obtains new buildings costing €85,000, machinery costing €120,000 and purchases five new trucks costing €50,000 each.

S & R Concrete Ltd has reserves of €35,000. The directors will invest €40,000 each and it will receive a grant of €75,000.

On 1 June it applied for a ten-year loan from M & M Finance Ltd. The loan was granted on 15 June.

You are required to calculate the amount of the loan required.

**2** (a) Name four services provided by banks for businesses.
(b) List three pieces of information that a private limited company must provide when opening a current account in a bank.
(c) State four factors that banks consider when granting a loan.
(d) F & M Ltd received a three-year loan of €15,000. Terms of the loan agreement were:
- capital repayments of €5,000 per year
- interest 12% APR.

Calculate the total interest payable over the three years.

# Business insurance

## Business risks

Businesses need profit to survive, hence most firms prefer to pay small sums of money for insurance and thereby avoid large losses. A businessperson must assess the risks involved in the firm and take out an insurance policy that gives protection according to the firm's needs.

There are many risks and here are some of the insurance policies to cover them.

- **Fire and special perils insurance** covers the stock and buildings against destruction and damage.
- **Employer's liability insurance** insures against injury caused to employees in the course of their work.
- **Product liability insurance** covers injury caused to any member of the public by the product that the business supplies.
- **Public liability insurance** insures against injury caused to a customer while on the business premises.

## COMPULSORY BUSINESS INSURANCE

There are insurance policies to cover many different risks but according to the law it is only compulsory for a business to have two types of insurance:

- **Vehicle insurance**
  If the business has delivery vans or cars it must have insurance on them.
- **PRSI**
  If the business has employees it must pay PRSI. This is a legal requirement.

# Worked Example

## Question

Office Fitters Ltd wants to insure the following: buildings €100,000; machinery €50,000; two vans at €15,000 each; stock €70,000; office cash €3,500.

They got the following quotation from Coverall Insurers Ltd: insurance for buildings and machinery €4 per €1,000 insured; vehicle insurance €900 per van; stock insurance €9 per €1,000 insured; cash insurance €10 per €500 insured. As new clients they are entitled to a 20% discount off the total premium.

Office Fitters Ltd agreed to take out this insurance on everything at replacement cost (as stated above) except for the buildings, which they insured for €75,000.

(a) Calculate the total amount of the premium paid by Office Fitters Ltd.
(b) In the event of damage to the buildings of €40,000, how much compensation would Office Fitters Ltd receive?
(c) Show how to record the payment of the total premium in the ledger on 2 February.

## Solution

**(a)**

| | | | |
|---|---|---|---|
| BUILDINGS | $\dfrac{€75,000}{€1,000}$ | X €4 = | €300 |
| MACHINERY | $\dfrac{€50,000}{€1,000}$ | X €4 = | €200 |
| VANS | €900 | X 2 = | €1,800 |
| STOCK | $\dfrac{€70,000}{€1,000}$ | X €9 = | €630 |
| CASH | $\dfrac{€3,500}{€500}$ | X €10 = | €70 |
| | | | €3,000 |
| less discount | | | €600 |
| **TOTAL PREMIUM** | | | **€2,400** |

**(b)** Average clause applies because the buildings are underinsured:

$$\frac{\text{sum insured}}{\text{actual value}} \quad X \quad \text{claim}$$

$$\frac{€75,000}{€100,000} \quad X \quad €40,000$$

$$= €30,000$$

**(c)**

| Dr | Bank Account | | | | | | Cr |
|---|---|---|---|---|---|---|---|
| Date | Details | F | Total | Date | Details | F | Total |
| | | | € | Feb | | | € |
| | | | | 2 | Insurance | | 2,400 |

| | Insurance Account | | | | | | |
|---|---|---|---|---|---|---|---|
| Feb | | | € | | | | € |
| 2 | Bank | | 2,400 | 31 | P+L | | 2,200 |
| | | | | | Balance | c/d | 200 |
| | | | 2,400 | | | | 2,400 |
| | Balance | b/d | 200 | | | | |

**TIP**

The €2,400 is shown on the credit (Cr) of the bank account as money is going out of the bank account. So the double-entry has to be on the debit (Dr) of the insurance account. As the payment was made in February, one month (€200) is carried as a balance into next year.

## Activity 18.1 Chapter Review

1. Write a note about each of the following insurance policies:
   (a) fire and special perils insurance
   (b) employer's liability insurance
   (c) product liability insurance
   (d) public liability insurance.

2. Write a note about each of the following compulsory insurance policies:
   (a) vehicle insurance
   (b) PRSI. What do the letters PRSI stand for?

3. Suggest a suitable money transfer facility to use to pay the following:
   (a) repayment of a car loan
   (b) paying staff wages
   (c) paying a telephone bill
   (d) paying suppliers.

## Activity 18.2 Calculate premium

1. Wheels Ltd wish to insure the following: showrooms €380,000; office equipment €25,000; three delivery vans valued at €18,000 each; stock of cars €160,000; cash held in the office €1,500. They get the following quotation for one year's insurance:
   - insurance for showrooms €3.50 per €1,000 value
   - insurance for equipment €3 per €1,000 value
   - van insurance €840 per van
   - stock insurance €12 per €1,000 value
   - cash insurance €9 per €500
   - new business introductory offer 15% off total premium.

   Calculate the premium.

2. Office Supplies Ltd wish to insure the following: warehouse €275,000; four forklifts valued at €18,000 each; computers €25,000; office equipment €65,000; cash held in the office €1,700. They get the following quotation for one year's insurance:
   - insurance for warehouse €2.50 per €1,000 value
   - forklift insurance €650 per forklift
   - insurance for computers €2 per €1,000 value
   - equipment insurance €11 per €1,000 value
   - cash insurance €11 per €500
   - new business introductory offer 15% off total premium.

   Calculate the premium.

Decor Ltd requested an insurance quotation from Shield Insurers Ltd for the following assets: buildings €150,000; machinery €80,000; five delivery vans valued at €20,000 each; stock €25,000; and cash in office €1,500.

Shield Insurers Ltd supplied the following quotation for one year's insurance.

Insurance for the buildings and machinery, €6 per €1,000 value.
Delivery van comprehensive cover €1,150 per van.
Stock insurance €13 per €1,000 value.
Cash insurance €15 per €500.

New business introductory offer 15% off total premium.

Decor Ltd accepted the quotation and took out insurance on everything at replacement cost (as stated above) except buildings, which they insured for €100,000. Decor Ltd paid the premium by cheque on 1 July of this year.

(a) Calculate the amount of the premium paid by Decor Ltd on 1 July.

(b) In the event of fire damage to the buildings of €60,000, how much compensation would Decor Ltd receive?

(c) The insurance account of Decor Ltd has an opening debit balance of €450. Record the payment of the premium to Shield Insurers Ltd on 1 July in the insurance account. Balance the insurance account on 31 December, showing clearly the amount to be transferred to the profit and loss account.

Try a test on this topic

▶ Find out about the different types of communication

▶ Learn how to prepare a business report

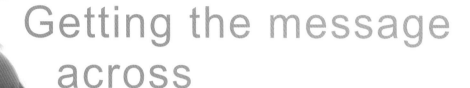

# Business communications

## Getting the message across

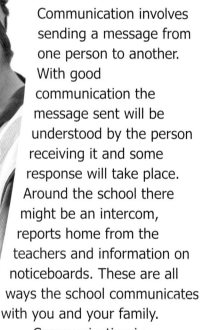

Communication involves sending a message from one person to another. With good communication the message sent will be understood by the person receiving it and some response will take place. Around the school there might be an intercom, reports home from the teachers and information on noticeboards. These are all ways the school communicates with you and your family.

Communication in business can be internal or external. Information exchanged within a business is known as **internal communication**, e.g. instructions between a manager and a subordinate or messages sent between colleagues. Communication between the business and outsiders is known as **external communication**, e.g. communication with suppliers, customers, potential customers, shareholders, the general public or the media.

This chapter will explain the three main types of communication: oral; written; and visual. Whichever method is selected will depend on a number of factors.

## CHOOSING A METHOD

The choice of a form of communication will be influenced by a number of factors:

- speed – how quickly must the message be delivered?
- reliability – is the message likely to be lost or misunderstood?
- cost – how expensive is the system going to be?
- security – must the message be kept secret?

Communication has many forms and functions but it is a two-way process where the person sending the message has to be sure the other person has received the right message.

# Types of communication

## oral

Oral communication in business can occur at meetings or on the telephone. This is a quick and informal way of communicating. Meetings are essentially an oral form of communication, but visual and written communication will also occur.

- Agenda: This lists the items that will be discussed at the meeting. It is usually sent in advance to the people who will attend the meeting.
- Minutes: This is a written record of what was said, or the actions that were agreed, by those attending the meeting.

## written

Written communication is slower than oral communication but at least you have a record of what you said. Written messages can take time to prepare and can make the sender take more care about what is being communicated. Written communication in business can take many forms.

- Emails are often short informal notes written in a casual tone.
- Letters are more formal. Within a business, letters can take many forms, e.g. a letter of appointment to a job, a letter of promotion, a letter of warning or a letter of dismissal. Letters, newsletters, contracts and brochures are also used in external communication with customers and suppliers.
- Reports are often used internally to give an update on the progress of a project. Reports have a standard format (described later in this chapter).
- Trading documents are another form of written communication that a business uses both internally and externally. These take the form of quotations, invoices, delivery dockets, credit notes and statements. They provide a written record of the buying and selling transactions that have taken place.

## visual

Visual communication can take the form of diagrams, charts or graphs. These are often easier to understand than lists of figures. There are three types you need to know: bar chart, trend graph and pie chart.

|  | Ulster | Munster | Leinster | Connacht |
|---|---|---|---|---|
| Sales | 2,000 | 3,000 | 1,000 | 6,000 |

The best way to show the above data is in a bar chart. For comparison purposes it is also shown below in a trend graph and pie chart.

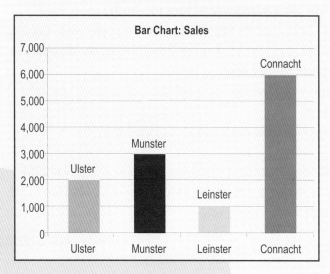

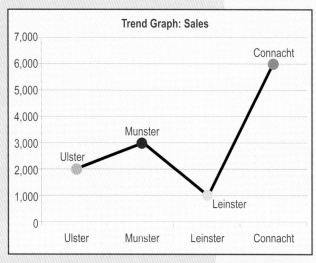

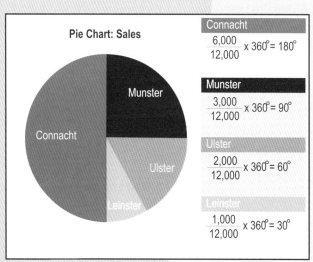

# COMMUNICATION AGENCIES

There are a number of companies that help businesses communicate with each other:

### An Post

An Post operates the national and international postal service for Ireland. The main services they provide for businesses are:

- **Publicity post:** An Post will deliver leaflets directly to the customers you wish to target in a specific area.
- **PostAim:** This is a 'mail-shot' where letters are sent to people whose names you know, e.g. customers and suppliers.
- **Business Reply Service:** This service allows people to post their orders to a company using a special envelope without the expense of buying a stamp.
- **Freepost:** This allows customers to write to a company free of charge by simply writing the word 'Freepost' in the address. No special envelope is required.

### Telecommunications Services

There are now several telecommunications companies operating in Ireland, e.g. Eircom, Vodafone, Meteor, O2. Between them they provide a variety of services to businesses.

- **Telephones and mobile phones**.
- **Freefone 1-800:** This service allows a customer to ring the company for free. The company pays for the call.
- **Fax:** This permits the electronic transfer of documents over the telephone line.
- **Internet:** This gives access to the World Wide Web and email.

*Chapter 19 Business Communications*

**PREPARING A REPORT**

Some sections of the question are just copied directly into the report, e.g. the addresses, what Ken outlined in the report, what Ken recommended.

The report itself is a little like a business letter.

**LAYOUT OF A REPORT**

Address of the person preparing the report

Date

Person getting the report

Introduction

Findings

Conclusion and recommendations

Final comment

Signature and job title

# Worked Example

## Question

Lisa Conneally, Bay View Road, Co. Clare had a new heating system installed in her home by Sunnyside Heating Ltd. She was dissatisfied with it and asked Ken McGrath, consultant engineer with Domestic Engineers Ltd, Atlantic Heights, Co. Clare, for his opinion. On 15 August 2010, he wrote a report to Lisa outlining the following:

- No insulation was installed around the boiler, which caused it to lose heat.
- The rattling under the floorboards is caused by badly fitted pipes.

Ken recommended installing insulation around the boiler and fitting new brackets on the pipes under the floorboards.
Write the report Ken sent to Lisa.

## Solution

Domestic Engineers Ltd
Atlantic Heights
Co. Clare

15 August 2010

To: Lisa Conneally
    Bay View Road, Co. Clare

Here is my report on the heating system in your bungalow as installed by Sunnyside Heating Ltd. Here are the main findings:

- No insulation was installed around the boiler, which caused it to lose heat.
- The rattling under the floorboards is caused by badly fitted pipes.

To improve the operation of the system I would recommend installing insulation around the boiler and fitting new brackets on the pipes under the floorboards.

Please contact me to discuss any aspect of this report.

Ken McGrath
Consultant Engineer

## Activity 19.1 Chapter Review

1. Write a note about each of the following types of communication:
   (a) internal communication
   (b) external communication
   (c) oral communication
   (d) written communication
   (e) visual communication.

2. What factors determine the choice of a form of communication?

3. Briefly describe each of these services provided by An Post for businesses:
   (a) publicity post
   (b) PostAim
   (c) Business Reply Service
   (d) Freepost.

4. Briefly describe how a business would use each of these telecommunications services:
   (a) mobile phones
   (b) freefone 1-800
   (c) fax
   (d) Internet.

## Activity 19.2 Graphs and charts

1. Show the following sales as a bar chart:

|  | Ulster | Munster | Leinster | Connacht |
|---|---|---|---|---|
| Sales | 4,000 | 5,000 | 2,500 | 3,000 |

2. Show the following government current expenditure in the form of a pie chart: health €3,000m; education €1,500m; social welfare €4,000m; national debt service €2,000m; agriculture €1,000m; other services €3,500m.

3. Show the following electricity bills as a line graph:

|  | January | February | March | April | May | June |
|---|---|---|---|---|---|---|
| Electricity | 200 | 240 | 220 | 160 | 140 | 120 |

## Activity 19.3 State Exam Practice

**1** Sportstyle Ltd has a number of shops throughout Leinster. It sells football jerseys of the top county teams. In 2003 sales of jerseys were as follows:

| Team name: | Meath | Dublin | Laois | Kildare | Offaly | Westmeath |
|---|---|---|---|---|---|---|
| Quantity: | 4,000 | 5,000 | 2,500 | 3,000 | 1,500 | 2,000 |

(a) Show the above information in the form of a bar chart or pie chart.

(b) At a price of €50 per jersey, calculate the total sales for 2003.

(JCOL, adapted)

**2** NPD Electric Ltd, 34 Live Wire Drive, Galway manufactures and distributes electrical appliances for the home. It sells its products in Ireland.

NPD Electric Ltd wishes to review its insurance policies and requires advice on its insurance requirements. It supplies the following information:

Its assets include: Premises, equipment, motor vehicles, stock of electrical appliances. It has 80 employees.

NPD Electric Ltd lodges its cash twice weekly in a bank ten kilometres away.

(a) Assume you are Martina Toban, Insurance Consultant, 10 Castle View, Roscommon. Prepare a report, on today's date, for the directors of NPD Electric Ltd, setting out the following:

    (i) Two types of insurance that NPD Electric Ltd is required to have by law.
    (ii) Four other relevant types of insurance you would advise it to have and the reasons for having these.
    (iii) The importance of having adequate insurance for NPD Electric Ltd.

(b) Martina advised the directors of NPD Electric Ltd that when calculating their insurance premium they must take into account the basic premium, loadings and deductions. The basic premium was €25,000, loadings were 30% of basic and deductions were 12% of basic plus loadings.

    (i) List one example of a loading and one example of a deduction that NPD Electric Ltd might have to take into account when calculating its premium.

    (ii) Calculate the total premium for NPD Electric Ltd.

(JCHL, adapted)

Try a test on this topic

# Chapter 20

## Channels of distribution

# Getting the goods to you

The channel of distribution is the path a product goes through from producer to wholesaler to retailer before finally reaching the consumer. Some products, such as fruit and vegetables, may go direct from the farmer (the producer) to the consumer. Tea, however, is grown (by the producer), blended and packed (by the wholesaler) and then displayed in a shop (by the retailer). We will look at each of these stages now.

## PRODUCERS

The producers are the people and firms that make the goods. There are three types:

**Primary producers**

These take materials from the land or sea or use the land or sea to make a product. The main industries involved in primary production are:
- agriculture
- forestry
- fishing
- aquaculture (fish farming)
- mining.

**Secondary producers**

These manufacture and process the raw materials supplied by the primary producers:
- new technology firms that produce electrical goods, chemicals and pharmaceuticals
- food, drink and tobacco firms
- traditional firms that make clothing, footwear, furniture, building materials.

**Tertiary producers**

These don't make any products. Instead they supply the services that businesses need to operate successfully:
- commercial services, which include banking, insurance, transport and communication firms
- direct services, which refers to solicitors, doctors, security firms, etc.

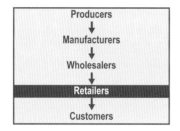

Producers
↓
Manufacturers
↓
Wholesalers
↓
**Retailers**
↓
Customers

Selling to consumers is known as retailing. Shops are the most visible and main form of retailing but this is changing. The advent of the Internet has meant that consumers can now do their shopping from the comfort and safety of their own homes.

## Functions of the retailer

- Stocks a wide variety of goods.
- Can give advice to the consumer on which product or service is most suitable.
- Has a location that makes it easy for the consumer to shop.
- Will notice consumer buying trends and give this feedback to the producer.

# Types of retailer

### independent retailers

These are usually small, family-run shops, such as grocery shops or tobacco, sweets and newsagent shops (TSNs). Sometimes they specialise in one particular product, e.g. butcher, shoe shop, public house. They offer a good personal service to their customers and rarely give credit.

### department stores

These are large shops selling a wide variety of consumer products, e.g. hardware, footwear, clothing, cosmetics, food and toys. The main department stores are Clerys, Brown Thomas, Arnotts and Debenhams.

### franchises

Many well-known stores operate under a franchise arrangement, e.g. McDonald's, Pizza Hut and Benetton.

### multiple stores

Any group of shops with many locations around the country can be called a multiple store. The term usually refers to supermarkets like Tesco, Superquinn and Dunnes but it can also include shops like Eason's. There are also international multiple retailers with branches in Ireland, e.g. Aldi and Lidl – two German food supermarket discount stores.

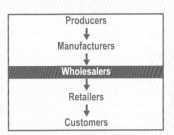

# WHOLESALERS

Wholesalers are often called the middleman in the channel of distribution. They act as a 'go-between', buying in large quantities from the manufacturer and selling in smaller quantities to the retailer. They offer services to both the manufacturer and the retailer.

```
Producers
   ↓
Manufacturers
   ↓
Wholesalers
   ↓
Retailers
   ↓
Customers
```

**Services to the manufacturer:**
- buying in bulk
- blending and packing the goods
- supplying the manufacturer with market information.

**Services to the retailer:**
- delivering the goods
- giving credit
- storing a selection of goods from different manufacturers for the retailer to choose from.

There are three types of wholesaler.

**Traditional wholesalers** travel around the country to shops to get orders. They usually give credit and deliver the goods to the shopkeeper. Eason's booksellers is an example of a traditional wholesaler of books and magazines.

**Cash-and-carry wholesalers** don't give credit and they don't deliver. In this case the shopkeepers go to the wholesaler and buy the goods they need. Musgrave is an example of a cash-and-carry wholesaler.

**Wholesale and symbol groups** consist of small local shops, e.g. Centra, Spar, Mace and Londis. They come together to compete with the larger supermarkets. They purchase in bulk for their members, deliver to them and mount advertising campaigns for the group.

## voluntary stores

These are independent retailers that have come together to compete with the multiples. They have similar product ranges and similar store layouts. Centra, Spar, Mace and Londis are examples. They are also called wholesale and symbol groups.

## supermarkets

These are self-service shops that operate on a cash sales basic.

Consumers now expect retailers to offer many different ways of purchasing goods and services. Of course, retailers are usually more than willing to oblige. The following are some recent trends.

# Modern trends in retailing

## Internet shopping

The Internet is growing in popularity for selling goods and services and almost all the big travel, grocery and clothing retailers now have an online shopping area. The integration of the traditional store with Internet selling is known as 'click and mortar', but the possibilities for selling online are not limited to these stores. Speciality stores, which only sell one product or service, also have a huge presence on the Internet and many of them don't have a traditional shop at all. This aspect of e-commerce has benefits for both the retailer and the consumer.

- The retailer is able to increase sales without the costs of running a shop.
- Orders can be filled more quickly, as fewer people are involved.
- Consumers are more in control.
- The shops are always open.

## vending machines

This is a rapidly growing retail area that offers many benefits.
Vending machines:
- don't take holidays. They are open 24 hours a day, all year round.
- offer a wide choice of products for sale, such as snack bars, hot drinks and bottled drinks.
- are an all-cash business. There are no debtors to chase for payment. The amount of cash taken in depends on the number of vending machines and where they are located.
- don't need advertising. The manufacturers of the products sold in the vending machines do the advertising that generates a demand for the products displayed.
- only need to be serviced twice a week, even in busy locations.

## convenience stores

These are open long hours, providing local consumers with a small choice of basic food and household products:
- Centra
- Spar
- Mace
- Londis.

## foreign-owned stores

In recent years there has been a growth in the number of foreign retailers trading in Ireland:
- Tesco
- Debenhams
- Aldi
- Lidl.

# Activity 20.1 Chapter Review

**1** What is the channel of distribution for:
   (a) apples?
   (b) coffee?
   (c) milk?
   (d) motor cars?

**2** Write a note about each of the following types of producer:
   (a) primary producers
   (b) secondary producers
   (c) tertiary producers.

**3** (a) What is retailing?
   (b) What are the functions of a retailer?

**4** Briefly describe each of these types of retailer, giving examples in each case.
   (a) Independent retailers.
   (b) Department stores.
   (c) Franchises.
   (d) Multiple stores.
   (e) Voluntary stores.
   (f) Supermarkets.

**5** What are the benefits of each of the following modern trends in retailing?
   (a) Internet shopping.
   (b) Vending machines.
   (c) Foreign-owned stores.
   (d) Convenience stores.

**6** (a) What is a wholesaler?
   (b) What services do wholesalers provide for manufacturers?
   (c) What services do wholesalers provide for retailers?

**7** Briefly describe each of these types of wholesaler, giving an example in each case.
   (a) Traditional wholesalers.
   (b) Cash-and-carry wholesalers.
   (c) Wholesale and symbol groups.

Jason mixed up the answers in his business studies test. He had all the correct answers but he put them in the wrong sentences.

Here is what he wrote:

Primary production is *where teachers, nurses and hairdressers are employed.*
Secondary production is *where raw materials are produced.*
The services industry is *where raw materials are turned into finished goods.*
The wholesaler is *a shop that sells airline tickets.*
A department store is *a slot machine where you can buy cans of orange.*
A shopping centre is *a retailer with branches around the country.*
A chain store is *a shop that sells newspapers.*
A vending machine is *a covered area where there are many shops.*
A travel agency is *a person who buys in bulk (large amounts) from the manufacturer.*
A newsagent is *one shop divided into many sections.*

(a) Write out each sentence fully, showing the correct answer in each sentence.

(b) Name two other types of retail shop that are not mentioned above and state the service that each of them provides.

(JCOL, adapted)

eTest.ie
Try a test on this topic

# Chapter 21

▶ Find out the difference between work and employment

▶ Read about the duties and responsibilities of employees

# People *at work*

## Work vs Employment

**Work** is any task or duty performed in order to produce goods or a service. Working for someone else and getting paid for this work is called **employment**.

You must be at least 16 years of age to get most jobs and most workers retire at 65 years of age. The average employee works 40 hours a week and is paid a wage less tax. Having a paid job means you can afford some luxuries, and money gives great independence.

Unemployed people suffer the loss of their income. Most people do not choose **unemployment** – it is forced on them. Some people are quickly able to find another job but others find they are unemployed for a long time, which can make it difficult to get back into a job. FÁS can help by providing valuable training. Learning new skills is often the best way to find a new job.

The **labour force** is the total number of people employed plus the number of people who are unemployed and available for work.

## CAUSES OF UNEMPLOYMENT

Recently we have seen a sharp rise in the number of people unemployed in Ireland. The causes of this unemployment are varied.

- Global recession.
- Firms moving to countries where wages are cheaper.
- Firms using machines to do work normally done by people.

| The Labour Force | | | |
|---|---|---|---|
| | EMPLOYED | UNEMPLOYED | LABOUR FORCE |
| 1983 | 1,100,000 | 180,800 | 1,280,800 |
| 2008 | 2,108,000 | 115,000 | 2,223,000 |

Being an employee is not terribly different from being at school – except at school you don't get paid money (instead your parents give you food, clothing and shelter). When you are in school you must arrive on time, follow directions and probably wear a uniform. Most jobs are a bit like that too.

# Doing an honest day's work

All employees have certain **responsibilities** and obligations. These are like the rules of working for the company. For example, employees must be punctual and able to follow instructions. They must also be polite and friendly with the other members of the staff. Nowadays many jobs require the worker to share duties and be part of a team. There is just no place in most companies for 'dead wood' and everyone is expected to do an honest day's work. Stealing, of course, could result in instant dismissal and workers must also respect the employer's property.

In return for for doing an honest day's work employees have certain **rights**. For example, they have the right to join a trade union. They also have the right to get holidays and maternity leave.

Over half the people employed in Ireland work in service industries like banking, insurance and transport. This is the real growth sector for jobs and where most school leavers find employment. Service companies do not make a product but instead supply a service to other businesses in Ireland that make products. For example, many people are employed in new technology computer firms.

Food, drink and tobacco firms and traditional firms like clothing and footwear producers also offer good employment opportunities. There are very few people now employed in agriculture and the number working here is dropping each year as people leave the land and work in cities in service and manufacturing companies.

Employees have the right to work in a safe environment and to get a fair wage. In return they have a responsibility to be on time for work, follow instructions and work honestly.

# MODERN TRENDS

### Job sharing

Job sharing means that two (or more) workers share one full-time position. It allows the worker have more time with his or her family and still earn a living and sustain a career.

### Flexitime

Instead of working the usual 40 hours from nine in the morning to five in the evening, the worker can start late some days and finish early other days. The only requirement is to complete 40 hours in the week.

### Teleworking

The employee has a home office and carries out his or her work as if on the company premises. This is suitable for jobs where the employee can use the phone or the Internet to do their work.

### Term time

In this case the employee only works during the school term. When the students are on their summer holidays the employee is given unpaid leave.

## Organisation chart

Many large firms can be divided into different departments where each section specialises in particular functions. The board of directors is elected by the shareholders. The board appoints the managing director. He or she appoints the managers for the different departments. These in turn appoint supervisors and hire workers as shown below.

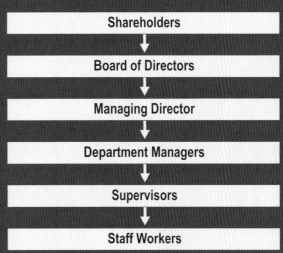

Shareholders
↓
Board of Directors
↓
Managing Director
↓
Department Managers
↓
Supervisors
↓
Staff Workers

# Self-employment

Of course not everyone likes working for an employer and they may start their own business. Many shopkeepers, hairdressers, mechanics, taxi drivers, carpenters and other tradespeople are self-employed, as well as many accountants, doctors and other professionals. The self-employed person will finance the business using his or her savings as well as any bank loans that can be acquired.

Self-employed people are their own bosses and they take all the risk of the business. They are **entrepreneurs**, risk takers. They get an idea for a business and they put together the finance, premises and staffing required to get the business up and running. So if the business is a success they get to keep the profit but if the business fails they suffer all the losses.

Self-employed people normally:
- work long hours
- take few holidays
- finance the business themselves
- take all the risk.

In return they have the satisfaction of knowing that whatever they achieve is their own. They are often highly motivated, since any profit the business makes belongs to them. If the firm gets big enough they can always hire additional workers and thereby share the responsibility.

## Activity 21.1 Chapter Review

**1** (a) What is the difference between work and employment?
(b) List *five* characteristics of an employee.
(c) What are the causes of unemployment?
(d) What is the labour force?

**2** (a) List *three* rights of an employee.
(b) List *three* responsibilities of an employee.
(c) Explain, giving examples, what is meant by 'service companies'.

**3** Write a note about each of the following modern trends in employment:
(a) job sharing
(b) flexitime
(c) teleworking
(d) term time.

**4** (a) In a company, who elects the board of directors?
(b) Who appoints the managing director?
(c) Who appoints the senior management team?
(d) List *five* departments you might find in a typical company.

**5** (a) What is self-employment?
(b) What sort of businesses do self-employed people form?
(c) List *four* characteristics of a self-employed person.
(d) Where do self-employed people get the money to start a business?
(e) Explain what is meant by the term 'entrepreneur'.

## Activity 21.2 State Exam Practice

**1** (a) In business, a sole trader is one of the following:
   (i) a person who checks the quality of new shoes
   (ii) a person who receives dividends
   (iii) a person who sells fish for a company
   (iv) a business run by its owner
   (v) a business which is always losing money.
   Write in your copy in full the most correct meaning of a sole trader from the above list.

(b) From the following figures draw a bar chart showing the sales of toys in Play Ltd, a toy store, for the last six months of last year.

| July | August | September | October | November | December |
|------|--------|-----------|---------|----------|----------|
| €2,000 | €1,000 | €3,000 | €4,000 | €6,000 | €8,000 |

(c) What was the total value of toys sold by the store for the whole six months?

(d) What was the average monthly sale of toys?

(e) Mary Moran is employed as a shop assistant at Play Ltd. She and all the other employees have certain duties and responsibilities towards their employer. In your copy, write out *three* of the duties or responsibilities that Mary would have.

**2** 'Emigration, unemployment and inflation are problems facing the Minister for Finance when the Government's annual budget is being prepared.'

(a) Explain *two* of the underlined words.

(b) Explain the difference between **work** and **employment**, giving one example of each.

(c) Eric Hughes, who is employed as a factory worker, has a number of responsibilities towards his employer. State *two* of those responsibilities.

(d) Self-employment (running your own business) has its rewards and also its risks. State *two* rewards and *two* risks of self-employment.

eTest.ie
Try a test on this topic

# Chapter 22

# Being an *employer*

## Giving someone a job

Thousands of people have jobs in Ireland, so it must be easy to get a job, right? Wrong! You may not realise it but giving someone a job is complicated and most employers are very careful about who they hire and what they agree to.

To avoid any confusion a **contract of employment** is usually drawn up between the employer and the employee.

This will contain things like details of pay, hours or work, holiday entitlements and sick pay.

A wise employer will keep **employee records**. The records will include personal and educational details about the worker, salary details and information about the different jobs the worker has done in the firm. This information is useful when making decisions about promotion.

When an employer hires a worker, he or she takes on certain responsibilities.

## EMPLOYERS' RESPONSIBILITIES

An employer must:
- allow the worker to join a trade union
- give the worker time off, e.g. maternity leave, holidays
- give women the same pay as men when doing the same work
- look after the employees' health and safety, making sure equipment is in good working order and providing protective clothing in certain jobs.

## EMPLOYERS' RIGHTS

An employer has the right to:
- decide who to hire
- expect an employee to do an honest day's work
- expect employees to follow health and safety directions
- fire employees who steal from the company.

Hiring a worker is not as easy as you might think. The procedure can be complicated and take several weeks. In this example, Peter Bradley is looking for a new sales representative. Ingrid Kelly applies for the job.

# Hiring staff

**COVER LETTER**

Rosses Point Crescent
Sligo

5 May 2010

Mr P. Bradley
It Suits Ltd
Sligo

Dear Mr Bradley

I wish to apply for the position of sales representative as advertised in today's Independent.

Having worked in Dublin for the past three years in Clerys I am keen to find a job in my home town. I am very interested in the clothing industry and believe I would fit in well in your company.

Please find enclosed a copy of my CV. I am available to meet you at any time that suits.

Yours sincerely

*Ingrid Kelly*

Ingrid Kelly

---

**CURRICULUM VITAE**

| | |
|---|---|
| **NAME:** | Ingrid Kelly |
| **ADDRESS:** | Rosses Point Crescent, Sligo |
| **EDUCATION:** | 1990–1999 St Kevin's NS |
| | 1999–2004 Sligo Community School |
| | 2004–2007 UCG |
| **WORK RECORD:** | 2003 Local Centra shop |
| | part-time cashier |
| | 2005 Burger King |
| | part-time counter staff |
| | 2007 Clerys, Dublin |
| | finance department administrator |
| **HOBBIES:** | Acting: member Sligo Drama Society |
| | Basketball: member local club |

## job description

First the employer makes out a job description. This details the work the employee will have to do. It shows the salary and any fringe benefits. It also lists the qualities, experience and age required (for certain jobs). Finally, it mentions how soon the firm needs this worker.

## job advertisement

The details for the advertisement are taken from the job description. Most firms need to advertise in newspapers or on the Internet but some will fill vacancies from among existing staff or their friends. The local FÁS office may also have a list of suitable candidates.

## curriculum vitae

Suppose you decide to apply for the job – what can you expect? The employer will go through the letters of application and pick out a few to interview. If you are among the lucky ones you will usually have to supply a curriculum vitae (CV) and a few references. The employer may telephone the referees and talk about you.

## CONTRACT

This agreement is dated 1 July 2010 and made between Ingrid Kelly and It Suits Ltd.

It is agreed that:

1. **EMPLOYMENT:** Ingrid will commence work on 1 July 2010 for an initial twelve months and thereafter until termination of this contract.
2. **DUTIES:** Ingrid will act as a sales representative for the company.
3. **PLACE OF WORK:** As required Ingrid will travel around Ireland visiting clothes shops.
4. **PAYMENT:** Ingrid will receive €500 basic per week plus ten per cent commission on sales.
5. **EXPENSES:** The company will reimburse Ingrid for all reasonable travelling and work-related expenses.
6. **TERMINATION:** One month's notice is required to terminate this contract.

Signed by:

*Peter Bradley*

Peter Bradley (MD)

*Ingrid Kelly*

Ingrid Kelly

## EMPLOYEE RECORD

| | |
|---|---|
| **NAME:** | Ingrid Kelly |
| **ADDRESS:** | Rosses Point Crescent, Sligo |
| **EDUCATION:** | 1990–1999 St Kevin's NS<br>1999–2004 Sligo Community School<br>2004–2007 UCG |
| **WORK RECORD:** | 2007 Clerys, Dublin<br>2010 joined It Suits Ltd<br>2010–2011 Finance Department<br>2012 Marketing Department |

## interview

At the interview the employer will ask you questions to get to know you better, such as:
- 'Tell me about yourself.'
- 'Why do you want this job?'
- 'What are your skills?'

## selection

After the interviews the employer may shortlist a few candidates and interview these a second time. Only after careful consideration will a candidate be chosen. The new employee will sign an employment contract and the firm will create an employee record.

## induction

The process is not over yet, however. Picking the right person for the job doesn't mean they will stay in the job. If you don't feel welcome in the job you will leave. High staff turnover is not good for a company and so some effort should be made to help the new worker settle into the job.

## CALCULATING WAGES

There are three methods of payment commonly used to calculate wages.

### Piece rate

This is a payment for each unit produced by an employee. This encourages staff to work 'flat out' to maximise their earnings. Workers in clothing and building firms are paid this way. For example, David works in the local service station. He is paid €2 for every car he cleans using the power hose. Last week he washed 50 cars and earned €100 (50 x €2).

### Time rate

Office workers are usually paid for the hours they work. The normal working week will contain 40 basic hours and any additional hours worked may be paid at overtime rates or given as time off. For example, Sarah gets an office job and is paid €14 an hour. Overtime is paid at time and a half, i.e. €21 an hour. Last week she worked 50 hours and was paid €770 (40 hours x €14 plus 10 hours x €21).

### Commission

This is a payment for every unit sold, or in some cases it may be a percentage of total sales. It is normally paid to salespeople. They often receive a basic salary plus commission on sales. For example, Orla sells carpets and is paid €200 each week plus 5% commission. Her sales last week were €6,000. Therefore, her wages were €500 (€200 plus 5% of €6,000).

# Worked Example

## Question

Hugh Jones worked 50 hours this week. He is paid €12 per hour for a basic 40-hour week and time and a half for any overtime worked. His tax credits are €30 per week. His rate of tax is 25%. PRSI is 5% of gross and his other deduction is pension, €30. Calculate his net pay and complete the payslip.

## Solution

## TIPS ?

**Gross pay**

| | |
|---|---|
| Basic: 40 hours x €12 | €480 |
| OT: 10 hours x €18 | €180 |
| **Total gross pay** | **€660** |

**PAYE**

| | |
|---|---|
| 25% of gross pay | €165 |
| Less tax credits | €30 |
| **PAYE** | **€135** |

**PRSI**

| | |
|---|---|
| **5% of gross pay** | **€33** |

**Wages Slip:** HUGH JONES

| PAY | € | DEDUCTIONS | € | NET PAY |
|---|---|---|---|---|
| Basic | 480.00 | PAYE | 135.00 | |
| Overtime | 180.00 | PRSI | 33.00 | **€462.00** |
| | | Pension | 30.00 | |
| **GROSS PAY** | 660.00 | **TOTAL DEDUCTIONS** | 198.00 | |

# Worked Example

## Question

**Doris:** basic pay €250; no overtime; PAYE €40; PRSI €20.

**Hugh:** basic pay €480; overtime €180; PAYE €135; PRSI €33; pension €30.

**Ingrid:** basic pay €100; commission €600; PAYE €110; PRSI €40; health insurance €12.12.

The employer's rate of PRSI is 10% of gross pay.

(a) Complete the wages and salaries book.

(b) Complete the cash analysis chart.

(c) Show the entries in the bank and wages accounts.

## TIPS ON ANSWERING THIS QUESTION

The wages and salaries book lists the employees and the details of their pay and deductions. Care should be taken with the calculations. Use your calculator where necessary.

## Solution

### (a) Wages and salaries book

| Date | Name | Basic Pay | OT/ Comm | Total Gross Pay | PAYE | PRSI | Other | Total Deductions | Net Pay | Employer's PRSI |
|------|------|-----------|----------|-----------------|------|------|-------|------------------|---------|-----------------|
| 1 Nov | Doris Burke | 250.00 | | 250.00 | 40.00 | 20.00 | | 60.00 | 190.00 | 25.00 |
| | Hugh Jones | 480.00 | 180.00 | 660.00 | 135.00 | 33.00 | 30.00 | 198.00 | 462.00 | 66.00 |
| | Ingrid Kelly | 100.00 | 600.00 | 700.00 | 110.00 | 40.00 | 12.12 | 162.12 | 537.88 | 70.00 |
| | TOTALS | 830.00 | 780.00 | 1,610.00 | 285.00 | 93.00 | 42.12 | 420.12 | 1,189.88 | 161.00 |

The cash analysis chart shows the notes and coins needed for each pay packet.

### (b) Cash analysis

| Name | Total | €50 | €20 | €10 | €5 | €2 | €1 | 50c | 20c | 10c | 5c | 2c | 1c |
|------|-------|-----|-----|-----|----|----|----|-----|-----|-----|----|----|----|
| Doris Burke | 190.00 | 3 | 2 | | | | | | | | | | |
| Hugh Jones | 462.00 | 9 | | 1 | | 1 | | | | | | | |
| Ingrid Kelly | 537.88 | 10 | 1 | 1 | 1 | 1 | | 1 | 1 | 1 | 1 | 1 | 1 |
| TOTALS | 1,189.88 | 22 | 3 | 2 | 1 | 2 | 0 | 1 | 1 | 1 | 1 | 1 | 1 |

### (c)

| Dr | | | Bank Account | | | | Cr |
|----|--|--|--------------|--|--|--|----|
| Date | Details | F | Total | Date | Details | F | Total |
| | | | € | Nov | | | € |
| | | | | 1 | Wages | | 1,189.88 |

| | | | Wages Account | | | | |
|--|--|--|---------------|--|--|--|--|
| Nov | | | € | | | | € |
| 1 | Bank | | 1,189.88 | | | | |

The bank account is credited (Cr) with the total wages bill as money is going out of the firm. The double-entry is on the debit (Dr) of the wages account.

1   What is contained in:
    (a) a contract of employment?
    (b) the employee record?

2   (a) List *three* rights of an employer.
    (b) List *three* responsibilities of an employer.

3   Write a note about each of the following stages of hiring staff:
    (a) job description
    (b) job advertisement
    (c) curriculum vitae
    (d) interview
    (e) selection
    (f) induction.

4   Explain, giving examples, the meaning of these methods of calculating wages:
    (a) piece rate
    (b) time rate
    (c) commission.

5   What is the difference between:
    (a) basic pay and overtime?
    (b) gross pay and net pay?
    (c) PAYE and PRSI?

## Activity 22.2 Calculate wages

**1** Calculate the net pay for each of these workers.

(a) Deirdre Kelly has a basic rate of €10 per hour. She works 39 hours at basic rate and eight hours overtime at time and a half. Her deductions are PAYE €96, PRSI €34 and health insurance €12.

(b) Valerie Poole is paid €3.40 for every dress she makes and €2.20 for every blouse. In one week she completes 50 dresses and 24 blouses. Her deductions are PAYE €87, PRSI €29 and pension €17.

(c) Cathal McCarthy is paid a basic salary of €800 a month and commission of 1% on every car he sells. Last month his car sales came to €65,000. His deductions are PAYE €1,820, PRSI €410 and pension €1,500.

**2** In these questions you have to work out the PAYE and PRSI before you find the net pay and complete a payslip. (*Payslips are provided in the workbook.*)

(a) Shane Dwyer is paid €12 per hour and last week he worked 21 hours. His tax credits are €50 per week. His rate of tax is 25%, PRSI is 5% of gross and his other weekly deduction is health insurance €12.

(b) Janette Kearns is paid €546 for a 39-hour week and €21 per hour for overtime. Last week she worked 47 hours. Her tax credits are €110 per week. Her rate of tax is 25%, PRSI is 5% of gross and her other weekly deduction is pension €25.

(c) Peter Brennan is paid €468 for a basic 39-hour week and €18 per hour overtime. Last week he worked 49 hours. His tax credits are €96 per week. His rate of tax is 25%, PRSI is 5% of gross and his other weekly deduction is union dues €3.

eTest.ie
Try a test on this topic

## Activity 22.3 Prepare payroll

**1**
- Lenny: basic pay €370; no overtime; PAYE €55; PRSI €28; health insurance €9.27.
- Aisling: basic pay €547; overtime €220; PAYE €146; PRSI €38; pension €12.50.
- Kevin: basic pay €190; commission €750; PAYE €184; PRSI €63; union dues €14.67.

The employer's rate of PRSI is 10% of gross pay.

*(Templates are provided in the workbook)*
(a) Complete the wages and salaries book.
(b) Complete the cash analysis chart.
(c) Show the entries in the bank and wages accounts.

**2**
- Clodagh: basic pay €460; no overtime; PAYE €66; PRSI €34; health insurance €9.26.
- Alex: basic pay €840; overtime €230; PAYE €187; PRSI €46; union dues €4.60.
- Brian: basic pay €240; commission €820; PAYE €197; PRSI €58; pension €14.68.

The employer's rate of PRSI is 10% of gross pay.

*(Templates are provided in the workbook)*
(a) Complete the wages and salaries book.
(b) Complete the cash analysis chart.
(c) Show the entries in the bank and wages accounts.

eTest.ie
Try a test on this topic

## Activity 22.4 State Exam Practice

Pauline Kelly, head mechanic in a local garage, resigned from her job and set up her own business called PK Motors. Pauline has employed Austin Martin as an assistant mechanic. *(A template is provided in the workbook for this question.)*

(a)  (i) State two rewards and two risks for Pauline as the owner of PK Motors.
     (ii) State two rights and two responsibilities Pauline has as an employer.
     (iii) Explain the importance to PK Motors of keeping employee records.

(b) Austin Martin will be paid a gross wage of €3,600 per month by PK Motors. He will pay income tax (PAYE) at the rate of 20% on the first €2,450 of his wage and 42% on the remainder. Austin Martin has a tax credit of €238 per month. The employee PRSI rate is 7.5% and the employer's PRSI rate is 12%.

   (i) Complete the wages book of PK Motors for this month.
   (ii) Calculate the total cost of employing Austin Martin for the month.

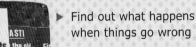

# Chapter 23

# *Industrial relations*

# Your representative in the workplace

A trade union is a group of workers who come together to protect and advance the interests of the members. By joining together the members are in a better position to negotiate with employers. Everyone has the right to join a trade union, except those people employed in the Gardaí or army. For example, if you get a job in a bank you will be invited to join the IBOA (Irish Bank Officials' Association) and if you get a job as a national schoolteacher you will be able to join the INTO (Irish National Teachers' Organisation).

The local union representative is the **shop steward**. He or she is elected by co-workers every year and has the following duties:

- provides members with information
- recruits new members
- tries to solve problems before a dispute arises
- negotiates agreements at local level and checks to make sure such agreements are kept.

## FUNCTIONS OF A TRADE UNION

The main functions and benefits of a trade union are to:

- negotiate better pay and working conditions with the employers
- provide legal advice to the members so they are protected against unfair dismissal or redundancy
- act as a pressure group in discussions with businesses and the government
- monitor the workplace to ensure the members are getting the legal rights they are entitled to, e.g. sick pay.

A strike is a withdrawal of labour and is the union's ultimate weapon. An **official strike** is one that the union head office supports. An **unofficial strike** is one that doesn't have this approval.

# When things go wrong

Workers suffer the loss of their income when they go on strike and therefore prefer to solve the dispute by negotiation. Disputes may be about:

- discrimination
- unsafe working conditions
- unfair dismissal
- membership of a union
- operation of trade union officials.

The shop steward and the management will resolve most disputes without any outside help. Some disputes, however, may be so complex that the shop steward has to call in the help of a full-time official from the union head office. This official will meet the management and discuss the disagreement. If the dispute is still not resolved, there may be a strike or a third party will be consulted.

## Steps in solving

### ALTERNATIVES TO STRIKES

An **all-out strike** is where all employees stop working. Before that there are some alternatives that employees may consider.

- A **go-slow** is where the workers stay at their employment but slow down production.
- A **work-to-rule** is where the workers only do the work as described in the job description.
- A **sit-in** is where the workers occupy the premises where they work; unions are rarely officially involved in a sit-in.

### 1

**Discuss with manager**
The worker discusses the problem with his or her immediate superior. If this doesn't solve the problem, then . . .

### 2

**Inform the shop steward**
The shop steward meets the **human resource manager**. The HR manager represents the company and works with the shop steward to try and resolve the problem. If this doesn't work, then . . .

## TYPES OF TRADE UNION

There are over 100 registered unions in Ireland and they can be grouped into the following areas:

**Craft unions:** The members complete a long apprenticeship to become highly skilled in a specific trade, e.g. actors join the Irish Actors' Equity Group and butchers join the Irish Master Butchers' Federation.

**Industrial unions:** The members of these all work in the same industry, e.g. IBOA is a finance union representing bank officials, while prison officers join the Prison Officers' Association (POA).

**General unions:** These unions cater for many different types of worker, e.g. cleaners, electricians, clothing workers and nurses. The main general unions are the Services, Industrial, Professional and Technical Union (SIPTU) and the Amalgamated Transport and General Workers Union (ATGWU).

**White collar unions:** These represent professional workers, e.g. teachers join the Association of Secondary Teachers in Ireland (ASTI), the Teachers' Union of Ireland (TUI) or the INTO. Civil servants join the Civil and Public Service Union (CPSU).

# a dispute

## 3

### Inform head office
The shop steward reports the problem to the union head office. Head office may now send out a union official to discuss the issue with the HR manager and try to find a solution to the problem. If this doesn't work, then . . .

## 4

### Still no agreement
Both sides may agree to call in the assistance of a third party. This is an outsider who tries to help find a solution to a dispute, e.g. the conciliator or the arbitrator.

### THIRD PARTIES TO A DISPUTE
In an effort to get both sides talking again, unions and employers often call in the help of a third party.

- The **conciliator** listens to both sides and encourages the two parties to enter into further negotiations.
- The **arbitrator** looks at the issues and makes a decision which both sides have agreed in advance to accept.

On the one hand we have the unions and on the other we have the employers. The unions want good conditions and fair wages for their members, and the employers want to remain competitive and keep costs down. To avoid conflicts both parties usually try to agree in advance on an acceptable wages level. This is called collective bargaining.

# Collective bargaining

Discussions between employers' organisations, trade unions and the government in relation to the level of wages is known as collective bargaining. The actions that are decided are called **National Wage Agreements**. These agreements give rise to **good industrial relations** where workers feel respected, there are fewer strikes and there is less conflict between managers and staff. However, each year there are always a few disagreements that lead to trade disputes.

## Irish Congress of Trade Unions (ICTU)

There are 64 trade unions affiliated to the ICTU and consequently it represents 750,000 workers and their families. One of the main functions of the Congress is to represent its members in the collective bargaining process.

## employers' organisations

In the same way as employees have trade unions to protect their rights, employers also group together to negotiate with trade unions. Here are some examples of the organisations employers form:

- Irish Business and Employers' Confederation (IBEC)
- Irish Small and Medium Enterprises Association (ISME)
- Construction Industry Federation (CIF)
- Small Firms Association (SFA)

| Trade Union | Membership |
| --- | --- |
| IBOA | 18,000 |
| ASTI | 17,000 |
| SIPTU | 220,000 |
| NUJ | 3,900 |
| CPSU | 13,000 |
| POA | 3,500 |

## Activity 23.1 Chapter Review

**1** Has every worker the right to join a trade union?

**2** Who is the local union representative in the workplace? List some of their duties.

**3** Who elects the shop steward?

**4** List three functions of a trade union.

**5** What is the difference between an official and an unofficial strike?

**6** List three reasons for trade disputes.

**7** Briefly describe each of these types of trade union and give an example of each:
   (a) craft unions
   (b) industrial unions
   (c) general unions
   (d) white collar unions.

**8** What are the alternatives to a strike?

**9** List and explain the steps in solving a dispute.

**10** Briefly describe the work of each of these third parties:
   (a) conciliator
   (b) arbitrator.

**11** What do the trade unions want for their members?

eTest.ie
Try a test on this topic

**12** What do employers want?

**13** Write a brief note to explain the National Wage Agreement.

**14** Briefly describe the work of each of these organisations:
   (a) Irish Congress of Trade Unions
   (b) Employers' Organisations.

**15** The following organisations are mentioned in the chapter. What do the initials stand for?
   (a) IBOA
   (b) POA
   (c) ASTI
   (d) IBEC
   (e) SFA
   (f) CPSU
   (g) SIPTU
   (h) TUI
   (i) ISME
   (j) INTO
   (k) ATGWU
   (l) ICTU
   (m) CIF.

## Activity 23.2 State Exam Practice

**1** (a) State three rights and three responsibilities of employers.

(b) Study the newspaper extract below and answer the questions that follow.

> Unions at Eircom are expected to serve strike notice on the company today after discussions to resolve a pay dispute collapsed. The unions must provide a week's notice of industrial action to management. The biggest union at the firm, the CWU, believes that the issue will go to the Labour Relations Commission when the notice is served. The CWU voted overwhelmingly in favour of industrial action after Eircom refused to pay workers a 2% increase due to them under the National Wage Agreement until they agreed to change their work practices.

(i) Name the two parties involved in the dispute.

(ii) What form of industrial action is being proposed?

(iii) Identify the third party who might help solve the dispute.

(c) (i) Other than pay, explain three possible reasons for industrial disputes.

(ii) Explain the following terms:
- arbitration
- conciliation
- shop steward
- human resource manager.

Try a test on this topic

**2** (a) The following table shows the number of strikes in Ireland for the period 1990–1994.

| Year | 1990 | 1991 | 1992 | 1993 | 1994 |
|---|---|---|---|---|---|
| Number of strikes | 49 | 54 | 38 | 48 | 32 |

(i) Illustrate the above information on a bar chart.

(ii) Calculate the average number of strikes for the period 1990–1994.

(iii) In what years were the numbers of strikes below the average for the period?

(b) Give three reasons why strikes take place.

(c) **Agriculture staff vote for action**

> Members of the Civil and Public Service Union in the offices of the Department of Agriculture have voted by four to one to implement industrial action because of what it calls the department's breach of an agreement on the employment of temporary staff. The action includes a ban on overtime, refusal to perform duties appropriate to higher grades and a ban on telephone and public office queries.

Study the newspaper report and answer the questions that follow.

(i) What was the dispute about?

(ii) Name the two parties in the dispute.

(iii) What forms of action did the union vote to take?

(iv) How might the dispute be settled? (JCHL, adapted)

▶ Find out how to carry out market research

▶ Learn about the different types of advertising and sales techniques

# Chapter 24

Sales and *marketing*

# Studying the market

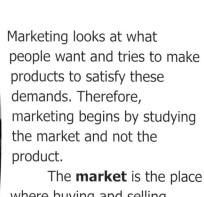

Marketing looks at what people want and tries to make products to satisfy these demands. Therefore, marketing begins by studying the market and not the product.

The **market** is the place where buying and selling occurs, e.g. the fish market, the fruit and vegetable market, the supermarket or the Internet (e-commerce). There is also a financial market which tries to get customers to buy financial services, e.g. open bank accounts and arrange personal loans, mortgages and insurance.

In each of these the sellers are looking for potential customers. These customers are the **target market** for the products or service. As a young person you are in the target market for chocolate manufacturers, drinks companies and publishers of teenage magazines. These are all trying to get you to buy their products.

## MARKET RESEARCH

Market research helps a firm find out about existing and potential markets. There are two types of research:

### Primary/field research

This involves going out to collect original information in the 'field'. Researchers use questionnaires and interview as many people as possible. Since they cannot get around to everyone they normally take a sample of their target market. A sample is a random collection of people who are interviewed for their opinions and preferences.

### Secondary/desk research

In this case the research will study published and other available material. This is not as expensive as field research although it does involve extensive use of the telephone and Internet. The main sources of published information are government statistics, EU publications, trade and technical magazines and websites.

Companies need to make their products different from each other so that the consumer can distinguish one product from another. They do this by advertising, using various selling techniques and by branding.

# Making your product different

One very effective way to make your product different is to use **branding.** The brand is the name of the product, e.g. Nike, Adidas. It identifies the product and people will call it by that name. Advertisements emphasise the brand name, e.g. 'Enjoy the taste of Coca-Cola'. Trademarks and company logos are also forms of branding by which a product can be identified, e.g. McDonald's distinctive 'M'. A logo is the company or product name written in a distinctive style.

Over €600 million is spent on advertising in Ireland each year. A wide range of **advertising media** is used. Most advertisements appear in the national press (newspapers), on the television and over the radio. Drinks companies are especially fond of advertising using outdoor posters and hoardings. Other media comprise 'free' local newspapers, magazines, leaflets, carrier bags and in-store promotions.

There are four types of advertising:
- **Informative advertising:** This gives the public basic information about the qualities of the product, e.g. sizes available, colours and where to buy it.
- **Persuasive advertising:** These advertisements try to convince the consumer that he or she really needs the product, e.g. you will not be clean unless you use NutriCream soap.
- **Competitive advertising:** This criticises the competitors and highlights the qualities of the producer's own product.
- **Collective advertising:** Many small firms pool their resources and advertise together. They can then mount a more effective advertising campaign on a larger budget.

| TOP TEN GROCERY BRANDS | |
|---|---|
| Brand | €m |
| Coca-Cola | 116 |
| Avonmore Fresh Milk | 94 |
| Premier Milk | 60 |
| Tayto Crisps | 59 |
| Lucozade Energy | 56 |
| 7-Up | 52 |
| Lyons Tea | 50 |
| Pampers | 50 |
| Denny Prepacked | 49 |
| Goodfellas | 45 |

# SELLING TECHNIQUES

## Loyalty cards

The consumer gets tokens or points or coupons and is rewarded for the amount purchased. This is used extensively by retailers to encourage loyalty. The tokens can be redeemed for gifts.

## Special offers

These reduce the price of the product or give some added value to make it more attractive to the consumer, e.g. 'Buy a burger, get a drink free'.

## Free samples

These are given out to promote new products. In this way the consumer can 'try before you buy'.

## Loss leaders

Many retailers reduce the price of some products to attract customers to their shops. The customer will normally buy more than these loss leaders and so the shop stays profitable.

## Sponsorship

Many sports and cultural events are sponsored by firms to promote their products. In return for a fee paid to the organisers, the company is given advertising space at the venue.

## Public relations (PR)

Public relations (PR) aims to improve the communications between a business and the public. This helps them maintain and increase sales. PR can affect a company's image by influencing:
- uniform and appearance of sales staff
- telephone and e-mail manner
- letter headings
- product packaging
- advertisements
- newspaper reports.

The **marketing mix** is the way a company combines what is called the 'four Ps' in order to make their product different from the competition. The **four Ps** are product, price, place and promotion. The aim is to find out what product to produce, what price to charge, where to sell the product and how to promote and advertise the product.

# The marketing mix

The four Ps are the elements that the marketing manager can control. The aim is to make decisions that focus the four Ps on the target market and thereby get the customers to buy the product or service on offer.

### Product decisions

The marketing team can influence:
- the brand name
- the quality of the product
- the styling of the product
- the packaging used
- after-sale repairs and support.

### Price decisions

Some decisions to be made here are:
- What will be the price of the product?
- Will there be a cash discount?
- Will there be a trade discount?
- Will there be a volume discount?
- Will customers in different parts of the country pay a different price?

### Place decisions

This is concerned with getting the product to the customer. Some examples of decisions here are:
- Where will customers be able to buy this product?
- Will we deliver to the customer?
- Which shops will stock the product?

### Promotion decisions

This is the way the company will tell the customer about the product, how to use it and where to buy it. Here are some examples of promotion decisions:
- the advertising strategy
- sales promotions
- publicity.

## Activity 24.1 Chapter Review

**1** (a) Give three examples of markets.

(b) What is meant by the term 'target market'?

(c) Explain the two types of market research.

**2** (a) List three examples of brand names.

(b) Why is the brand name important?

(c) List the main advertising media.

**3** Briefly describe each of these types of advertising and give an example in each case:

(a) informative advertising

(b) persuasive advertising

(c) competitive advertising

(d) collective advertising.

**4** (a) List and explain three selling techniques.

(b) What is PR?

(c) What effect can PR have on a company?

**5** (a) What is the marketing mix?

(b) Briefly describe each element of the marketing mix.

## Activity 24.2 State Exam Practice

**1** William mixed up the answers in his Business Studies test. He had all the correct answers but he put them in the wrong sentences. Here is what he wrote.

1. A market is *a reduced price offer to a customer.*
2. A questionnaire is *giving the public information about a product.*
3. Market research is *all the potential customers for a product or service.*
4. Money off is *collecting information about a market.*
5. Informative advertising is *where a firm gives money to a sports club to organise a competition.*
6. A special offer is *given to a particular good or range of goods so that it will become well known among the public.*
7. A brand name is *given to consumers for every €10 they spend in certain shops. Also called tokens, a certain number of them may be exchanged for a free gift.*
8. A target market is *giving extra value for money, such as three for the price of two.*
9. A coupon is *a list of questions consumers are asked.*
10. Sponsorship is *a place where goods are bought and sold.*

Write out each sentence fully, showing the correct answer in each sentence.

(JCOL, adapted)

**2** Peter Sports Ltd sells footballs throughout Munster. In one year the number of footballs sold in each county was as follows.

| Clare | Cork | Kerry | Limerick | Tipperary | Waterford |
|-------|------|-------|----------|-----------|-----------|
| 2,000 | 4,000 | 4,500 | 1,500 | 2,500 | 1,000 |

(a) Using graph paper, draw a bar chart showing the above information.

(b) At €20 a football, what were the total sales for the year? (Show your workings.)

Peter Sports Ltd is also producing a new range of football boots that they hope to sell all over Munster.

(c) Write out **two** reasons why companies advertise their goods or services.

(d) State **three** methods that Peter Sports Ltd might use to advertise the football boots. Give one reason in favour of each method you mention.

(JCOL, adapted)

**3** (a) State **four** factors that a business should consider before deciding to produce a new product.

(b) Explain **two** methods of obtaining information about a market.

(c) Knockair is a low-cost airline flying from Knock Airport to ten European capitals. The company is launching a new route from Knock to Paris. Flights, available seven days a week, will depart at 6.30 a.m. This new route will commence on 1 June and will cost €15, one way, plus government taxes. Booking is online at www.knockair.com.

  (i) Draft a suitable advertisement for this new route that could be inserted in a national newspaper.

  (ii) State **three** methods, other than newspapers and the Internet, of advertising a low-cost airline.

(JCHL, adapted)

eTest.ie
Try a test on this topic

▶ Learn the factors to consider when choosing a method of delivery

▶ Find out about the different ways of delivering goods

# Chapter 25

# Delivery systems

# Choosing a method of delivery

The transport and delivery of raw materials and finished goods costs millions of euro each year. Goods now have a **carbon footprint**, i.e. the amount of fuel that has been used to get the product from its place of origin to you, the customer. Firms are increasingly aware of the need to keep their transport costs down. But there are other factors that may overrule this.

The four factors to consider when choosing a method of delivering goods are cost, distance, speed and reliability.

Anything that greatly increases the **cost** will reduce a product's competitiveness. For example, air transport is very expensive and is often only used to transport expensive goods.

Exporting a long **distance** is expensive: the goods are loaded onto a ship or plane and unloaded at the port or airport. Then they may be loaded onto a truck or train and unloaded again at the new destination. To save money goods may be placed into containers, as these are easy to transfer between the different methods of transport.

Producers usually operate within strict deadlines and **speed** is important. They need fast systems that will permit them to meet delivery dates. Road congestion and air, rail or ship timetables have to be worked around.

It is essential to choose a method that has good **reliability**. It would be unwise to select a method of transport that breaks down frequently no matter how cheap it might be, since this might result in a firm missing its deadlines and losing orders.

The main methods of delivering goods within Ireland are by road or rail. To deliver goods outside Ireland we have to use air or sea.

# Delivering the goods

## roads

Road transport is the most common means of delivering goods in Ireland. Motorways offer a direct route from one city to another, bypassing smaller towns. Of course traffic jams can cause costly delays.

Many firms prefer to buy their own fleet of delivery vans. The main costs of running a fleet of delivery vans are insurance, diesel fuel, drivers' wages, repairs and annual service. But the advantages often make it worthwhile.
- They can advertise their products or services on the vans.
- They have greater security.
- They have more control over their delivery schedules.
- There will be less damage to the products caused by handling.

## rail

This may be quicker than road delivery over long distances. However, goods can only be delivered from station to station on fixed routes. Railways operate to a regular timetable and are ideal for bulky loads such as cement.

Iarnród Éireann Freight provides many types of freight services, from the delivery of a single letter to a full trainload of cargo. It has a wide network of freight depots located all around the country and it uses both road and rail to ensure quick and safe delivery of cars, containers and kegs of beer. It also has the Fastrack service, which provides a same-day delivery of parcels and letters.

## air

This is the fastest form of transport. Over three million people use Irish airports each year, while another three million travel by sea. Because air transport is expensive, the goods transported usually have a high value, e.g. jewellery, spare parts and fresh fish.

In recent years there has been an increase in the use of air transport. There are a number of reasons for this:
- It is less expensive now due to increased competition.
- More airports have been opened.
- Modern planes can carry greater loads.

## sea

Around ten ships leave Irish ports every day for Britain and the Continent. Sea transport is ideal for bulky loads over long distances. Both 'roll-on, roll-off' (RO-RO) and 'lift-on, lift-off' (LO-LO) trailers travel this way. Many trailers use the 'land bridge' to the Continent, i.e. they get a ferry to Britain, drive to a southern British port and get another ferry or use the Channel Tunnel to the Continent.

- Rosslare Port is Ireland's busiest ferry port. It is operated by Iarnród Éireann and is the closest point in Ireland to the UK.

- Dublin Port is another busy port but it is situated right in the centre of Dublin. The new Port Tunnel gives easier access to the port.

## pipelines

We make extensive use of pipelines to transport gas, oil and water. Gas is piped from the natural gas fields off the south coast of Ireland as far north as Dundalk. Pipelines are also used to deliver airport fuel from Dublin Port to Dublin Airport. These pipelines are expensive to set up but cheap to operate. However, they are only suitable for certain types of product.

## canals

Although Ireland has an extensive canal and river network it is not used for transporting goods. Canals and rivers are a big tourist attraction, however, generating much revenue from the hire of boats for cruising and fishing.

# COMPARING TRANSPORT SYSTEMS

When comparing transport systems we need to consider the following:

- Air transport is more expensive than sea transport and is only suitable for products with a high value. Bulky products will be transported by sea, e.g. coal and anything in containers.
- Over short distances (less than 300km) road transport is cheaper than rail transport.
- Having a return load greatly reduces costs.
- Transport by sea is slow and subject to weather conditions.
- Rail transport is fast but only operates station to station and is tied to a timetable.
- Road transport is fast but is subject to poor roads and congestion.

The costs involved in road transport can be put into two groups:

### Fixed costs

The fixed costs are the annual costs of running the vehicles, e.g. motor tax, insurance and annual repairs. These costs do not change with the amount of driving. Find the total of these costs and divide this total by the number of days the company is open for each year. This gives you the fixed costs for one day.

### Variable costs

These are the daily costs of running the vehicle, e.g. diesel and toll charges. The more the vehicle is used, the greater the variable costs.

### Cost of delivery

Add the fixed costs for one day to the total variable costs and you get the cost of delivery.

# Worked Example

## Question

(a) Calculate the cost of the round trip from Cavan to Cork, given the following information.
- (i) The annual motor tax is €480.
- (ii) The annual van insurance is €750.
- (iii) The annual maintenance costs are €270.
- (iv) It is 300km from Cavan to Cork.
- (v) The driver is paid €100 per day.
- (vi) The van covers 12km per litre of diesel.
- (vii) Diesel costs 96 cent a litre.
- (viii) The company is open 250 days a year.

(b) Express the total cost of the return journey as a percentage of the invoice value of the goods, given as €3,080. Give one reason why it is important to know this percentage.

## Solution

**(a)**

| Fixed costs | € |
| --- | --- |
| Motor tax | 480 |
| Insurance | 750 |
| Maintenance | 270 |
| Total fixed costs | 1,500 |
| **Amount for day (€1,500 / 250)** | **€6** |

| Variable costs | € |
| --- | --- |
| Distance: 300km x 2 = 600km | |
| Diesel used: 600km / 12 = 50 litres | |
| Fuel costs (50 litres x 96 cent) | 48 |
| Labour costs | 100 |
| Total variable costs | 148 |
| Fixed costs for day | 6 |
| **Cost of journey** | **€154** |

**(b)**

$$\frac{\text{Cost of journey}}{\text{Invoice value of goods}} = \frac{154}{3,080} \times \frac{100}{1} = 5\%$$

It costs 5% of the value of the goods to deliver the goods. Therefore, the firm should ensure that its profit on sales is greater than 5%.

## Activity 25.1 Chapter Review

**1** Write a note about each of the following factors to consider when choosing a method of delivery:
(a) cost
(b) distance
(c) speed
(d) reliability.

**2** Explain, giving examples, the benefits of using each of these types of transport:
(a) road
(b) rail
(c) air
(d) sea
(c) pipelines
(d) canals.

**3** Suggest a suitable method of transport in each of these cases.
(a) Delivering cement from Dundalk to Cork.
(b) Delivering urgently needed spare parts from Detroit (USA) to Limerick.
(c) Delivering new cars from Genoa (Italy) to Rosslare.
(d) Delivering gas from Kinsale to Dublin.

## Activity 25.2 Calculate the cost of road delivery

**1** Calculate the cost of the round trip from Larne to Portlaoise, given the following information.
(i) The annual motor tax is €540.
(ii) The annual van insurance is €680.
(iii) The annual maintenance costs are €290.
(iv) It is 288km from Larne to Portlaoise.
(v) The driver is paid €90 per day.
(vi) The van covers 10km per litre of diesel.
(vii) Diesel costs 98 cent a litre.
(viii) The company is open 250 days a year.

**2** Calculate the cost of the round trip from Wexford to Clifden, given the following information.
(i) The annual motor tax is €470.
(ii) The annual van insurance is €1,130.
(iii) The annual maintenance costs are €460.
(iv) It is 330km from Wexford to Clifden.
(v) The driver is paid €85 per day.
(vi) The van covers 11km per litre of diesel.
(vii) Diesel costs 99 cent a litre.
(viii) The company is open 300 days a year.

## Activity 25.3 State Exam Practice

**1** (a) Name **three** factors which a business would consider when choosing a transport system to deliver goods to its customers. Explain the importance of each factor.

(b) Most Irish companies use road transport to deliver goods.
(i) Give **two** advantages of using road transport.
(ii) Give **two** disadvantages of using road transport.

(c) Express Couriers Ltd delivers goods overnight to firms around the country. Its vans travel at an average speed of 56 kilometres per hour. The van drivers must take one hour's rest after every four hours of driving.

A firm in Carlow has requested Express Couriers Ltd to deliver an urgent packet to a shop in Tralee, a distance of 252 kilometres. The packet must be delivered before 9.00 a.m. the following day.

Calculate the latest time that a van driver from Express Couriers Ltd can set off from Carlow to deliver the packet by 9.00 a.m. in Tralee.

(d) Toll roads, quality bus corridors, distance tables, bypasses, bicycle lanes, tachographs, ferries, pipelines and fork-lift trucks are terms relating to transport and delivery systems. Explain **four** of these terms.

(JCOL, adapted)

**2** (a) Give **three** reasons why a business might use its own delivery vans.

(b) Explain **three** factors that should be taken into account when deciding on the type of delivery system to be used by a business.

(c) Champ Ltd, Sligo asks you to calculate the total cost of a journey (round trip) from Sligo to Dublin and back again to Sligo on 29 May from the following data.

(i) The distance from Sligo to Dublin is 217km.
(ii) The diesel van can cover 14km per litre of diesel.
(iii) The cost of diesel is 99 cent per litre.
(iv) The van driver's wages are €95 per day.
(v) The annual motor tax is €560.
(vi) The annual motor insurance is €1,400.
(vii) The annual repairs are €700.
(viii) Champ Ltd operates 300 working days of the year.

(JCHL, adapted)

# Chapter 26

# Stages in a business transaction

# Trading on credit

When you buy goods in a shop you normally pay cash straight away. The only document involved is a receipt.

In business, things are a little more complicated. The reason is that when businesses trade with each other they often do it as a **credit transaction**, i.e. the goods are sold and delivered but no cash is paid until weeks or months later. The reason the buyer has so long to pay is to give him or her time to sell the goods and get cash. Then the supplier can be paid.

Buying and selling goods involves communication between two businesses. In order to keep track of the transactions, a business will issue a number of documents. These give both the buyer and the seller a written record of the transaction and the documents are usually filed for future reference. They also help to avoid any error in processing the order. Below is a list of the business documents issued in the course of a credit transaction.

| seller | | buyer |
|---|---|---|
| | ◄·········· **Enquiry** | The buyer (customer) begins by making an enquiry. If desired an order is placed and later payment is made. |
| The seller waits until an enquiry is received. Then the quotation is sent and if an order is received a whole process begins. The documents sent by the seller are shown in red. | **Quotation** ············► | |
| | ◄·········· **Order** | |
| | **Invoice** ···············► | |
| | **Delivery docket** ·······► | |
| | **Credit note** ············► | |
| | **Debit note** ············► | |
| | **Statement** ············► | |
| | ◄·········· **Payment** | |
| | **Receipt** ·················► | |

*Chapter 26 Stages in a Business Transaction*   159

# LETTER OF ENQUIRY

A letter of enquiry is sent from the buyer to the seller to find out about the prices of goods available. A buyer may send many letters of enquiry to different sellers. The seller with the best conditions of sale will be selected.

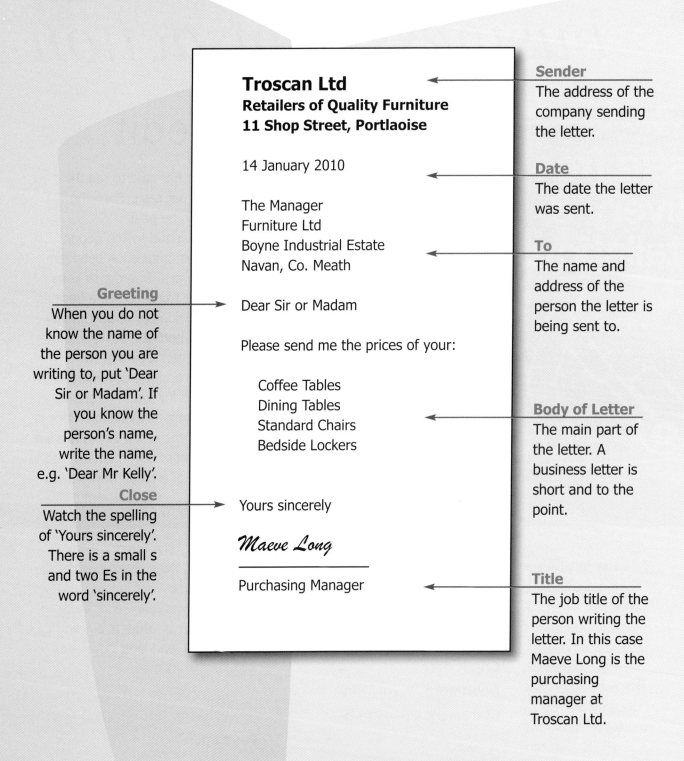

**Sender**
The address of the company sending the letter.

**Troscan Ltd**
**Retailers of Quality Furniture**
**11 Shop Street, Portlaoise**

14 January 2010

**Date**
The date the letter was sent.

The Manager
Furniture Ltd
Boyne Industrial Estate
Navan, Co. Meath

**To**
The name and address of the person the letter is being sent to.

**Greeting**
When you do not know the name of the person you are writing to, put 'Dear Sir or Madam'. If you know the person's name, write the name, e.g. 'Dear Mr Kelly'.

Dear Sir or Madam

Please send me the prices of your:

Coffee Tables
Dining Tables
Standard Chairs
Bedside Lockers

**Body of Letter**
The main part of the letter. A business letter is short and to the point.

**Close**
Watch the spelling of 'Yours sincerely'. There is a small s and two Es in the word 'sincerely'.

Yours sincerely

*Maeve Long*
_____
Purchasing Manager

**Title**
The job title of the person writing the letter. In this case Maeve Long is the purchasing manager at Troscan Ltd.

# QUOTATION

A quotation is sent by the supplier to customers who have enquired about goods for sale. It gives details about the goods they have in stock, such as prices, delivery dates, VAT and terms of trade. Some suppliers may have price lists or catalogues they willl send out instead of a quotation.

---

### QUOTATION

No. 253

**Furniture Ltd**
**Boyne Industrial Estate**
**Navan, Co. Meath**

19 January 2010

Ms Maeve Long
Purchasing Manager
Troscan Ltd
Retailers of Quality Furniture
11 Shop Street, Portlaoise

| Model No. | Description | Price Each |
|---|---|---|
| | | € |
| CT123 | Coffee Tables | 120.00 |
| DT324 | Dining Tables | 250.00 |
| SC751 | Standard Chairs | 25.00 |
| BL822 | Bedside Lockers | 50.00 |

Trade discount: 20% on all goods
VAT: 10% on all goods
Carriage paid; For acceptance within 30 days

E&OE

---

# COMPARING QUOTATIONS

A customer will compare the quotations in relation to price, carriage and terms of trade before deciding on the best deal.

---

### Carriage
This is the transport arrangement for the delivery of the goods.
- **Carriage paid:** In this case the supplier will deliver the goods free.
- **FOR (free on rail):** The supplier will pay for the delivery of the goods by train to the station nearest to the customer.
- **Ex works:** The price quoted does not include delivery. You must make your own arrangements to collect the goods from the factory or pay the supplier to deliver.
- **CWO (cash with order):** In this case the customer must pay for the goods when ordering.
- **COD (cash on delivery):** This means the buyer must pay for the goods when they are delivered.

---

### Terms of trade
This gives details about the discount.
- **Trade discount:** This is a discount given to regular customers who are 'in the trade', i.e. when the buyer and seller are in the same line of business. This discount is a deduction from the list price, made by the supplier so that the retailer can make a profit when the goods are sold at the list price.
- **Cash discount:** This is given to customers who pay up promptly: '5% seven days' means that you will get a 5% discount if you pay within a week.

# ORDER

The order is sent by the customer to the supplier, indicating the goods the customer wishes to purchase. Many suppliers have a standard order form that customers complete.

## ORDER

### No. 98

**Troscan Ltd**
**Retailers of Quality Furniture**
**11 Shop Street, Portlaoise**

25 January 2010

The Manager
Furniture Ltd
Boyne Industrial Estate
Navan, Co. Meath

Please supply the following goods:

| Quantity | Description | Price Each |
|----------|-------------|------------|
| | | € |
| 40 | Coffee Tables (CT123) | 120.00 |
| 30 | Dining Tables (DT324) | 250.00 |
| 80 | Standard Chairs (SC751) | 25.00 |
| 12 | Bedside Lockers (BL822) | 50.00 |

Signed:

*Maeve Long*

Purchasing Manager

E&OE

## Checking credit rating

When an order is received, the sales office must check the customer's credit rating. Regular customers who pay within a reasonable time will have no trouble getting credit. Other customers may have to pay cash on delivery or cash with order. New customers must be investigated and a decision made whether to give them credit or not. These customers may be required to give references of other suppliers they deal with. This will show whether the supplier can trust them or not.

The seller will look for:
- a reference from the customer's bank (a bank reference)
- a reference from another company the customer does business with (a trade reference).

## Checking stock

The seller must check to see if the goods ordered are in stock. Otherwise, part of the order may have to be left out. In this case, the supplier may be tempted to include items not ordered by the customer. It is up to the customer to ensure that the goods delivered are the goods ordered. If the supplier is out of stock, this means a loss of sale for that item as the customer may be able to go elsewhere and get the goods. Suppliers can easily lose customers by not having sufficient quantities of a product in stock.

## Stock control

To avoid running out of stock, a firm should operate a proper stock control system with the following policies.

- **Decide suitable stock levels:** The amount of stock stored will depend on the size of the stock room. It is also costly to buy stock. At certain times more stock is needed as the supplier knows to expect sales.
- **Decide reorder quantities and reorder times:** If new stock can be delivered quickly, the supplier may decide to order little and often. This is the basis of the 'just in time' stock system.
- **Carry out stocktaking regularly:** Many firms have computerised stock control systems that give them a regular update of their stock position.

## Errors in documents

Since errors may occur in drafting business documents they usually include the phrase E&OE ('Errors and omissions excepted'). This gives the company issuing the document the right to correct any errors they discover later.

## What happens next?

Once the seller is satisfied that the customer is creditworthy and that the goods are in stock, the delivery can be arranged and the invoice can be posted out to the customer.

The delivery docket is signed by the customer. The customer keeps a copy and a duplicate copy is returned by the delivery person to the supplier to prove the goods were delivered.

---

### DELIVERY DOCKET

No. 153

**Furniture Ltd
Boyne Industrial Estate
Navan, Co. Meath**

8 February 2010

Ms Maeve Long
Purchasing Manager
Troscan Ltd
Retailers of Quality Furniture
11 Shop Street, Portlaoise

| Quantity | Description |
|---|---|
| 40 | Coffee Tables |
| 30 | Dining Tables |
| 80 | Standard Chairs |
| 12 | Bedside Lockers |

Received the above goods in good condition.

Signed _____

---

A customer will compare the delivery docket with the order to make sure the goods that have been delivered are the ones that were originally ordered.

# INVOICE

The invoice is sent by the supplier to the customer. The final figure is the amount the customer owes. The invoice shows the trade discount given (if any), the VAT charged and the terms of trade.

## INVOICE

No. 167

**Furniture Ltd**
**Boyne Industrial Estate**
**Navan, Co. Meath**

8 February 2010

Ms Maeve Long
Purchasing Manager
Troscan Ltd
Retailers of Quality Furniture
11 Shop Street, Portlaoise

| Quantity | Description | Code | Price Each | Total |
|----------|-------------|------|------------|-------|
| | | | € | € |
| 40 | Coffee Tables | CT123 | 120.00 | 4,800.00 |
| 30 | Dining Tables | DT324 | 250.00 | 7,500.00 |
| 80 | Standard Chairs | SC751 | 25.00 | 2,000.00 |
| 12 | Bedside Lockers | BL822 | 50.00 | 600.00 |
| | | | Total (excluding VAT) | 14,900.00 |
| | | | 20% Trade discount | 2,980.00 |
| | | | Subtotal | 11,920.00 |
| | | | 10% VAT | 1,192.00 |
| | | | Total (including VAT) | 13,112.00 |

E&OE

## What happens next?

When Maeve Long gets this invoice she should:
- check the accuracy of the figures
- check that she is getting the agreed discount
- compare the invoice with the order to ensure she is getting what she ordered
- file it for future reference.

# CREDIT NOTE

This is given by the supplier to the customer. There are two occasions when it is used:
- when a customer returns goods.
- when a customer has been overcharged.

## CREDIT NOTE

No. 76

**Furniture Ltd**
**Boyne Industrial Estate**
**Navan, Co. Meath**

10 February 2010

Ms Maeve Long
Purchasing Manager
Troscan Ltd
Retailers of Quality Furniture
11 Shop Street, Portlaoise

| Quantity | Description | Code | Price Each | Total |
|----------|-------------|------|------------|-------|
| | | | € | € |
| 1 | Coffee Tables | CT123 | 120.00 | 120.00 |
| 1 | Dining Tables | DT324 | 250.00 | 250.00 |
| | | | Total (excluding VAT) | 370.00 |
| | | | 20% Trade discount | 74.00 |
| | | | Subtotal | 296.00 |
| | | | 10% VAT | 29.60 |
| | | | Total (including VAT) | 325.60 |

E&OE

# DEBIT NOTE

A debit note is given by the supplier to the customer:
- when some item has been omitted from the invoice
- when a customer has been undercharged.

# STATEMENT OF ACCOUNT

The statement is sent by the supplier at the end of the month. It gives a summary of the transactions that have occurred with a particular customer over the previous month. A 'balance forward' figure is the amount the customer owed previously. Any invoices are shown in the debit column and any credit notes or cheques received are listed in the credit column. The balance column shows a running balance and is reduced or increased depending on whether the entries are in the debit or credit columns. The final figure shows the amount the customer now owes the supplier.

Before sending out this statement Furniture Ltd should:
- check that the calculations are correct
- check that all transactions have been invoiced
- check that the terms are correct
- file a copy for future reference.

## STATEMENT

No. 174

**Furniture Ltd**
**Boyne Industrial Estate**
**Navan, Co. Meath**

26 February 2010

Ms Maeve Long
Purchasing Manager
Troscan Ltd
Retailers of Quality Furniture
11 Shop Street, Portlaoise

| Date | Description | Debit | Credit | Balance |
|------|-------------|-------|--------|---------|
|      |             | €     | €      | €       |
| 1 Feb | Balance forward | | | 250.00 |
| 8 Feb | Invoice | 13,112.00 | | 13,362.00 |
| 10 Feb | Credit Note | | 325.60 | 13,036.40 |
| 17 Feb | Cheque | | 500.00 | 12,536.40 |

E&OE

---

**What is effective purchasing?**
An effective purchaser will:
- get at least three quotations
- compare the prices and the terms carefully
- make sure that what is ordered is received in the correct quantity
- promptly return any damaged goods.

## PAYMENT

The customer is now expected to pay the amount due. This is normally paid by cheque. Most will pay promptly to avail of any discounts.

| | | |
|---|---|---|
| | 20 Feb 20 10 | **Allied Irish Banks** |
| Pay | Furniture Ltd | or order |
| | Twelve thousand, five hundred and thirty-six | € 12,536.40 |
| | euro and 40 cent | Maeve Long |
| | | Maeve Long |

00601   93 7436   66228844

## RECORDING THE PAYMENT

The cheque payment is recorded in the bank account. Enter the €12,536.40 on the credit side of the account.

| Dr | | | | Bank Account | | | Cr |
|---|---|---|---|---|---|---|---|
| Date | Details | F | Total | Date | Details | F | Total |
| | | | € | Feb 20 | Furniture Ltd | | € 12,536.40 |

| **Furniture Ltd** Boyne Industrial Estate, Navan, Co.Meath | | No.: 151 |
|---|---|---|
| Date: | 24 Feb 2010 | |
| Received From: | Maeve Long | |
| The sum of: | Twelve thousand, five hundred and thirty-six euro and 40 cent | |
| | | € 12,536.40 |
| With Thanks | Signed: Noel Thompson | |

## RECEIPT

Once the cheque is received the supplier will issue a receipt. This concludes the transaction.

*Templates for these questions are provided in the workbook.*

**1** On 15 May Mr John Kelly, the Principal of St Cronan's School, Wicklow, writes a letter of enquiry to Wise Furniture Ltd, Wise Avenue, Dundalk. He wants details about the tables and chairs that Wise Furniture Ltd supplies. Write the letter sent by Mr Kelly.

**2** On 12 November Ms Paula Toomey, the purchasing manager of Powertown Ltd, Bridge Street, Cavan, writes a letter of enquiry to Ace Electrics Ltd, Bloonfield Industrial Estate, Athlone. She wants details about the fridges and cookers that Ace Electrics Ltd supplies. Write the letter sent by Ms Toomey.

**3** Music Wholesalers Ltd, Bridge Street, Galway supplies guitars to music shops around Ireland. On 5 March Music Wholesalers Ltd send a quotation for the following goods to Billy Stafford, Purchasing Manager, Alto Ltd, Catherine Street, Limerick.

| | |
|---|---|
| Malaga Guitars | Model MJ35 @ €45 each |
| Orlando Guitars | Model OA67 @ €90 each |

From the above details, complete quotation no. 67.

**4** Computer Wholesalers Ltd, College Street, Waterford supplies computers to shops around Ireland. On 14 April Computer Wholesalers Ltd send a quotation for the following goods to Jen Conroy, Purchasing Manager, PC Ireland Ltd, Morgan Street, Cork.

| | |
|---|---|
| Mini Laptops | Model ML64 @ €150 each |
| Desktops | Model DT97 @ €340 each |
| Printers | Model P52 @ €45 each |

From the above details, complete quotation no. 259.

**5** Billy Stafford is the purchasing manager at Alto Ltd, Catherine Street, Limerick. On 27 April he orders the following goods from Music Wholesalers Ltd, Bridge Street, Galway.

| | |
|---|---|
| 10 Malaga Guitars | Model MJ35 @ €45 each |
| 18 Orlando Guitars | Model OA67 @ €90 each |

From the above details, complete order no. 241.

**6** Jen Conroy is the purchasing manager at PC Ireland Ltd, Morgan Street, Cork. On 16 May she orders the following goods from Computer Wholesalers Ltd, College Street, Waterford.

| | |
|---|---|
| 15 Mini Laptops | Model ML64 @ €150 each |
| 20 Desktops | Model DT97 @ €340 each |
| 18 Printers | Model P52 @ €45 each |

From the above details, complete order no. 169.

## Activity 26.2 Delivery docket, invoice, credit note

*Templates for these questions are provided in the workbook.*

**1** Paul Gearon works as a van driver for Haircare Wholesalers Ltd, Cranmore Industrial Estate, Sligo. On 12 March he loaded 10 flat irons, 15 hairdryers and 25 gift sets into his van and delivered them to Mane Hair Ltd, Main Street, Letterkenny. Draft the delivery docket he brought with him.

**2** On 4 April O'Donoghues Song Supplies, Mitchell Street, Tipperary, sent an invoice, no. 251, to Cronin's Music Shop, Bowers Lane, Killarney for the following goods: 20 copies of *Irish Songs* at €4 each, 60 copies of *Country Songs* at €3 each and 10 copies of *Gaelic Songs* at €12 each. Trade discount is 20% and VAT is 10%. Draft the invoice sent on 4 April.

**3** On 9 April Cronin's Music Shop, Bowers Lane, Killarney returned 3 copies of *Gaelic Songs* (faulty covers) at €12 each to O'Donoghues Song Supplies, Mitchell Street, Tipperary. Trade discount is 20% and VAT is 10%. Draft the credit note sent by O'Donoghues Song Supplies on 10 April.

**4** On 26 May Baby Supplies Ltd, Castle Street, Thurles sent an invoice, no. 364, to Bouncy Ltd, School Street, Wexford for the following goods: 15 travel cots at €72 each, 20 car seats at €84 each and 4 twin pushchairs at €215 each. Trade discount is 20% and VAT is 10%. Draft the invoice sent on 26 May.

**5** On 28 May Bouncy Ltd, School Street, Wexford returned 2 faulty travel cots (faulty netting) at €72 each to Baby Supplies Ltd, Castle Street, Thurles. Trade discount is 20% and VAT is 10%. Draft the credit note sent by Baby Supplies Ltd on 28 May.

**6** On 22 June Digital Supplies Ltd, Great Water Industrial Estate, Longford sent an invoice, no. 418, to Techie Ltd, Blackhall Street, Mullingar for the following goods: 12 cameras at €64 each, 15 22" flat-screen TVs at €172 each and 9 mini camcorders at €59 each. Trade discount is 20% and VAT is 10%. Draft the invoice sent on 22 June.

**7** On 30 June Techie Ltd, Blackhall Street, Mullingar returned 2 faulty cameras (faulty lens) at €64 each to Digital Supplies Ltd, Great Water Industrial Estate, Longford. Trade discount is 20% and VAT is 10%. Draft the credit note sent by Digital Supplies Ltd on 1 July.

**8** On 8 July Scooter Supplies Ltd, Swords, Co. Dublin, sent an invoice, no. 517, to Lucan Bikes Ltd, Main Street, Lucan for the following goods: 30 helmets at €46 each, 15 biker pants at €38 each and 20 biker jackets at €43 each. Trade discount is 20% and VAT is 10%. Draft the invoice sent on 8 July.

**9** On 12 July Lucan Bikes Ltd, Main Street, Lucan returned 2 faulty helmets (faulty straps) at €46 each to Scooter Supplies Ltd, Swords, Co. Dublin. Trade discount is 20% and VAT is 10%. Draft the credit note sent by Scooter Supplies Ltd on 13 July.

## Activity 26.3 Statement

*Templates for these questions are provided in the workbook.*

**1** Seller: Bath Supplies Ltd, Main Street, Athlone.
Buyer: BrayBuild Ltd, Seaview Avenue, Bray, Co. Wicklow.

On 1 April, BrayBuild Ltd owed Bath Supplies Ltd €3,500.

The following transactions took place during the month of April.
　　10 April　Bath Supplies Ltd received a cheque from BrayBuild Ltd for €1,800.
　　15 April　Bath Supplies Ltd sent an invoice no. 43 to BrayBuild Ltd, €6,000 + VAT 20%
　　24 April　Bath Supplies Ltd sent a credit note no. 28 to BrayBuild Ltd, €1,300 + VAT 20%

From the above details, complete the statement no. 59.

**2** Seller: Carco Ltd, Castle Street, Carlow.
Buyer: Donegal Garage Ltd, Killybegs Avenue, Donegal.

On 1 May, Donegal Garage Ltd owed Carco Ltd €2,600.

The following transactions took place during the month of May.
　　11 May　Carco Ltd sent an invoice no. 289 to Donegal Garage Ltd, €3,500 + VAT 20%
　　18 May　Carco Ltd received a cheque from Donegal Garage Ltd for €2,200.
　　24 May　Carco Ltd sent a credit note no. 124 to Donegal Garage Ltd, €900 + VAT 20%

From the above details, complete the statement no. 317.

**3** Seller: A1 Supplies Ltd, Main Street, Athlone.
Buyer: KerryBooks Ltd, Seaview Avenue, Co. Kerry.

On 1 June, KerryBooks Ltd owed A1 Supplies Ltd €1,800.

The following transactions took place during the month of June.
　　15 June A1 Supplies Ltd sent an invoice no. 241 to KerryBooks Ltd, €4,300 + VAT 20%
　　24 June A1 Supplies Ltd sent a credit note no. 97 to KerryBooks Ltd, €800 + VAT 20%
　　29 June A1 Supplies Ltd received a cheque from KerryBooks Ltd for €2,600

From the above details, complete the statement no. 264.

*Templates for these questions are provided in the workbook.*

**1** Patricia Blake works in the sales department of Time Wholesalers Ltd. On 10 March 2010, she receives the following order.

---

### ORDER
No. 219

**Dolmen Ltd**
**Department Store**
**12–18 Main Street, Dundalk**

7 March 2010

The Sales Manager
Time Wholesalers Ltd
Carlton Industrial Estate
Drogheda, Co. Louth

Please supply the following goods:

| Quantity | Description | Price Each |
|---|---|---|
| | | € |
| 90 | Men's Watches (WTM 74) | 40.00 |
| 70 | Ladies' Watches (WTL 92) | 60.00 |
| 30 | Alarm Clocks (CTA 58) | 26.50 |
| 80 | Digital Watches (WCD 36) | 22.50 |

Signed:

*Sarah Parsons*

Purchasing Manager

E&OE

---

The goods ordered are in stock, except for the alarm clocks. All the other items (men's watches, ladies' watches and digital watches) are available.

From the above details, complete the invoice no. 1477. Note that trade discount on all the goods is 15% and VAT on all the goods is 20%.

(JCOL, adapted)

*Templates for these questions are provided in the workbook.*

**2** On 28 May 2009, Bright Paints Ltd, Décor Avenue, Brush Row, Galway received an order no. 3 from Martin Ltd, 10 Green Valley, Loughrea, Co. Galway for the following goods:

| | | |
|---|---|---|
| 50 | Ten-litre drums of white paint | @ €60 per drum |
| 50 | Five-litre drums of cream paint | @ €80 per drum |
| 15 | Five-litre drums of wood preservative | @ €50 per drum |

All the goods ordered were in stock, except for the wood preservative.

Bright Paints Ltd issued invoice no. 42 for the goods in stock on 1 June 2010.
The invoice included the following terms: trade discount 30% and VAT 21%.

On receiving the goods and invoice no. 42 on 4 June 2010, Martin Ltd paid the amount due in full.

Bright Paints Ltd issued receipt no. 67, signed by Molly Bright, on 15 June 2010.

(a) What procedures would you recommend to Bright Paints Ltd when preparing and processing receipts?
(b) Complete invoice no. 42 and receipt no. 67 issued by Bright Paints Ltd.

(JCHL, adapted)

**3** The following details refer to the sale of goods on credit by Kenny Ltd, Main Street, Galway to Brown Ltd, Claremorris, Co. Mayo for the month of April 2010.

On 1 April 2010, Brown Ltd owed Kenny Ltd €2,500.

The following transactions took place during the month of April.
10/4/2010 Kenny Ltd received a cheque no. 34 from Brown Ltd ......€1,750
23/4/2010 Kenny Ltd sent an invoice no. 22 to Brown Ltd ..............€7,000 + VAT 21%
29/4/2010 Kenny Ltd sent a credit note no. 78 to Brown Ltd ..........€1,800 + VAT 21%

On 30 April 2010, Kenny Ltd sent a statement of account no. 91 to Brown Ltd.

(a) Outline how Kenny Ltd should treat outgoing statements of account.
(b) Complete the statement of account no. 91.

(JCHL, adapted)

**4** The following quotation was received by Martin Banner, purchasing manager of Homefit Ltd on 12 May 2010.

---

## QUOTATION

No. 456

**Doors for all Occasions Ltd**
**Wood Lane, Limerick**

8 May 2010

The Purchasing Manager
Homefit Ltd
Kilkee, Co. Clare

Dear Mr. Banner

Thanks for your enquiry of 2 May 2010. I enclose the following quotation which I hope will be to your satisfaction.

| Model No. | Description | Price Each |
|---|---|---|
| | | € |
| 50 | Exterior Teak Doors | 200.00 |
| 100 | Interior Pine Doors | 60.00 |

Terms: Trade Discount 20%
The above goods are subject to VAT at 21%.
I look forward to receiving your order.

Yours sincerely
*Joan Shannon*
Sales Manager

---

(a) (i) Explain each of the following terms: VAT, trade discount.

 (ii) What procedures would you recommend to Doors for all Occasions Ltd when preparing and processing quotations?

 (iii) Martin Banner considers himself to be an effective purchasing manager. What does effective purchasing involve?

 Martin Banner completed an order (no. 100) for 50 exterior teak doors and 100 interior pine doors. These were delivered on 18 May 2010. When Martin examined the doors, he found that five of the exterior teak doors were badly scratched. His complaint to Joan Shannon, Sales Manager, was accepted and she sent him a credit note no. 23 for the five exterior teak doors on 1 June 2010.

(b) Complete the credit note no. 23 issued on 1 June 2010.
 (JCHL, adapted)

# Chapter 27

# Purchases and *purchases returns*

# Recording cash purchases

Cash purchases are recorded in the ledger using record book three. Three accounts are created: the purchases account, the VAT account and the cash account.

**Consider this transaction:**
You purchase €2,000 worth of goods plus 20% VAT on January 8 and pay by cash.

If you study the accounts you will see that the €2,000 is entered on the debit (left) of the purchases account, and €200 is entered on the debit (left) of the VAT account.

This information is also recorded on the credit. This is known as double-entry bookkeeping. Study the cash account and you will see the same €2,200 but this time it is shown on the credit (right) of the account.

**Summary**
Notice that:
- in total €2,200 is written on the debit (left) and on the credit (right)
- the word in the details column is the name of the other account
- the date is the same in each account
- we do not need to record the name of the supplier.

| Dr | Purchases Account | | | | | | Cr |
|------|---------|---|-------|------|---------|---|---|
| Date | Details | F | € | Date | Details | F | € |
| Jan 8 | Cash | | 2,000 | | | | |

| Dr | VAT Account | | | | | | Cr |
|------|---------|---|-----|------|---------|---|---|
| Date | Details | F | € | Date | Details | F | € |
| Jan 8 | Cash | | 200 | | | | |

| Dr | Cash Account | | | | | | Cr |
|------|---------|---|---|------|-----------|---|-------|
| Date | Details | F | € | Date | Details | F | € |
| | | | | Jan 8 | Purchases | | 2,200 |

# Recording credit purchases

Making credit purchases means buying goods from your supplier now and paying for them later. The supplier becomes a creditor – someone you owe money to. The supplier's name, the date and the amount of money must be recorded. The source document for this information is the invoice that is sent by the supplier.

## Consider this transaction:

On 5 March Doogans Ltd purchase desks and bookshelves on credit and receive the following invoice:

### INVOICE
No. 87

**Clarkes Ltd**
**Carlow**

5 March 2010

Doogans Ltd
Donegal

| Quantity | Description | Code | Price Each | Total |
|----------|-------------|------|------------|-------|
|          |             |      | €          | €     |
| 5 | Office desks | OD654 | 200 | 1,000 |
| 3 | Bookshelves | B987 | 100 | 300 |
|   |  | | **Net (excluding VAT)** | **1,300** |
|   |  | | 20% VAT | 260 |
|   |  | | **Total (including VAT)** | **1,560** |

E&OE

## Dealing with faulty goods:

The goods are delivered and one of the desks is returned as it has a faulty drawer. Clarkes Ltd then issue the following credit note:

### CREDIT NOTE
No. 54

**Clarkes Ltd**
**Carlow**

9 March 2010

Doogans Ltd
Donegal

| Quantity | Description | Code | Price Each | Total |
|----------|-------------|------|------------|-------|
|          |             |      | €          | €     |
| 1 | Office desks | OD654 | 200 | 200 |
|   | (faulty drawer) | | | |
|   |  | | **Net (excluding VAT)** | **200** |
|   |  | | 20% VAT | 40 |
|   |  | | **Total (including VAT)** | **240** |

E&OE

## The invoice:

Study the invoice above and find:
- the net, €1,300
- the VAT, €260
- the total, €1,560.

All of these must be noted along with the name of the supplier: Clarkes Ltd.

## The credit note:

Study the credit note above and find:
- the net, €200
- the VAT, €40
- the total, €240.

All of these must be noted along with the name of the supplier: Clarkes Ltd.

## Purchases Day Book

| Mar | | F. | No. | Net €| VAT €| Total €|
|-----|------------|-----|-----|-------|------|-------|
| 5 | Clarkes Ltd | CL | 87 | 1,300 | 260 | 1,560 |

## Purchases Returns Day Book

| | | | | | | |
|---|-------------|-----|-----|-----|-----|-----|
| 9 | Clarkes Ltd | CL | 54 | 200 | 40 | 240 |

## GENERAL LEDGER

**Purchases Account**

| Dr | | | | | | | Cr |
|------|-------------|-----|-------|------|---------|-----|-----|
| Date | Details | F | € | Date | Details | F | € |
| Mar 5 | Clarkes Ltd | PB | 1,300 | | | | |

**Purchases Returns Account**

| | | | | | | | |
|------|---------|-----|-----|-------|-------------|-----|-----|
| | | | | Mar 5 | Clarkes Ltd | PR | 200 |

**VAT Account**

| | | | | | | | |
|-------|-------------|-----|-----|-------|-------------|-----|-----|
| Mar 5 | Clarkes Ltd | PB | 260 | Mar 5 | Clarkes Ltd | PR | 40 |
| | | | | 31 | Balance | c/d | 220 |
| | | | 260 | | | | 260 |
| Apr 1 | Balance | b/d | 220 | | | | |

## CREDITORS LEDGER

**Clarkes Ltd Account**

| | | | | | | | |
|-------|---------------|-----|-------|-------|-----------|-----|-------|
| Mar 5 | Purchases ret. | PR | 240 | Mar 5 | Purchases | PB | 1,560 |
| 31 | Balance | c/d | 1,320 | | | | |
| | | | 2,040 | | | | 2,040 |
| | | | | Apr 1 | Balance | b/d | 1,320 |

## Trial Balance as on 31 March

| | | | Debit € | Credit € |
|---|-----------------|---|-------|-------|
| | Purchases | | 1,300 | |
| | Purchases returns | | | 200 |
| | VAT | | 220 | |
| | Clarkes Ltd | | | 1,320 |
| | | | 1,520 | 1,520 |

## Record book 2: the day books

Record book two records the details of the purchase. The net (€1,300), VAT (€260), total (€1,560), the name of the supplier (Clarkes Ltd) and the invoice number (87) are recorded as shown. The source document for this information is the invoice. Similarly, the details for the returns are recorded in the purchases returns day book. The source document is the credit note.

## Record book 3: the ledger

Record book three is used to record a summary of the purchase. The net (€1,300), VAT (€260) and total (€1,560) are all recorded. First, show the €1,300 on the debit (left) of the purchases account and show the VAT associated with this purchase (€260) on the debit of the VAT account. Then show the total (€1,560) of this transaction on the credit (right) of Clarkes Ltd account. Now do the same with the returns. Show the net (€200) on the credit (right) of the purchases returns account and the VAT (€40) on the credit of the VAT account. Then show the total (€240) on the debit of Clarkes Ltd account. Balance the VAT and Clarkes Ltd accounts as shown.

Notice that there is a general ledger to list the purchases, returns and VAT accounts, while the creditors ledgers lists the suppliers (creditors) accounts.

## Record book 2: the trial balance

Now return to record book two to draw up a trial balance. This is a list of the balances from the accounts. The balances are shown in the debit or credit column depending on where they are in the accounts. The two columns are then totalled. The trial balance is a good way to check the accuracy of your work, as the two totals should be the same.

# Recording several purchases

## Question

The following transactions took place during the month of May:

May 4    Purchased goods on credit from Pattons Ltd, Invoice No. 34, €1,400 + VAT 20%

      10    Returned goods to Pattons Ltd, Credit Note No. 14, €300

      15    Purchased goods on credit from Quinns Ltd, Invoice No. 86, €3,600 + VAT 20%

      21    Purchased goods on credit from Reids Ltd, Invoice No. 73, €2,300 + VAT 20%

      27    Returned goods to Reids Ltd, Credit Note No. 34, €500

**You are required to:**

(a) show the entries in the purchases day book and the purchases returns day book

(b) post to the ledger

(c) balance the accounts on 31 May, and extract a trial balance as on that date.

## Record book 2: the day books

Record book two is used to record the purchases and the returns. In the purchases day book note:

- €1,680 (the amount owed to Pattons)
- €4,320 (the amount owed to Quinns)
- €2,760 (the amount owed to Reids)
- €7,300 (net purchases)
- €1,460 (VAT on purchases).

In the purchases returns day book note:

- €360 (the amount returned to Pattons)
- €600 (the amount returned to Reids)
- €800 (net returns)
- €160 (VAT on the returns).

## Record book 3: the general ledger

Record book three is used to record a summary of the purchases. The net purchases (€7,300) is shown on the debit of the purchases account and the VAT on purchases (€1,460) is shown on the debit of the VAT account. The net returns (€800) is shown on the credit of the purchases returns account and the VAT on returns (€160) is shown on the credit of the VAT account. The VAT account is then balanced.

## Solution

### Purchases Day Book

| May | | F. | No. | Net €| VAT €| Total €|
|---|---|---|---|---|---|---|
| 4 | Pattons Ltd | CL | 34 | 1,400 | 280 | 1,680 |
| 15 | Quinns Ltd | CL | 86 | 3,600 | 720 | 4,320 |
| 21 | Reids Ltd | CL | 73 | 2,300 | 460 | 2,760 |
| | | | | 7,300 | 1,460 | 8,760 |

### Purchases Returns Day Book

| | | | | | | |
|---|---|---|---|---|---|---|
| 10 | Pattons Ltd | CL | 14 | 300 | 60 | 360 |
| 27 | Reids Ltd | CL | 34 | 500 | 100 | 600 |
| | | | | 800 | 160 | 960 |

### GENERAL LEDGER

**Purchases Account**

| Dr | | | | | | | Cr |
|---|---|---|---|---|---|---|---|
| Date | Details | F | € | Date | Details | F | € |
| May 31 | Sundry creditors | PB | 7,300 | | | | |

**Purchases Returns Account**

| | | | | | | | |
|---|---|---|---|---|---|---|---|
| | | | | May 31 | Sundry creditors | PR | 800 |

**VAT Account**

| | | | | | | | |
|---|---|---|---|---|---|---|---|
| May 31 | Sundry creditors | PB | 1,460 | May 31 | Sundry creditors | PR | 160 |
| | | | | 31 | Balance | c/d | 1,300 |
| | | | 1,460 | | | | 1,460 |
| Jun 1 | Balance | b/d | 1,300 | | | | |

## CREDITORS LEDGER

**Dr**      **Pattons Ltd Account**      **Cr**

| Date | Details | F | € | Date | Details | F | € |
|------|---------|---|-----|------|---------|---|-----|
| May 10 | Purchases ret. | PR | 360 | May 4 | Purchases | PB | 1,680 |
| 31 | Balance | c/d | 1,320 | | | | |
| | | | 1,680 | | | | 1,680 |
| | | | | Jun 1 | Balance | b/d | 1,320 |

**Quinns Ltd Account**

| Date | Details | F | € | Date | Details | F | € |
|------|---------|---|-----|------|---------|---|-----|
| | | | | May 15 | Purchases | PB | 4,320 |

**Reids Ltd Account**

| Date | Details | F | € | Date | Details | F | € |
|------|---------|---|-----|------|---------|---|-----|
| May 27 | Purchases ret. | PR | 600 | May 21 | Purchases | PB | 2,760 |
| 31 | Balance | c/d | 2,160 | | | | |
| | | | 2,760 | | | | 2,760 |
| | | | | Jun 1 | Balance | b/d | 2,160 |

### Record book 3: the creditors ledger

Record book three is used to record the purchases and the returns. The €1,680 purchased from Pattons Ltd is shown on the credit of Pattons account and the goods returned to Pattons (€360) are shown on the debit of this account. The balance of €1,320 is the money we owe Pattons Ltd. Similar entries are made for Quinns Ltd and Reids Ltd. The accounts show we owe €4,320 to Quinns Ltd and €2,160 to Reids Ltd.

Notice that all the creditor's accounts are listed in the creditors ledger. These are the suppliers of the firm and putting them together makes it easier to find them if there are any queries about their accounts.

### Trial Balance as on 31 May

| | Debit € | Credit € |
|---|---|---|
| Purchases | 7,300 | |
| Purchases returns | | 800 |
| VAT | 1,300 | |
| Pattons Ltd | | 1,320 |
| Quinns Ltd | | 4,320 |
| Reids Ltd | | 2,160 |
| | 8,600 | 8,600 |

### Record book 2: the trial balance

Now return to record book two to draw up a trial balance. This is a list of the balances from the accounts. The balances are shown in the debit or credit column depending on where they are in the accounts. The two columns are then totalled. The trial balance is a good way to check the accuracy of your work, as the two totals should be the same.

**Dr**      **Purchases Account**      **Cr**

| Date | Details | F | € | Date | Details | F | € |
|------|---------|---|-----|------|---------|---|-----|
| Jan 8 | Cash | CB | 2,400 | | | | |
| Jan 9 | Sundry creditors | PB | 6,800 | | | | |

### Note

The purchases account on the left appeared in the ledger of John Gahan. It has both cash and credit purchases.
- On 8 January, Gahan purchased goods and paid by cash, €2,400.
- On 9 January, Gahan purchased goods on credit from various suppliers (creditors), €6,800.

## Activity 27.1 Chapter Review

1. (a) What is a cash purchase?
   (b) What is a credit purchase?
   (c) Why do we need to record credit transactions?
   (d) When you buy goods on credit what document does the supplier send you?
   (e) When you return goods what document does the supplier send you?

2. Which record book is used for:
   (a) the day books?
   (b) the ledger accounts?
   (c) the trial balance?

3. (a) What is listed in the trial balance?
   (b) If you do your work correctly what should happen with the trial balance totals?

## Activity 27.2 Recording credit purchases

In the case of the following invoice and credit note you are required to:
(a) show the entries in the purchases day book and the purchases returns day book
(b) post to the ledger
(c) balance the accounts on 30 April, and extract a trial balance as on that date.

### INVOICE
No. 231

**Grants Ltd**
**Galway**

23 April 2010

Tierneys Ltd
Tipperary

| Quantity | Description | Code | Price Each | Total |
|---|---|---|---|---|
| | | | € | € |
| 7 | Electric Kettles | EK635 | 60 | 420 |
| 4 | Toasters | T869 | 20 | 80 |
| | | Net (excluding VAT) | | 500 |
| | | 20% VAT | | 100 |
| | | Total (including VAT) | | 600 |

E&OE

### CREDIT NOTE
No. 168

**Grants Ltd**
**Galway**

26 April 2010

Tierneys Ltd
Tipperary

| Quantity | Description | Code | Price Each | Total |
|---|---|---|---|---|
| | | | € | € |
| 1 | Electric Kettle | EK635 | 60 | 60 |
| | (faulty cable) | | | |
| | | Net (excluding VAT) | | 60 |
| | | 20% VAT | | 12 |
| | | Total (including VAT) | | 72 |

E&OE

# Activity 27.3 Purchases

**1** The following transactions took place during the month of June:

Jun 12 Purchased goods on credit from Clancys Ltd, invoice no. 67, €3,500 + VAT 20%
    14 Returned goods to Clancys Ltd, credit note no. 25, €400
    19 Purchased goods on credit from Mahonys Ltd, invoice no. 241, €2,800 + VAT 20%
    25 Purchased goods on credit from Hogans Ltd, invoice no. 364, €4,600 + VAT 20%
    28 Returned goods to Hogans Ltd, credit note no. 97, €700

You are required to:
(a) show the entries in the purchases day book and the purchases returns day book
(b) post to the ledger
(c) balance the accounts on 30 June, and extract a trial balance as on that date.

**2** The following transactions took place during the month of July:

Jul 11 Purchased goods on credit from Ryans Ltd, invoice no. 357, €2,700 + VAT 20%
    10 Returned goods to Ryans Ltd, credit note no. 75, €600
    19 Purchased goods on credit from Walsh's Ltd, invoice no. 248, €5,600 + VAT 20%
    25 Purchased goods on credit from Quinns Ltd, invoice no. 68, €3,900 + VAT 20%
    28 Returned goods to Walsh's Ltd, credit note no. 147, €400

You are required to:
(a) show the entries in the purchases day book and the purchases returns day book
(b) post to the ledger
(c) balance the accounts on 31 July, and extract a trial balance as on that date.

**3** The following transactions took place during the month of August:

Aug 12 Purchased goods on credit from Keanes Ltd, invoice no. 97, €1,200 + VAT 20%
    10 Returned goods to Keanes Ltd, credit note no. 64, €100
    19 Purchased goods on credit from Lynch's Ltd, invoice no. 54, €3,400 + VAT 20%
    25 Purchased goods on credit from Burkes Ltd, invoice no. 37, €2,700 + VAT 20%
    28 Returned goods to Burkes Ltd, credit note No. 28, €300

You are required to:
(a) show the entries in the purchases day book and the purchases
    returns day book
(b) post to the ledger
(c) balance the accounts on 31 August, and extract a trial
    balance as on that date.

**4** The following transactions took place during the month of September:

Sep 12  Purchased goods on credit from Scanlons Ltd, invoice no. 74, €1,900 + VAT 20%
    14  Returned goods to Scanlons Ltd, credit note no. 41, €250
    19  Purchased goods on credit from Conways Ltd, invoice no. 82, €4,600 + VAT 20%
    25  Purchased goods on credit from Durkans Ltd, invoice no. 63, €3,700 + VAT 20%
    28  Returned goods to Durkans Ltd, credit note no. 43, €550

You are required to:
(a) show the entries in the purchases day book and the purchases returns day book
(b) post to the ledger
(c) balance the accounts on 30 September, and extract a trial balance as on that date.

**5** The following transactions took place during the month of October:

Oct 11  Purchased goods on credit from Malones Ltd, invoice no. 576, €1,600 + VAT 20%
    10  Returned goods to Malones Ltd, credit note no. 465, €150
    19  Purchased goods on credit from Duffys Ltd, invoice no. 168, €940 + VAT 20%
    25  Purchased goods on credit from Healys Ltd, invoice no. 257, €2,400 + VAT 20%
    28  Returned goods to Duffys Ltd, credit note no. 67, €180

You are required to:
(a) show the entries in the purchases day book and the purchases returns day book
(b) post to the ledger
(c) balance the accounts on 31 October, and extract a trial balance as on that date.

**6** The following transactions took place during the month of November:

Nov 12  Purchased goods on credit from Bennetts Ltd, invoice no. 73, €760 + VAT 20%
    10  Returned goods to Bennetts Ltd, credit note no. 24, €80
    19  Purchased goods on credit from Caseys Ltd, invoice no. 86, €2,700 + VAT 20%
    25  Purchased goods on credit from Dooleys Ltd, invoice no. 42, €1,300 + VAT 20%
    28  Returned goods to Dooleys Ltd, credit note no. 16, €250

You are required to:
(a) show the entries in the purchases day book and the purchases returns day book
(b) post to the ledger
(c) balance the accounts on 30 November, and extract
a trial balance as on that date.

eTest.ie
Try a test on this topic

# Sales and sales returns

# Recording cash sales

Cash sales are recorded in the ledger using record book three. Two accounts are created: the sales account and the cash account.

**Consider this transaction:**
You sell €3,000 worth of goods plus 20% VAT on January 9 and pay by cash.

| Dr | | | Sales Account | | | | Cr |
| Date | Details | F | € | Date | Details | F | € |
| --- | --- | --- | --- | --- | --- | --- | --- |
| | | | | Jan 9 | Cash | | 3,000 |

| Dr | | | VAT Account | | | | Cr |
| Date | Details | F | € | Date | Details | F | € |
| --- | --- | --- | --- | --- | --- | --- | --- |
| | | | | Jan 9 | Cash | | 300 |

| Dr | | | Cash Account | | | | Cr |
| Date | Details | F | € | Date | Details | F | € |
| --- | --- | --- | --- | --- | --- | --- | --- |
| Jan 9 | Sales | | 3,300 | | | | |

If you study the sales account you will see the €3,000 on the credit (right) of the sales account and €300 on the credit of the VAT account.

This information is also recorded on the debit. This is known as double-entry bookkeeping. Study the cash account and you will see that the €3,300 is entered on the debit (left) of the cash account.

**Summary**
Notice that:
- in total €3,300 is written on the debit (left) and on the credit (right)
- the word in the details column is the name of the other account
- the date is the same in each account
- we do not need to record the name of the customer.

# Recording credit sales

Credit sales means that you sell goods today and the customer pays you later. The customer becomes a debtor – someone who owes you money. The customer's name, the date and the amount of money are all noted. The source document for this information is the copy of the invoice that you send to the customer.

**Consider this transaction:**

On 4 February Ganleys Ltd sell dishwashers and washing machines on credit and send the following invoice:

**Dealing with faulty goods:**

The goods are delivered and one of the washing machines is returned as it has a faulty door. Ganleys Ltd then issue the following credit note:

### INVOICE
No. 164

**Ganleys Ltd**
**Galway**

4 February 2010

Kirbys Ltd
Kildare

| Quantity | Description | Code | Price Each | Total |
|---|---|---|---|---|
| | | | € | € |
| 4 | Dishwashers | DW49 | 200 | 800 |
| 3 | Washing machines | WM37 | 300 | 900 |
| | | Net (excluding VAT) | | 1,700 |
| | | 20% VAT | | 340 |
| | | Total (including VAT) | | 2,040 |

E&OE

### CREDIT NOTE
No. 71

**Ganleys Ltd**
**Galway**

8 February 2010

Kirbys Ltd
Kildare

| Quantity | Description | Code | Price Each | Total |
|---|---|---|---|---|
| | | | € | € |
| 1 | Washing machine (faulty door) | WM37 | 300 | 300 |
| | | Net (excluding VAT) | | 300 |
| | | 20% VAT | | 60 |
| | | Total (including VAT) | | 360 |

E&OE

**The invoice:**

Study the invoice above and find:
- the net, €1,700
- the VAT, €340
- the total, €2,040.

All of these must be noted along with the name of the customer: Kirbys Ltd.

**The credit note:**

Study the credit note above and find:
- the net, €300
- the VAT, €60
- the total, €360.

All of these must be noted along with the name of the customer: Kirbys Ltd.

| Sales Day Book | | | | | | |
|---|---|---|---|---|---|---|
| | | F. | No. | Net | VAT | Total |
| Feb | | | | € | € | € |
| 4 | Kirbys Ltd | DL | 164 | 1,700 | 340 | 2,040 |
| **Sales Returns Day Book** | | | | | | |
| 8 | Kirbys Ltd | DL | 71 | 300 | 60 | 360 |

### GENERAL LEDGER

| Dr | | | Sales Account | | | | Cr |
|---|---|---|---|---|---|---|---|
| Date | Details | F | € | Date | Details | F | € |
| | | | | Feb 4 | Kirbys Ltd | SB | 1,700 |

**Sales Returns Account**

| Feb 8 | Kirbys Ltd | SR | 300 | | | | |
|---|---|---|---|---|---|---|---|

**VAT Account**

| Feb 8 | Kirbys Ltd | SR | 60 | Feb 4 | Kirbys Ltd | SB | 340 |
|---|---|---|---|---|---|---|---|
| 28 | Balance | c/d | 280 | | | | |
| | | | 340 | | | | 340 |
| | | | | Mar 1 | Balance | b/d | 280 |

### DEBTORS LEDGER

**Kirbys Ltd Account**

| Feb 4 | Sales | SB | 2,040 | Feb 8 | Sales returns | SR | 360 |
|---|---|---|---|---|---|---|---|
| | | | | 28 | Balance | c/d | 1,680 |
| | | | 2,040 | | | | 2,040 |
| Mar 1 | Balance | b/d | 1,680 | | | | |

| Trial Balance as on 28 February | | | Debit | Credit |
|---|---|---|---|---|
| | | | € | € |
| | Sales | | | 1,700 |
| | Sales returns | | 300 | |
| | VAT | | | 280 |
| | Kirbys Ltd | | 1,680 | |
| | | | 1,980 | 1,980 |

## Record book 2: the day books

Record book two is used to record the details of the sale. The net (€1,700), VAT (€340) and total (€2,040), the name of the customer (Kirbys Ltd) and the invoice number (164) are recorded as shown. The source document for this information is the invoice. Similarly, the details for the returns are recorded in the sales returns day book as shown. The source document is the credit note.

## Record book 3: the ledger

Record book three is used to record a summary of the sale. The net (€1,700), VAT (€340) and total (€2,040) are all recorded. First, show the €1,700 on the credit (right) of the sales account and show the VAT associated with this sale (€340) on the credit of the VAT account. Then show the total (€2,040) of this transaction on the debit (left) of Kirbys Ltd account. Now do the same with the returns. Show the net (€300) on the debit (left) of the sales returns account and the VAT (€60) on the debit of the VAT account. Then show the total (€360) on the credit of Kirbys Ltd account. Balance the VAT and Kirbys Ltd accounts as shown.

Notice that there is a general ledger to list the sales, returns and VAT accounts, while the debtors ledger lists the customers' (debtors') accounts.

## Record book 2: the trial balance

Now return to record book two to draw up a trial balance. This is a list of the balances from the accounts. The balances are shown in the debit or credit column depending on where they are in the accounts. The two columns are then totalled. The trial balance is a good way to check the accuracy of your work, as the two totals should be the same.

# Recording several sales

## Question

The following transactions took place during the month of March:

Mar 2 Sold goods on credit to Lavins Ltd, Invoice No. 56, €2,000 + VAT 20%

11 Lavins Ltd returned goods, Credit Note No. 34, €400

16 Sold goods on credit to Mahons Ltd, Invoice No. 57, €3,000 + VAT 20%

23 Sold goods on credit to Nolans Ltd, Invoice No. 58, €4,000 + VAT 20%

29 Nolans Ltd returned goods, Credit Note No. 35, €300

**You are required to:**

(a) show the entries in the day books

(b) post to the ledger

(c) balance the accounts on 31 March, and extract a trial balance as on that date.

## Record book 2: the day books

Record book two is used to record the sales and the returns. In the sales day book note:

- €2,400 (the amount Lavin owes us)
- €3,600 (the amount Mahon owes us)
- €4,800 (the amount Nolan owes us)
- €9,000 (net sales)
- €1,800 (VAT on sales)

In the purchases returns day book note:

- €480 (the amount returned by Lavins)
- €360 (the amount returned by Nolans)
- €700 (net returns)
- €140 (VAT on the returns)

## Record book 3: the general ledger

Record book three is used to record a summary of the sales. The net sales (€9,000) is shown on the credit of the sales account and the VAT on sales (€1,800) is shown on the credit of the VAT account. The net returns (€700) is shown on the debit of the sales returns account and the VAT on returns (€140) is shown on the debit of the VAT account. The VAT account is then balanced.

## Solution

### Sales Day Book

|  |  | F. | No. | Net | VAT | Total |
|---|---|---|---|---|---|---|
| Mar |  |  |  | € | € | € |
| 2 | Lavins Ltd | DL | 56 | 2,000 | 400 | 2,400 |
| 16 | Mahons Ltd | DL | 57 | 3,000 | 600 | 3,600 |
| 23 | Nolans Ltd | DL | 58 | 4,000 | 800 | 4,800 |
|  |  |  |  | 9,000 | 1,800 | 10,800 |

### Sales Returns Day Book

| 11 | Lavins Ltd | DL | 34 | 400 | 80 | 480 |
|---|---|---|---|---|---|---|
| 29 | Nolans Ltd | DL | 35 | 300 | 60 | 360 |
|  |  |  |  | 700 | 140 | 840 |

### GENERAL LEDGER

**Dr**      **Sales Account**      **Cr**

| Date | Details | F | € | Date | Details | F | € |
|---|---|---|---|---|---|---|---|
|  |  |  |  | Mar 31 | Sundry debtors | SB | 9,000 |

**Sales Returns Account**

| Mar 31 | Sundry debtors | SR | 700 |  |  |  |  |
|---|---|---|---|---|---|---|---|

**VAT Account**

| Mar 31 | Sundry debtors | SR | 140 | Mar 31 | Sundry debtors | SB | 1,800 |
|---|---|---|---|---|---|---|---|
| 31 | Balance | c/d | 1,660 |  |  |  |  |
|  |  |  | 1,800 |  |  |  | 1,800 |
|  |  |  |  | Apr 1 | Balance | b/d | 1,660 |

## DEBTORS LEDGER

**Lavins Ltd Account**

| Date | Details | F | € | Date | Details | F | € |
|---|---|---|---|---|---|---|---|
| Mar 2 | Sales | SB | 2,400 | Mar 11 | Sales returns | SR | 480 |
| | | | | 31 | Balance | c/d | 1,920 |
| | | | 2,400 | | | | 2,400 |
| Apr 1 | Balance | b/d | 1,920 | | | | |

**Mahons Ltd Account**

| Date | Details | F | € | Date | Details | F | € |
|---|---|---|---|---|---|---|---|
| Mar 16 | Sales | SB | 3,600 | | | | |

**Nolans Ltd Account**

| Date | Details | F | € | Date | Details | F | € |
|---|---|---|---|---|---|---|---|
| Mar 23 | Sales | SB | 4,800 | Mar 29 | Sales returns | SR | 360 |
| | | | | 31 | Balance | c/d | 4,440 |
| | | | 4,800 | | | | 4,800 |
| Apr 1 | Balance | b/d | 4,440 | | | | |

**Record book 3: the debtors ledger**

Record book three is used to record the sales and the returns. The €2,400 sales to Lavins Ltd is shown on the debit of Lavins account and the goods returned by Lavin (€480) are shown on the credit of this account. The balance of €1,920 is the money Lavin owes us. Similar entries are made in the accounts of Mahons Ltd and Nolans Ltd. The accounts show Mahons Ltd owe us €3,600 and Nolans Ltd owe us €4,440.

Notice that all the debtor's accounts are listed in the debtors ledger. These are the customers of the firm and putting them together makes it easier to find them if there are any queries about their accounts.

### Trial Balance as on 31 March

| | Debit € | Credit € |
|---|---|---|
| Sales | | 9,000 |
| Sales returns | 700 | |
| VAT | | 1,660 |
| Lavins Ltd | 1,920 | |
| Mahons Ltd | 3,600 | |
| Nolans Ltd | 4,440 | |
| | 10,660 | 10,660 |

**Record book 2: the trial balance**

Now return to record book two to draw up a trial balance. This is a list of the balances from the accounts. The balances are shown in the debit or credit column depending on where they are in the accounts. The two columns are then totalled. The trial balance is a good way to check the accuracy of your work, as the two totals should be the same.

In order to make a profit, goods are sold at a higher price than they were bought at:

**Cost price + profit = selling price**

The extent of the profit can be measured by calculating the mark-up and margin using these formulae:

$$\text{Mark-up} = \frac{\text{Profit}}{\text{Cost price}} \times 100$$

$$\text{Margin} = \frac{\text{Profit}}{\text{Selling price}} \times 100$$

**Question**

A firm sells goods for €250. The cost of the goods was €200. Calculate the mark-up and the margin.

**Solution**

$$\text{Mark-up} = \frac{\text{Profit}}{\text{Cost price}} \times 100$$

$$= \frac{50}{200} \times 100 = 25\%$$

$$\text{Margin} = \frac{\text{Profit}}{\text{Selling price}} \times 100$$

$$= \frac{50}{250} \times 100 = 20\%$$

## Activity 28.1 Recording credit sales

In the case of the following invoice and credit note you are required to:
(a) show the entries in the sales day book and the sales returns day book
(b) post to the ledger
(c) balance the accounts on 31 May, and extract a trial balance as on that date.

| INVOICE | | | | |
|---|---|---|---|---|
| No. 754 | | | | |
| **Kerrs Ltd** | | | | |
| **Kerry** | | | | |
| 15 May 2010 | | | | |
| Dunnes Ltd | | | | |
| Donegal | | | | |
| Quantity | Description | Code | Price Each | Total |
| | | | € | € |
| 6 | Desks | D654 | 240 | 1,440 |
| 4 | Chairs | C238 | 90 | 360 |
| | | Net (excluding VAT) | | 1,800 |
| | | 20% VAT | | 360 |
| | | Total (including VAT) | | 2,160 |
| E&OE | | | | |

| CREDIT NOTE | | | | |
|---|---|---|---|---|
| No. 539 | | | | |
| **Kerrs Ltd** | | | | |
| **Kerry** | | | | |
| 19 May 2010 | | | | |
| Dunnes Ltd | | | | |
| Donegal | | | | |
| Quantity | Description | Code | Price Each | Total |
| | | | € | € |
| 1 | Desk | D654 | 240 | 240 |
| | (faulty drawer) | | | |
| | | Net (excluding VAT) | | 240 |
| | | 20% VAT | | 48 |
| | | Total (including VAT) | | 288 |
| E&OE | | | | |

## Activity 28.2 Calculating mark-up and margin

1  A firm sells goods for €250. The cost of the goods was €200. Calculate the mark-up and the margin.

2  A firm sells goods for €520. The cost of the goods was €440. Calculate the mark-up and the margin.

3  A firm sells goods for €3,100. The cost of the goods was €2,500. Calculate the mark-up and the margin.

4  A firm sells goods for €9,980. The cost of the goods was €8,000. Calculate the mark-up and the margin.

5  A firm sells goods for €1,840. The cost of the goods was €1,040. Calculate the mark-up and the margin.

# Activity 28.3 Sales

**1** The following transactions took place during the month of December:

Dec 3 Sold goods on credit to Kelly Ltd, invoice no. 754, €5,500 + VAT 20%
12 Kelly Ltd returned goods, credit note no. 645, €300
16 Sold goods on credit to Gahan Ltd, invoice no. 755, €4,600 + VAT 20%
24 Sold goods on credit to Coyne Ltd, invoice no. 756, €7,300 + VAT 20%
29 Gahan Ltd returned goods, credit note no. 646, €400

You are required to:
(a) show the entries in the day books
(b) post to the ledger
(c) balance the accounts on 31 December, and extract a trial balance as on that date.

**2** The following transactions took place during the month of January:

Jan 8 Sold goods on credit to Shaw Ltd, invoice no. 357, €5,300 + VAT 20%
10 Shaw Ltd returned goods, credit note no. 75, €700
17 Sold goods on credit to Barry Ltd, invoice no. 358, €3,800 + VAT 20%
25 Sold goods on credit to Cleary Ltd, invoice no. 359, €6,700 + VAT 20%
26 Barry Ltd returned goods, credit note no. 76, €900

You are required to:
(a) show the entries in the day books
(b) post to the ledger
(c) balance the accounts on 31 January, and extract a trial balance as on that date.

**3** The following transactions took place during the month of February:

Feb 2 Sold goods on credit to Keanes Ltd, invoice no. 97, €4,200 + VAT 20%
8 Keanes Ltd returned goods, credit note no. 64, €200
14 Sold goods on credit to Lynch's Ltd, invoice no. 98, €5,400 + VAT 20%
23 Sold goods on credit to Burkes Ltd, invoice no. 99, €4,800 + VAT 20%
27 Burkes Ltd returned goods, credit note no. 65, €600

You are required to:
(a) show the entries in the day books
(b) post to the ledger
(c) balance the accounts on 28 February, and extract a trial
balance as on that date.

## Activity 28.4 Purchases and sales

**1** The following transactions took place during the month of March:

Mar 7   Purchased goods on credit from Scott Ltd, invoice no. 74, €2,700 + VAT 20%

    14   Returned goods to Scott Ltd, credit note no. 41, €300

    17   Sold goods on credit to Quinn Ltd, invoice no. 82, €5,800 + VAT 20%

    23   Purchased goods on credit from Roche Ltd, invoice no. 63, €1,300 + VAT 20%

    28   Quinn Ltd returned goods, credit note no. 43, €400

You are required to:

(a) show the entries in the day books

(b) post to the ledger

(c) balance the accounts on 31 March, and extract a trial balance as on that date.

**2** The following transactions took place during the month of April:

Apr 3   Sold goods on credit to Power Ltd, invoice no. 576, €3,200 + VAT 20%

    9   Power Ltd returned goods, credit note no. 465, €550

    18   Purchased goods on credit from Moore Ltd, invoice no. 168, €1,400 + VAT 20%

    25   Purchased goods on credit from Smyth Ltd, invoice no. 257, €2,700 + VAT 20%

    28   Returned goods to Smyth Ltd, credit note no. 67, €320

You are required to:

(a) show the entries in the day books

(b) post to the ledger

(c) balance the accounts on 30 April, and extract a trial balance as on that date.

**3** The following transactions took place during the month of May:

May 8   Purchased goods on credit from Taylor Ltd, invoice no. 73, €970 + VAT 20%

    10   Returned goods to Taylor Ltd, credit note no. 24, €80

    16   Sold goods on credit to Jones Ltd, invoice no. 86, €2,900 + VAT 20%

    25   Sold goods on credit to Mullan Ltd, invoice no. 87, €1,200 + VAT 20%

    29   Mullan Ltd returned goods, credit note no. 16, €400

You are required to:

(a) show the entries in the day books

(b) post to the ledger

(c) balance the accounts on 31 May, and extract a trial balance as on that date.

Try a test on this topic

# Analysed cash book

# Understanding the cash book

The cash book is used to record cash that comes in and out of a business. Two lists are created: one for cash received and one for cash paid.

**Money in**
Money received is shown on the debit side. In our example, the firm received €12,000 cash from sales. The firm also received €15,000 from the issue of shares (capital).

**Money out**
Money paid out is shown on the credit side. In our example, the firm paid €4,000 for advertising, €6,000 to a supplier (Hayes Ltd) and €4,800 for purchases.

| Dr | | | | | | Analysed Cash Book | | | | | | | | Cr |
|---|---|---|---|---|---|---|---|---|---|---|---|---|---|---|
| Date | Details | F | Bank | Sales | VAT | Other | Date | Details | F | Bank | Purchases | VAT | Creditors | Advertising |
| Mar | | | € | € | € | € | Mar | | | € | € | € | € | € |
| 11 | Balance | b/d | 600 | | | | 15 | Advertising | 4 | 4,000 | | | | 4,000 |
| 19 | Sales | | 12,000 | 10,000 | 2,000 | | 16 | Hayes Ltd | 5 | 6,000 | | | 6,000 | |
| 23 | Capital | | 15,000 | | | 15,000 | 21 | Purchases | 6 | 4,800 | 4,000 | 800 | | |
| | | | | | | | 31 | Balance | c/d | 24,800 | | | | |
| | | | 37,600 | 10,000 | 2,000 | 15,000 | | | | 37,600 | 4,000 | 800 | 6,000 | 4,000 |
| Apr 1 | Balance | b/d | 24,800 | | | | | | | | | | | |

**The balance**
The €600 opening balance is the money the firm has at the start of the month. The €24,800 closing balance is the money the firm has at the end of the month.

**Overheads**
Overheads are the expenses of running a business. They are recorded on the credit side of the cash book, e.g. advertising, insurance, rent and electricity.

*Chapter 29 Analysed Cash Book*　**189**

# Sample question and solution

Ross Ltd had the following balances in its general journal on 1 May.

| General Journal | | Dr € | Cr € |
|---|---|---|---|
| May 1 | Machinery | 120,000 | |
| | Debtor: Cooney Ltd | 5,000 | |
| | Bank overdraft | | 2,000 |
| | Ordinary share capital | | 123,000 |
| | Assets, liabilities and share capital of Ross Ltd | 125,000 | 125,000 |

(a) Post the balances in the above general journal to the relevant ledger accounts.

(b) Record the following bank transactions for the month of May and post to the ledger.
Note: Analyse the bank transactions using the following money column headings:
**Debit (Receipts) side:** Bank; Sales; VAT; Debtors; Capital.
**Credit (Payments) side:** Bank; Purchases; VAT; Advertising.

  May  2  Shareholders invested €40,000 and this was lodged.
  7  Cash sales lodged, €36,000 (€30,000 + €6,000 VAT).
  9  Paid advertising (cheque no. 1), €1,000.
  23  Cooney Ltd paid €3,000 and this was lodged (receipt no. 1).
  29  Purchases for resale (cheque no. 2), €20,000 + 20% VAT.

(c) Balance the accounts on 31 May and extract a trial balance as on that date.

## Solution

| Dr | | | | | | | Analysed Cash Book | | | | | | | Cr |
|---|---|---|---|---|---|---|---|---|---|---|---|---|---|---|
| Date | Details | F | Bank | Sales | VAT | Debtors | Capital | Date | Details | F | Bank | Purchases | VAT | Advertising |
| May | | | € | € | € | € | € | May | | | € | € | € | € |
| 2 | Capital | | 40,000 | | | | 40,000 | 1 | Balance | b/d | 2,000 | | | |
| 7 | Sales | | 36,000 | 30,000 | 6,000 | | | 9 | Advertising | 1 | 1,000 | | | 1,000 |
| 23 | Cooney Ltd | 1 | 3,000 | | | 3,000 | | 21 | Purchases | 2 | 24,000 | 20,000 | 4,000 | |
| | | | | | | | | 31 | Balance | c/d | 52,000 | | | |
| | | | 79,000 | 30,000 | 6,000 | 3,000 | 40,000 | | | | 79,000 | 20,000 | 4,000 | 1,000 |
| Apr 1 | Balance | b/d | 52,000 | | | | | | | | | | | |

## Record book 1

Record book one is used to record the bank transactions. Notice that the opening balance, €2,000 is shown on the credit as it is an overdraft.

*Open for Business*

## GENERAL LEDGER

**Dr**     **Machinery Account**     **Cr**

| Date | Details | F | € | Date | Details | F | € |
|------|---------|---|---|------|---------|---|---|
| May 1 | Balance | b/d | 120,000 | | | | |

**Advertising Account**

| Date | Details | F | € | Date | Details | F | € |
|------|---------|---|---|------|---------|---|---|
| May 9 | Bank | CB | 1,000 | | | | |

**Sales Account**

| Date | Details | F | € | Date | Details | F | € |
|------|---------|---|---|------|---------|---|---|
| | | | | May 7 | Bank | CB | 30,000 |

**Purchases Account**

| Date | Details | F | € | Date | Details | F | € |
|------|---------|---|---|------|---------|---|---|
| May 21 | Bank | CB | 20,000 | | | | |

**VAT Account**

| Date | Details | F | € | Date | Details | F | € |
|------|---------|---|---|------|---------|---|---|
| May 21 | Bank | CB | 4,000 | May 7 | Bank | CB | 6,000 |
| 31 | Balance | c/d | 2,000 | | | | |
| | | | 6,000 | | | | 6,000 |
| | | | | Jun 1 | Balance | b/d | 2,000 |

**Ordinary Share Capital Account**

| Date | Details | F | € | Date | Details | F | € |
|------|---------|---|---|------|---------|---|---|
| 31 | Balance | c/d | 163,000 | May 1 | Balance | b/d | 123,000 |
| | | | | 2 | Bank | CB | 40,000 |
| | | | 163,000 | | | | 163,000 |
| | | | | Jun 1 | Balance | b/d | 163,000 |

## DEBTORS LEDGER

**Cooney Ltd Account**

| Date | Details | F | € | Date | Details | F | € |
|------|---------|---|---|------|---------|---|---|
| May 1 | Balance | b/d | 5,000 | May 23 | Bank | CB | 3,000 |
| | | | | 31 | Balance | c/d | 2,000 |
| | | | 5,000 | | | | 5,000 |
| Jun 1 | Balance | b/d | 2,000 | | | | |

## Trial Balance as on 28 February 2010

| | Debit € | Credit € |
|---|---|---|
| Machinery | 120,000 | |
| Advertising | 1,000 | |
| Sales | | 30,000 |
| Purchases | 20,000 | |
| VAT | | 2,000 |
| Ordinary share capital | | 163,000 |
| Cooney Ltd | 2,000 | |
| Bank | 52,000 | |
| | 195,000 | 195,000 |

## Record book 3

### 1. Refer to the general journal.

Open a ledger account for each general journal figure: machinery, Cooney Ltd and ordinary share capital. The figure for bank is entered in the cash book. If the figure is debit in the general journal, it is debit in the ledger. If it is credit in the general journal, it is credit in the ledger. Write 'balance' in the details column of each account.

### 2. Refer to the cash book.

Credit entries in the cash book are posted to the debit in the ledger and debit entries are posted to the credit in the ledger. Thus, the €1,000 advertising is shown on the debit of the advertising account. The €20,000 paid for purchases is shown on the debit of the purchases account. Similarly, the VAT of €4,000 is shown on the debit of the VAT account. On the other hand, the sales of €30,000, VAT of €6,000 and €3,000 received from Cooney, are all shown on the credit in the ledger.

### 3. Balance VAT, OSC and Cooney accounts.

The other accounts only have one entry in them and do not need balancing.

## Record book 2

Now use record book two to draw up a trial balance. This is a list of the balances from the accounts above in record book three. The balances are shown in the debit or credit column depending on where they are in the accounts. The two columns are then totalled and if you have done your work correctly the two totals should be the same.

**1**    (a)   Record the following bank transactions for the month of June and post to the ledger.
Note: Analyse the bank transactions using the following money column headings:
**Debit (Receipts) side:** Bank; Sales; VAT; Debtors; Capital.
**Credit (Payments) side:** Bank; Purchases; VAT; Wages.

| Jun | 1 | Shareholders invested €90,000 and this was lodged |
|---|---|---|
| | 6 | Cash sales lodged, €48,000 (€40,000 + €8,000 VAT) |
| | 8 | Paid wages (cheque no. 1), €3,000 |
| | 22 | Quinn Ltd paid €5,000 and this was lodged (receipt no. 1) |
| | 28 | Purchases for resale (cheque no. 2), €30,000 + 20% VAT |

     (b)   Balance the accounts on 30 June and extract a trial balance as on that date.

**2**    (a)   Record the following bank transactions for the month of July and post to the ledger.
Note: Analyse the bank transactions using the following money column headings:
**Debit (Receipts) side:** Bank; Sales; VAT; Debtors; Capital.
**Credit (Payments) side:** Bank; Purchases; VAT; Advertising.

| Jul | 1 | Shareholders invested €75,000 and this was lodged |
|---|---|---|
| | 5 | Cash sales lodged, €60,000 (€50,000 + €10,000 VAT) |
| | 7 | Kelly Ltd paid €2,000 and this was lodged (receipt no. 1) |
| | 21 | Paid advertising (cheque no. 1), €8,000 |
| | 27 | Purchases for resale (cheque no. 2), €35,000 + 20% VAT |

     (b)   Balance the accounts on 31 July and extract a trial balance as on that date.

**3**    (a)   Record the following bank transactions for the month of August and post to the ledger.
Note: Analyse the bank transactions using the following money column headings:
**Debit (Receipts) side:** Bank; Sales; VAT; Debtors; Capital.
**Credit (Payments) side:** Bank; Purchases; VAT; Wages.

| Aug | 3 | Shareholders invested €50,000 and this was lodged |
|---|---|---|
| | 8 | Purchases for resale (cheque no. 1), €45,000 + 20% VAT |
| | 10 | Paid wages (cheque no. 2), €9,000 |
| | 24 | Mooney Ltd paid €6,000 and this was lodged (receipt no. 1) |
| | 30 | Cash sales lodged, €24,000 (€20,000 + €4,000 VAT) |

     (b)   Balance the accounts on 31 August and extract a trial balance as on that date.

**1**  Clancy Ltd had the following balances in its general journal on 1 September.

| Trial Balance as on 1 September | | Dr | Cr |
|---|---|---|---|
| | | € | € |
| Sep 1 | Premises | 100,000 | |
| | Debtor: Maguire Ltd | 10,000 | |
| | Bank overdraft | | 8,000 |
| | Ordinary share capital | | 102,000 |
| | | 110,000 | 110,000 |

(a)  Post the balances in the above general journal to the relevant ledger accounts.

(b)  Record the following transactions for the month of September and post to the ledger.
Note: Analyse the bank transactions using the following money column headings:
**Debit (Receipts) side:** Bank; Sales; VAT; Debtors; Capital.
**Credit (Payments) side:** Bank; Purchases; VAT; Advertising.

Sep  3  Shareholders invested €50,000 and this was lodged
7  Paid advertising (cheque no. 1), €5,000
10  Cash sales lodged, €12,000 (€10,000 + €2,000 VAT)
23  Maguire Ltd paid €4,000 and this was lodged (receipt no. 1)
28  Purchases for resale (cheque no. 2), €30,000 + 20% VAT

(c)  Balance the accounts on 30 September and extract a trial balance as on that date.

**2**  Ryan Ltd had the following balances in its general journal on 1 October.

| Trial Balance as on 1 October | | Dr | Cr |
|---|---|---|---|
| | | € | € |
| Oct 1 | Equipment | 150,000 | |
| | Debtor: Colbert Ltd | 25,000 | |
| | Bank overdraft | | 5,000 |
| | Ordinary share capital | | 170,000 |
| | | 175,000 | 175,000 |

(a)  Post the balances in the above general journal to the relevant ledger accounts.

(b)  Record the following bank transactions for the month of October and post to the ledger.
Note: Analyse the bank transactions using the following money column headings:
**Debit (Receipts) side:** Bank; Sales; VAT; Debtors; Capital.
**Credit (Payments) side:** Bank; Purchases; VAT; Wages.

Oct  2  Shareholders invested €30,000 and this was lodged
7  Purchases for resale (cheque no. 1), €15,000 + 20% VAT
9  Paid wages (cheque no. 2), €15,000
23  Colbert Ltd paid €7,000 and this was lodged (receipt no. 1)
29  Cash sales lodged, €72,000 (€60,000 + €12,000 VAT)

(c)  Balance the accounts on 31 October and extract a trial balance as on that date.

**3** Cody Ltd had the following balances in its general journal on 1 November.

| Trial Balance as on 1 September | | Dr | Cr |
|---|---|---|---|
| | | € | € |
| Nov 1 | Equipment | 100,000 | |
| | Creditor: Moore Ltd | | 7,000 |
| | Bank | 5,000 | |
| | Ordinary share capital | | 98,000 |
| | | 105,000 | 105,000 |

(a) Post the balances in the above general journal to the relevant ledger accounts.

(b) Record the following transactions for the month of November and post to the ledger.
Note: Analyse the bank transactions using the following money column headings:
**Debit (Receipts) side:** Bank; Sales; VAT; Capital.
**Credit (Payments) side:** Bank; Purchases; VAT; Light and Heat; Creditors.

Nov 2 Shareholders invested €50,000 and this was lodged
8 Paid light and heat (cheque no. 1), €5,000
12 Cash sales lodged, €30,000 (€25,000 + €5,000 VAT)
24 Paid Moore Ltd (cheque no. 2), €3,000
27 Purchases for resale (cheque no. 3), €14,000 + 20% VAT

(c) Balance the accounts on 30 November and extract a trial balance as on that date.

**4** O'Grady Ltd had the following balances in its general journal on 1 December.

| Trial Balance as on 1 December | | Dr | Cr |
|---|---|---|---|
| | | € | € |
| Dec 1 | Equipment | 164,000 | |
| | Creditor: O'Neill Ltd | | 7,000 |
| | Bank | 13,000 | |
| | Ordinary share capital | | 170,000 |
| | | 177,000 | 177,000 |

(a) Post the balances in the above general journal to the relevant ledger accounts.

(b) Record the following bank transactions for the month of December and post to the ledger.
Note: Analyse the bank transactions using the following money column headings:
**Debit (Receipts) side:** Bank; Sales; VAT; Capital.
**Credit (Payments) side:** Bank; Purchases; VAT; Wages; Creditors.

Dec 3 Shareholders invested €40,000 and this was lodged
6 Purchases for resale (cheque no. 1), €16,000 + 20% VAT
8 Paid wages (cheque no. 2), €14,000
20 Cash sales lodged, €54,000 (€45,000 + €9,000 VAT)
28 Paid O'Neill Ltd (cheque no. 3), €4,000

(c) Balance the accounts on 31 December and extract a trial balance as on that date.

Try a test on this topic

# Chapter 30

# Petty cash book

# What is petty cash?

Petty cash refers to the small expenses of running a business, e.g. an employee who is asked to post a letter for the business can claim the cost of the stamp.

## Petty Cash Voucher

Ref. no. 38

Date: 9 April

| Details | Amount |
|---------|--------|
| Computer paper | 15.00 |
| Paper clips and folders | 12.00 |
| | 27.00 |

Signature: *Tony Gibson*

Passed by: *Susan Brennan*

### The imprest

The petty cashier is the person appointed to pay the petty cash expenses. He or she is given cash, known as the imprest. The petty cash expenses are paid out of this imprest. At the end of each month the imprest is restored, i.e. the finance manager gives the petty cashier enough money to return the imprest to its original amount.

### Petty cash voucher

An employee who wishes to make a claim for expenses must complete a petty cash voucher. This contains the date, the reason for the claim and the amount claimed.

### Advantages

The advantages of this system are:
- the company has a record of small payments (the vouchers)
- the company can control small payments
- the financial manager is not constantly interrupted by claims for many small sums of money.

# Sample question and solution

## Question

Prepare a petty cash book from the following information to show analysis columns for motor, postage, stationery and sundries. The imprest is €300 and the cashier restores the imprest at the end of the month.

| | | |
|---|---|---|
| May 1 | Balance (imprest) on hand, €300 |
| 3 | Paper, €12 (voucher no. 51) |
| 9 | Postage, €27 (voucher no. 52) |
| 13 | Envelopes (stationery), €14 (voucher no. 53) |
| 19 | Petrol, €62 (voucher no. 54) |
| 23 | Cleaning, €74 (voucher no. 55) |
| 27 | Motor oil, €21 (voucher no. 56) |
| 29 | Postage, €16 (voucher no. 57) |

## Solution

| Dr | | | | | | Petty Cash Book | | | | | | | Cr |
|---|---|---|---|---|---|---|---|---|---|---|---|---|---|
| Date | Details | F | Total | | | Date | Details | F | Total | Motor | Postage | Stationery | Sundries |
| May | | | € | | | May | | | € | € | € | € | € |
| 1 | Balance | b/d | 300 | | | 3 | Paper | 51 | 12 | | | 12 | |
| | | | | | | 9 | Postage | 52 | 27 | | 27 | | |
| | | | | | | 13 | Envelopes | 53 | 14 | | | 14 | |
| | | | | | | 19 | Petrol | 54 | 62 | 62 | | | |
| | | | | | | 23 | Cleaning | 55 | 74 | | | | 74 |
| | | | | | | 27 | Motor oil | 56 | 21 | 21 | | | |
| | | | | | | 29 | Postage | 57 | 16 | | 16 | | |
| | | | | | | 31 | Balance | c/d | 74 | | | | |
| | | | 300 | | | | | | 300 | 83 | 43 | 26 | 74 |
| Jun 1 | Balance | | 74 | | | | | | | | | | |
| | Bank | | 226 | | | | | | | | | | |

| Dr | | | Motor Expenses Account | | | | Cr |
|---|---|---|---|---|---|---|---|
| Date | Details | F | € | Date | Details | F | € |
| May 31 | Petty cash | | 83 | | | | |
| | | | Postage Expenses Account | | | | |
| May 31 | Petty cash | | 43 | | | | |
| | | | Stationery Expenses Account | | | | |
| May 31 | Petty cash | | 26 | | | | |
| | | | Sundries Expenses Account | | | | |
| May 31 | Petty cash | | 74 | | | | |

### Record book 1

Use record book one to prepare the petty cash book as shown above. The imprest is recorded on the debit and the expenses are listed on the credit.

### Record book 3

The total of each expense is recorded in ledger accounts in record book three as shown on the left.

## Activity 30.1 Preparing the petty cash book

**1** Prepare a petty cash book from the following information to show analysis columns for motor, postage, stationery and sundries. The imprest is €250 and the cashier restores the imprest at the end of the month.

| Jun | 1 | Balance (imprest) on hand, €250 |
|-----|-----|--------------------------------|
| | 3 | Cleaning, €65 (voucher no. 60) |
| | 9 | Postage, €14 (voucher no. 61) |
| | 13 | Envelopes (stationery), €18 (voucher no. 62) |
| | 17 | Motor oil, €32 (voucher no. 63) |
| | 18 | Postage, €8 (voucher no. 64) |
| | 23 | Paper, €25 (voucher no. 65) |
| | 29 | Petrol, €58 (voucher no. 66) |

**2** Prepare a petty cash book from the following information to show analysis columns for motor, postage, stationery and sundries. The imprest is €150 and the cashier restores the imprest at the end of the month.

| Jul | 1 | Balance (imprest) on hand, €150 |
|-----|-----|--------------------------------|
| | 8 | Petrol, €43 (voucher no. 80) |
| | 12 | Cleaning, €24 (voucher no. 81) |
| | 14 | Paper, €9 (voucher no. 82) |
| | 18 | Postage, €6 (voucher no. 83) |
| | 24 | Envelopes (stationery), €5 (voucher no. 84) |
| | 26 | Motor oil, €15 (voucher no. 85) |
| | 28 | Postage, €8 (voucher no. 86) |

**3** Prepare a petty cash book from the following information to show analysis columns for motor, postage, stationery and sundries. The imprest is €300 and the cashier restores the imprest at the end of the month.

| Aug | 1 | Balance (imprest) on hand, €300 |
|-----|-----|--------------------------------|
| | 3 | Paper, €14 (voucher no. 42) |
| | 7 | Cleaning, €80 (voucher no. 43) |
| | 13 | Motor oil, €25 (voucher no. 44) |
| | 18 | Postage, €15 (voucher no. 45) |
| | 19 | Postage, €16 (voucher no. 46) |
| | 22 | Envelopes (stationery), €23 (voucher no. 47) |
| | 27 | Petrol, €56 (voucher no. 48) |

eTest.ie
Try a test on this topic

**1** Rita Whyte is the office manager in Quinlan Ltd. She uses a petty cash book to keep an account of small office expenses. She begins each month with an imprest of €250.

On 1 September 2008, the petty cash book had a balance on hand of €250. The following were her petty cash transactions during September:

Sep 2 She paid €15 for postage – petty cash voucher no. 31

4 She bought writing paper (stationery) for €11 – petty cash voucher no. 32

8 She paid €20 to a local charity for raffle tickets – petty cash voucher no. 33

9 She bought envelopes (stationery) for €18 – petty cash voucher no. 34

11 She paid €17 to the window cleaner – petty cash voucher no. 35

16 She paid €16 for cleaning materials for the office – petty cash voucher no. 36

18 She paid €14 for repairs to a filing cabinet – petty cash voucher no. 37

21 She paid €25 for cleaning of office – petty cash voucher no. 38

22 She paid €32 for repairs to an office desk – petty cash voucher no. 39

25 She paid €8 to post a large packet to a customer – petty cash voucher no. 40

28 She paid €15 for toll charges – petty cash voucher no. 41

29 She bought copying paper (stationery) for €23 – petty cash voucher no. 42

(a) Write up the petty cash book for the month of September using the following analysis columns: Postage, Stationery, Cleaning, Repairs, Other.

(b) Total each analysis column and balance the petty cash book at the end of September.

**2** Michael Dillon is the office manager in Cubes Ltd. He uses a petty cash book to keep an account of small office expenses. He begins each month with an imprest of €400.
The following were his petty cash transactions during May:

May 1 Balance (imprest) on hand €400

3 He bought writing paper (stationery) for €11 – petty cash voucher no. 50

4 He paid €18 for postage – petty cash voucher no. 51

5 He bought writing paper (stationery) for €32 – petty cash voucher no. 52

9 He paid €30 to a local charity for a sponsored walk – petty cash voucher no. 53

11 He bought envelopes (stationery) for €27 – petty cash voucher no. 54

12 He paid €57 for repairs to computer desk – petty cash voucher no. 55

17 He paid €26 to SPD Couriers Ltd (postage) – petty cash voucher no. 56

19 He paid €15 for a taxi to collect a customer – petty cash voucher no. 57

20 He paid €35 for cleaning of office – petty cash voucher no. 58

23 He paid €30 for repairs to a printer – petty cash voucher no. 59

26 He purchased copying paper (stationery) for €54 – petty cash voucher no. 60

27 He paid train fare €40 for sales manager – petty cash voucher no. 61

31 He paid €24 for postage – petty cash voucher no. 62

(a) Write up the petty cash book for the month of May using the following analysis columns: Postage, Stationery, Repairs, Travel, Sundries.

(b) Total each analysis column and balance the petty cash book at the end of May.

# General *journal*

# Buying assets

So far you have studied:
- the purchase on credit of goods for resale
- the sale on credit of goods for resale
- cash purchases of goods for resale
- cash sales of goods for resale.

In each case you can see how these are concerned with goods for resale. However, sometimes a business may buy an asset that it does not intend to resell, e.g. a furniture shop might buy a van. This will be used in the business to collect furniture from suppliers and deliver furniture to customers. It is not treated in the same way as the purchase and sale of tables and chairs (goods for resale).

| General Journal | | | Dr | Cr |
|---|---|---|---|---|
| Apr | | | € | € |
| 3 | Delivery van | | 15,000 | |
| | Vantastic Ltd | | | 15,000 |
| | (purchase of van on credit) | | | |

**Delivery Van Account**

| Dr | | | | | | | | Cr |
|---|---|---|---|---|---|---|---|---|
| Date | Details | F | € | Date | Details | F | € | |
| Apr 3 | Vantastic Ltd | | 15,000 | | | | | |

**Vantastic Ltd Account**

| Dr | | | | | | | | Cr |
|---|---|---|---|---|---|---|---|---|
| Date | Details | F | € | Date | Details | F | € | |
| | | | | Apr 3 | Delivery van | | 15,000 | |

**Question**
Furniture Supplies Ltd buys a new delivery van on credit from Vantastic Ltd, €15,000.

**Record book 2** The general journal shows how the transaction will appear in the ledger: debit delivery van account, €15,000 and credit Vantastic Ltd, €15,000. Notice there is a narration (in brackets) describing the purchase.

**Record book 3** Use record book three to show the ledger accounts for the double-entry. The delivery van account is debited with €15,000 and the Vantastic Ltd account is credited with the €15,000.

**General Journal**

| | | | Dr | Cr |
|---|---|---|---|---|
| May | | | € | € |
| 7 | Tom Fallon | | 3,400 | |
| | Delivery van | | | 3,400 |
| | (sold van on credit) | | | |

**Delivery Van Account**

| Dr | | | | | | Cr | |
|---|---|---|---|---|---|---|---|
| Date | Details | F | € | Date | Details | F | € |
| | | | | May 7 | Tom Fallon | | 3,400 |

**Tom Fallon Account**

| Dr | | | | | | Cr | |
|---|---|---|---|---|---|---|---|
| Date | Details | F | € | Date | Details | F | € |
| May 7 | Delivery van | | 3,400 | | | | |

**Question**

Furniture Supplies Ltd sells an old delivery van on credit to Tom Fallon, €3,400.

**Record book 2** The general journal shows how the transaction will appear in the ledger: debit Tom Fallon account, €3,400 and credit delivery van, €3,400. Notice there is a narration (in brackets) describing the sale.

**Record book 3** Use record book three to show the ledger accounts for the double-entry. The delivery van account is credited with €3,400 and the Tom Fallon account is debited with the €3,400.

## Activity 31.1 General journal

**1** On 1 June, Kellys Bakery Ltd buys new machinery on credit from Dunnes Ltd, €24,000. Show how this is recorded in the general journal, and post to the ledger.

**2** On 2 July, Garden Supplies Ltd sells an old computer on credit to Egans Ltd, €1,300. Show how this is recorded in the general journal, and post to the ledger.

**3** On 3 August, Athlone Fitness Centre Ltd buys new sports equipment on credit from Foleys Ltd, €9,000. Show how this is recorded in the general journal, and post to the ledger.

**4** On 4 September, Slaney Insurance Co Ltd sells old office furniture on credit to Gordons Ltd, €15,000. Show how this is recorded in the general journal, and post to the ledger.

**5** On 5 October, Boylan's Supermarket Ltd buys new fridges on credit from Hughes Ltd, €36,000. Show how this is recorded in the general journal, and post to the ledger.

eTest.ie
Try a test on this topic

# Chapter 32

## Worked *example*

# Putting it together

This chapter contains elements of a number of topics we have already studied:

- credit sales and purchase
- cash transactions.

This chapter brings you through a worked example to help you become familiar with the type of question asked in the examination.

**1** **Post the balances from the general journal into the ledger.** Use record book three for the ledger accounts. For each entry in the general journal create a ledger account. If the figure is debit in the general journal it is debit in the ledger.

**2** **Post the relevant figures from the day books into the ledger.** Post the net, VAT and total from the day books to the ledger.

**3** **Record the bank transactions in the cash book.** Money received is listed on the debit side and money spent is listed on the credit side.

**4** **Post the relevant figures from the cash book into the ledger.** Debit figures will be posted to the credit of the ledger and credit figures will be posted to the debit of the ledger.

**5** **Balance the accounts and extract a trial balance.** Write out the account names in the trial balance. Now take the final figure from each account and list it debit or credit in the trial balance, depending on where it is in the account.

# Sample question and solution

## Question

Cullen Ltd had the following balances in its general journal on 1 October.

| General Journal | | Dr | Cr |
|---|---|---|---|
| | | € | € |
| Oct 1 | Buildings | 100,000 | |
| | Debtor: Keogh Ltd | 23,000 | |
| | Bank overdraft | | 3,000 |
| | Ordinary share capital | | 120,000 |
| | Assets, liabilities and share capital of Cullen Ltd | 123,000 | 123,000 |

(a) Post the balances in the above general journal to the relevant ledger accounts.

(b) Post the relevant figures from the sales and purchases books below to the ledger.

| Sales Day Book | | | | | | |
|---|---|---|---|---|---|---|
| | | F. | No. | Net | VAT | Total |
| Oct | | | | € | € | € |
| 4 | Moore Ltd | DL | 132 | 20,000 | 2,000 | 22,000 |
| **Purchases Day Book** | | | | | | |
| 7 | Brady Ltd | CL | 89 | 9,000 | 900 | 9,900 |

(c) Record the following bank transactions for the month of October and post to the ledger.

Note: Analyse the bank transactions using the following money column headings:

**Debit (Receipts) side:** Bank; Sales; VAT; Debtors.

**Credit (Payments) side:** Bank; Purchases; VAT; Creditors; Insurance.

Oct 5     Cash sales lodged, €44,000 (€40,000 + €4,000 VAT)

8     Purchases for resale (cheque no. 1), €20,000 + 10% VAT

9     Keogh Ltd paid its account in full and this was lodged (receipt no. 7)

12     Paid Brady Ltd (cheque no. 2), €5,000

23     Moore Ltd paid €14,000 and this was lodged (receipt no. 8)

29     Paid insurance (cheque no. 3), €3,000

(d) Balance the accounts on 31 October and extract a trial balance as on that date.

## Solution

| Dr | | | | | | Analysed Cash Book | | | | | | | | Cr |
|---|---|---|---|---|---|---|---|---|---|---|---|---|---|---|
| Date | Details | F | Bank | Sales | VAT | Debtors | Date | Details | F | Bank | Purchases | VAT | Creditors | Insurance |
| Oct | | | € | € | € | € | Oct | | | € | € | € | € | € |
| 5 | Sales | | 44,000 | 40,000 | 4,000 | | 1 | Balance | b/d | 3,000 | | | | |
| 9 | Keogh Ltd | 7 | 23,000 | | | 23,000 | 8 | Purchases | 1 | 22,000 | 20,000 | 2,000 | | |
| 23 | Moore Ltd | 8 | 14,000 | | | 14,000 | 12 | Brady Ltd | 2 | 5,000 | | | 5,000 | |
| | | | | | | | 29 | Insurance | 3 | 3,000 | | | | 3,000 |
| | | | | | | | 31 | Balance | c/d | 48,000 | | | | |
| | | | 81,000 | 40,000 | 4,000 | 37,000 | | | | 81,000 | 20,000 | 2,000 | 5,000 | 3,000 |
| Nov 1 | Balance | b/d | 48,000 | | | | | | | | | | | |

*Open for Business*

## GENERAL LEDGER

**Dr**             **Buildings Account**             **Cr**

| Date | Details | F | € | Date | Details | F | € |
|---|---|---|---|---|---|---|---|
| Oct 1 | Balance | b/d | 100,000 | | | | |

### Insurance Account

| Date | Details | F | € | Date | Details | F | € |
|---|---|---|---|---|---|---|---|
| Oct 29 | Bank | CB | 3,000 | | | | |

### Sales Account

| Date | Details | F | € | Date | Details | F | € |
|---|---|---|---|---|---|---|---|
| Oct 31 | Balance | c/d | 60,000 | Oct 4 | Moore Ltd | SB | 20,000 |
| | | | | 5 | Bank | CB | 40,000 |
| | | | 60,000 | | | | 60,000 |
| | | | | Nov 1 | Balance | b/d | 60,000 |

### Purchases Account

| Date | Details | F | € | Date | Details | F | € |
|---|---|---|---|---|---|---|---|
| Oct 7 | Brady Ltd | PB | 9,000 | Oct 31 | Balance | c/d | 29,000 |
| 8 | Bank | CB | 20,000 | | | | |
| | | | 29,000 | | | | 29,000 |
| Nov 1 | Balance | b/d | 29,000 | | | | |

### VAT Account

| Date | Details | F | € | Date | Details | F | € |
|---|---|---|---|---|---|---|---|
| Oct 7 | Brady Ltd | PB | 900 | Oct 4 | Moore Ltd | SB | 2,000 |
| 8 | Bank | CB | 2,000 | 5 | Bank | CB | 4,000 |
| 31 | Balance | c/d | 3,100 | | | | |
| | | | 6,000 | | | | 6,000 |
| | | | | Nov 1 | Balance | b/d | 3,100 |

### Ordinary Share Capital Account

| Date | Details | F | € | Date | Details | F | € |
|---|---|---|---|---|---|---|---|
| | | | | Oct 1 | Balance | b/d | 120,000 |

## CREDITORS LEDGER

### Brady Ltd Account

| Date | Details | F | € | Date | Details | F | € |
|---|---|---|---|---|---|---|---|
| Oct 12 | Bank | CB | 5,000 | Oct 7 | Purchases | PB | 9,900 |
| 31 | Balance | c/d | 4,900 | | | | |
| | | | 9,900 | | | | 9,900 |
| | | | | Nov 1 | Balance | b/d | 4,900 |

## DEBTORS LEDGER

### Moore Ltd Account

| Date | Details | F | € | Date | Details | F | € |
|---|---|---|---|---|---|---|---|
| Oct 4 | Sales | SB | 22,000 | Oct 23 | Bank | CB | 14,000 |
| | | | | 31 | Balance | c/d | 8,000 |
| | | | 22,000 | | | | 22,000 |
| Nov 1 | Balance | b/d | 8,000 | | | | |

### Keogh Ltd Account

| Date | Details | F | € | Date | Details | F | € |
|---|---|---|---|---|---|---|---|
| Oct 1 | Balance | b/d | 23,000 | Oct 9 | Bank | CB | 23,000 |

## Trial Balance as on 31 October

| | | Debit € | Credit € |
|---|---|---|---|
| Buildings | | 100,000 | |
| Insurance | | 3,000 | |
| Sales | | | 60,000 |
| Purchases | | 29,000 | |
| VAT | | | 3,100 |
| Ordinary share capital | | | 120,000 |
| Brady Ltd | | | 4,900 |
| Moore Ltd | | 8,000 | |
| Bank | | 48,000 | |
| | | 188,000 | 188,000 |

## Record book 3

### 1. Refer to the general journal.

Open a ledger account for each general journal figure: buildings, Keogh Ltd and ordinary share capital. The figure for bank is entered in the cash book. If the figure is debit in the general journal, it is debit in the ledger. If it is credit in the general journal, it is credit in the ledger. Write 'balance' in the details column of each account.

### 2. Refer to the cash book.

Credit entries in the cash book are posted to the debit in the ledger and debit entries are posted to the credit in the ledger. Thus, the €3,000 insurance is shown on the debit of the insurance account. The €20,000 paid for purchases is shown on the debit of the purchases account. Similarly, the VAT of €2,000 is shown on the debit of the VAT account. The €5,000 paid to Brady Ltd is shown on the debit of Brady Ltd account. On the other hand the sales of €40,000, VAT of €4,000, €23,000 received from Keogh Ltd and €14,000 received from Moore Ltd are all shown on the credit in the ledger.

### 3. Balance the accounts.

Balance the accounts with two or more entries.

## Record book 2

Now use record book two to draw up a trial balance. This is a list of the balances from the accounts above in record book three. The balances are shown in the debit or credit column depending on where they are in the accounts. Total the two columns. If you have done your work correctly the two totals should be the same.

**1** Foley Ltd had the following balances in its general journal on 1 November.

| General Journal | | Dr | Cr |
|---|---|---|---|
| | | € | € |
| Nov 1 | Equipment | 120,000 | |
| | Debtor: Duffy Ltd | 30,000 | |
| | Bank overdraft | | 10,000 |
| | Ordinary share capital | | 140,000 |
| | Assets, liabilities and share capital of Foley Ltd | 150,000 | 150,000 |

(a) Post the balances in the above general journal to the relevant ledger accounts.

(b) Post the relevant figures from the sales and purchases books below to the ledger.

| | | F. | No. | Net | VAT | Total |
|---|---|---|---|---|---|---|
| | **Sales Day Book** | | | | | |
| Nov | | | | € | € | € |
| 5 | Lyons Ltd | DL | 114 | 30,000 | 3,000 | 33,000 |
| | **Purchases Day Book** | | | | | |
| 9 | Cronin Ltd | CL | 65 | 14,000 | 1,400 | 15,400 |

(c) Record the following bank transactions for the month of November and post to the ledger.
Note: Analyse the bank transactions using the following money column headings:
**Debit (Receipts) side:** Bank; Sales; VAT; Debtors.
**Credit (Payments) side:** Bank; Purchases; VAT; Creditors; Advertising.

Nov  3   Cash sales lodged, €22,000 (€20,000 + €2,000 VAT)
      7   Purchases for resale (cheque no. 1), €12,000 + 10% VAT
     11   Duffy Ltd paid its account in full and this was lodged (receipt no. 1)
     17   Paid Cronin Ltd (cheque no. 2), €8,000
     24   Lyons Ltd paid €19,000 and this was lodged (receipt no. 2)
     28   Paid advertising (cheque no. 3), €4,000

(d) Balance the accounts on 30 November and extract a trial balance as on that date.

**2** Dunne Ltd had the following balances in its general journal on 1 December.

| General Journal | | Dr | Cr |
|---|---|---|---|
| | | € | € |
| Dec 1 | Machinery | 90,000 | |
| | Debtor: McCarthy Ltd | 5,000 | |
| | Bank overdraft | | 15,000 |
| | Ordinary share capital | | 80,000 |
| | Assets, liabilities and share capital of Dunne Ltd | 95,000 | 95,000 |

(a) Post the balances in the above general journal to the relevant ledger accounts.
(b) Post the relevant figures from the sales and purchases books below to the ledger.

| Sales Day Book | | F. | No. | Net | VAT | Total |
|---|---|---|---|---|---|---|
| Dec | | | | € | € | € |
| 5 | Keogh Ltd | DL | 114 | 14,000 | 2,800 | 16,800 |
| **Purchases Day Book** | | | | | | |
| 9 | Maguire Ltd | CL | 65 | 8,000 | 1,600 | 9,600 |

(c) Record the following bank transactions for the month of December and post to the ledger.
Note: Analyse the bank transactions using the following money column headings:
**Debit (Receipts) side:** Bank; Sales; VAT; Debtors.
**Credit (Payments) side:** Bank; Purchases; VAT; Creditors; Insurance.
Dec 3 Cash sales lodged, €48,000 (€40,000 + €8,000 VAT)
   7 Purchases for resale (cheque no. 11), €7,000 + 20% VAT
   11 McCarthy Ltd paid its account in full and this was lodged (receipt no. 8)
   17 Paid Maguire Ltd (cheque no. 12), €5,000
   24 Keogh Ltd paid €12,000 and this was lodged (receipt no. 9)
   28 Paid insurance (cheque no. 13), €2,500
(d) Balance the accounts on 31 December and extract a trial balance as on that date.

eTest.ie
Try a test on this topic

**3** Long Ltd had the following balances on 1 May.

Buildings, €148,000

Debtor: Short Ltd, €42,000

(a) Enter these balances in the general journal, find the ordinary share capital balance and post these balances to the relevant ledger accounts.

(b) Post the relevant figures from the purchases and purchases returns books below to the ledger accounts.

| Purchases Day Book | | | | | | |
|---|---|---|---|---|---|---|
| | | F. | No. | Net | VAT | Total |
| May | | | | € | € | € |
| 9 | Smyth Ltd | CL | 97 | 12,000 | 1,620 | 13,620 |
| Purchases Returns Day Book | | | | | | |
| 18 | Smyth Ltd | CL | 16 | 4,000 | 540 | 4,540 |

(c) Record the following bank transactions for the month of November and post to the ledger.
Note: Analyse the bank transactions using the following money column headings:
**Debit (Receipts) side:** Bank; Sales; VAT; Debtors; Capital.
**Credit (Payments) side:** Bank; Purchases; VAT; Wages.

May  1   Shareholder invested €40,000 and this was lodged (receipt no. 14)

6   Cash sales lodged, €68,100 (€60,000 + €8,100 VAT)

12   Short Ltd paid its account in full and this was lodged (receipt no. 15)

17   Purchases for resale (cheque no. 26), €24,000 + 13.5% VAT

30   Paid wages (cheque no. 27), €14,000

(d) Balance the accounts on 31 May and extract a trial balance as on that date.

**4** Kelly Ltd is a retail store.

(a) Record the following credit transactions in the purchases and purchases returns books of Kelly Ltd for the month of April. Post relevant figures from the books to the ledger accounts.

Apr 3 Purchased goods on credit from Nee Ltd invoice no. 12 €16,000 + VAT 13.5%

Apr 9 Purchased goods on credit from Hay Ltd invoice no. 67 €22,600 + VAT 13.5%

Apr 15 Returned goods to Nee Ltd credit note no. 5 € 7,000 + VAT 13.5%

(b) Record the following bank transactions for the month of April in the analysed cash book of Kelly Ltd. Post relevant figures to the ledger accounts.
Note: Analyse the bank transactions using the following money headings:
**Debit (Receipts) Side:** Bank; Sales; VAT; Share; Capital.
**Credit (Payments) Side:** Bank; Purchases; VAT; Light and Heat; Creditors.

Apr   1   Shareholder invested €150,000 and this was lodged (receipt no. 24)

2   Purchases for resale (cheque no. 45) €70,000 + VAT 13.5%

13   Paid electricity bill (cheque no. 46) €1,700

19   Cash sales lodged €90,800 (€80,000 + VAT €10,800)

28   Paid Hay Ltd (cheque no. 47) €17,500

(c) Balance the accounts on 30 April and extract a trial balance as at that date.

# Presentation of *ledger accounts*

## Are you traditional or modern?

There are two ways of presenting ledger accounts: the traditional 'T' shape account; or the modern continuous balance method.

| Dr | Cash Account | | | | | | Cr |
|---|---|---|---|---|---|---|---|
| Date | Details | F | € | Date | Details | F | € |
| Jan 1 | Balance | b/d | 100 | Jan 5 | Mortgage | GL | 500 |
| 3 | Wages | GL | 700 | 7 | Petrol | GL | 60 |
| | | | | 8 | Balance | c/d | 240 |
| | | | 800 | | | | 800 |
| Jan 9 | Balance | b/d | 240 | | | | |

**Traditional**

The traditional 'T' account is shown in record book three. The cash account on the left is an example of the traditional layout. Money received is listed on the debit and money paid is listed on the credit. It is not until the very end that you get to see what the balance is in the account.

**Modern**

The modern way to show a ledger account is to use record book two. The same cash account we looked at above is shown on the left in the continuous format. Notice that there is a 'running balance' so you get to see the balance in the account as each transaction is entered. Money received, like the wages, increases the running balance and money paid out, like the mortgage and petrol, reduces the running balance. The final figure is the balance in the account.

| | Cash Account | | | | | |
|---|---|---|---|---|---|---|
| Date | Details | F | Dr | Cr | Balance | |
| Jan | | | € | € | € | |
| 1 | Balance | b/d | | | 100 | |
| 3 | Wages | GL | 700 | | 800 | |
| 5 | Mortgage | GL | | 500 | 300 | |
| 7 | Petrol | GL | | 60 | 240 | |

## Activity 33.1 Convert accounts

**1**

| Dr | Cash Account | | | | | | | Cr |
|---|---|---|---|---|---|---|---|---|
| Date | Details | F | € | Date | Details | F | € |
| Jan 1 | Balance | b/d | 200 | Jan 4 | Mortgage | GL | 800 |
| 4 | Wages | GL | 900 | 6 | Groceries | GL | 120 |
| | | | | 7 | Balance | c/d | 180 |
| | | | 1,100 | | | | 1,100 |
| Jan 8 | Balance | b/d | 180 | | | | |

Show this account in the continuous balance format. Use record book two for your answer.

**2**

| | Bank Account | | | | |
|---|---|---|---|---|---|
| | | F | Dr | Cr | Balance |
| Feb | | | € | € | € |
| 1 | Balance | b/d | | | 1,200 |
| 4 | Sales | GL | 3,400 | | 4,600 |
| 6 | Rent | GL | | 900 | 3,700 |
| 9 | Sales | GL | 2,300 | | 6,000 |

Show this account in the traditional 'T' format. Use record book three for your answer.

**3**

| Dr | Bank Account | | | | | | | Cr |
|---|---|---|---|---|---|---|---|---|
| Date | Details | F | € | Date | Details | F | € |
| Mar 1 | Balance | b/d | 500 | Mar 5 | Purchases | GL | 1,700 |
| 2 | Sales | GL | 4,200 | 6 | Insurance | GL | 1,400 |
| | | | | 8 | Balance | c/d | 1,600 |
| | | | 4,700 | | | | 4,700 |
| Mar 9 | Balance | b/d | 1,600 | | | | |

Show this account in the continuous balance format. Use record book two for your answer.

**4**

| | Cash Account | | | | |
|---|---|---|---|---|---|
| | | F | Dr | Cr | Balance |
| Apr | | | € | € | € |
| 1 | Balance | b/d | | | 600 |
| 3 | Wages | GL | 1,200 | | 1,800 |
| 7 | Rent | GL | | 700 | 1,100 |
| 9 | Groceries | GL | | 110 | 990 |

Show this account in the traditional 'T' format. Use record book three for your answer.

Try a test on this topic

# Chapter 34

▶ Find out the difference between your debtors and your creditors

▶ Learn how to keep control of your debtors and your creditors

# Control accounts

# Get control

Control accounts are used to summarise and check the accuracy of credit transactions. There are two types of control account that you need to study: debtors' control account; and creditors' control account. Both accounts are prepared in record book three.

| Dr | Debtors Control Account | | | | | | | Cr |
|---|---|---|---|---|---|---|---|---|
| Date | Details | F | € | Date | Details | F | € |
| 30 | Sales | | 26,000 | Jun 30 | Sales returns | | 5,000 |
| | | | | 30 | Cash | | 17,000 |
| | | | | 30 | Balance | c/d | 4,000 |
| | | | 26,000 | | | | 26,000 |
| Jul 1 | Balance | b/d | 4,000 | | | | |

### Debtors' Control Account

Debtors are customers that you sell to on credit. They owe you money. The debtors' control account checks the sales ledger. The total sales for the month is listed on the debit. The total sales returns and total cash received from debtors are listed on the credit.

| Dr | Creditors Control Account | | | | | | | Cr |
|---|---|---|---|---|---|---|---|---|
| Date | Details | F | € | Date | Details | F | € |
| Jun 30 | Purchases returns | | 2,000 | Jun 30 | Purchases | | 14,000 |
| 30 | Cash | | 9,000 | | | | |
| 30 | Balance | c/d | 3,000 | | | | |
| | | | 14,000 | | | | 14,000 |
| | | | | Jul 1 | Balance | b/d | 3,000 |

### Creditors' Control Account

Creditors are suppliers you purchase from on credit. You owe them money. The creditors' control account checks the purchases ledger. The total purchases figure is listed on the credit. The total purchases returns and the total cash paid to suppliers are both listed on the debit.

## Activity 34.1 Control accounts

**1** From the following information complete and balance the debtors' control account for the month of June:

        Total credit sales for June, €32,000

        Total sales returns, €5,000

        Total cash received from debtors, €26,000

**2** From the following information complete and balance the debtors' control account for the month of July:

        Total credit sales for July, €53,000

        Total sales returns, €4,000

        Total cash received from debtors, €41,000

**3** From the following information complete and balance the debtors' control account for the month of August:

        Total credit sales for August, €16,000

        Total sales returns, €2,000

        Total cash received from debtors, €9,000

**4** From the following information complete and balance the creditors' control account for the month of September:

        Total credit purchases for September, €29,000

        Total purchases returns, €3,000

        Total cash paid to creditors, €17,000

**5** From the following information complete and balance the creditors' control account for the month of October:

        Total credit purchases for October, €46,000

        Total purchases returns, €4,000

        Total cash paid to creditors, €35,000

**6** From the following information complete and balance the creditors' control account for the month of November:

        Total credit purchases for November, €64,000

        Total purchases returns, €6,000

        Total cash paid to creditors, €48,000

Try a test on this topic

# Chapter 35

# Trading account

# Modern layout

The trading account is used to find the gross profit for a business. In simple terms, sales less cost of sales gives you profit. However, it gets more complicated because a business will have opening and closing stocks.

## Question

From the following information prepare a trading account for the year ended 31 December.

|  | € |
|---|---|
| Sales | 280,000 |
| Opening stock | 50,000 |
| Purchases | 160,000 |
| Carriage in | 7,000 |
| Closing stock | 40,000 |

## Solution

### Trading Account for the year ended 31 December

|  |  | € | € |
|---|---|---|---|
| Sales |  |  | 280,000 |
| *Less cost of sales* |  |  |  |
| Opening stock |  | 50,000 |  |
| + Purchases |  | 160,000 |  |
| + Carriage in |  | 7,000 |  |
|  |  | 217,000 |  |
| - Closing stock |  | 40,000 |  |
| Cost of sales |  |  | 177,000 |
| **GROSS PROFIT** |  |  | **103,000** |

## Record book 2

Use record book two to prepare the trading account. Most students find it difficult to remember which column the figures go in. If you study the layout you will see that the reason we go into the middle column is to have somewhere to find the cost of sales figure. Once we have the cost of sales (€177,000) we need to place it so that we can subtract it from the sales. Thus, the €177,000 must go in the right column under the €280,000 to give the profit of €103,000.

## Cost of sales

Cost of sales is the cost of the goods you sell. Suppose you buy a bike for €177 and sell it for €280. The cost of sales is €177. So your profit is sales less cost of sales, i.e. 280−177=103. Just add a few zeros and you will see this is similar to the example on the left.

# Traditional layout

### Record book 3

The traditional way to prepare a trading account is to use record book three. Using this method a series of ledger accounts are opened and the balances are then posted to the trading account.

**GENERAL LEDGER**

Dr      **Sales Account**      Cr

| Date | Details | F | € | Date | Details | F | € |
|------|---------|---|------|------|---------|---|------|
| Dec 31 | Trading | | 280,000 | Dec 31 | Balance | b/d | 280,000 |

**Purchases Account**

| Date | Details | F | € | Date | Details | F | € |
|------|---------|---|------|------|---------|---|------|
| Dec 31 | Balance | b/d | 160,000 | Dec 31 | Trading | | 160,000 |

**Carriage In Account**

| Date | Details | F | € | Date | Details | F | € |
|------|---------|---|------|------|---------|---|------|
| Dec 31 | Balance | b/d | 7,000 | Dec 31 | Trading | | 7,000 |

**Stock Account**

| Date | Details | F | € | Date | Details | F | € |
|------|---------|---|------|------|---------|---|------|
| Jan 1 | Balance | b/d | 50,000 | Dec 31 | Trading | | 50,000 |
| Dec 31 | Trading (deduct) | | 40,000 | | | | |

**Trading Account for the year ended 31 December**

| Details | | F | € | Details | | F | € |
|---------|--|---|------|---------|--|---|------|
| Opening stock | | | 50,000 | Sales | | | 280,000 |
| + Purchases | | | 160,000 | | | | |
| + Carriage in | | | 7,000 | | | | |
| | | | 217,000 | | | | |
| - Closing stock | | | 40,000 | | | | |
| | | | 177,000 | | | | |
| Gross profit | | c/d | 103,000 | | | | |
| | | | 280,000 | | | | 280,000 |
| | | | | Gross profit | | b/d | 103,000 |

## Activity 35.1 Preparing the trading account

**1** From the following information prepare a trading account for the year ended 31 December.

|                | €       |
|----------------|--------:|
| Sales          | 120,000 |
| Opening stock  | 12,000  |
| Purchases      | 53,000  |
| Carriage in    | 7,000   |
| Closing stock  | 11,000  |

**2** From the following information prepare a trading account for the year ended 31 December.

|                | €       |
|----------------|--------:|
| Sales          | 240,000 |
| Opening stock  | 43,000  |
| Purchases      | 110,000 |
| Carriage in    | 26,000  |
| Closing stock  | 38,000  |

**3** From the following information prepare a trading account for the year ended 31 December.

|                | €       |
|----------------|--------:|
| Sales          | 320,000 |
| Opening stock  | 64,000  |
| Purchases      | 130,000 |
| Carriage in    | 35,000  |
| Closing stock  | 59,000  |

**4** From the following information prepare a trading account for the year ended 31 December.

|                | €       |
|----------------|--------:|
| Opening stock  | 54,000  |
| Closing stock  | 63,000  |
| Sales          | 360,000 |
| Purchases      | 190,000 |
| Carriage in    | 42,000  |

**5** From the following information prepare a trading account for the year ended 31 December.

|                | €       |
|----------------|--------:|
| Sales          | 260,000 |
| Purchases      | 125,000 |
| Opening stock  | 53,000  |
| Closing stock  | 34,000  |
| Carriage in    | 28,000  |

**6**   From the following information prepare a trading account for the year ended 31 December.

|                | €       |
|----------------|---------|
| Sales          | 120,000 |
| Purchases      | 52,000  |
| Carriage in    | 7,000   |
| Opening stock  | 12,000  |
| Closing stock  | 11,000  |

**7**   From the following information prepare a trading account for the year ended 31 December.

|                | €       |
|----------------|---------|
| Purchases      | 105,000 |
| Carriage in    | 17,000  |
| Sales          | 240,000 |
| Opening stock  | 25,000  |
| Closing stock  | 32,000  |

**8**   From the following information prepare a trading account for the year ended 31 December.

|                | €       |
|----------------|---------|
| Carriage in    | 26,000  |
| Opening stock  | 53,000  |
| Sales          | 380,000 |
| Purchases      | 135,000 |
| Closing stock  | 62,000  |

**9**   From the following information prepare a trading account for the year ended 31 December.

|                | €       |
|----------------|---------|
| Opening stock  | 23,000  |
| Closing stock  | 34,000  |
| Sales          | 375,000 |
| Purchases      | 146,000 |
| Carriage in    | 53,000  |

Try a test on this topic

**10**  From the following information prepare a trading account for the year ended 31 December.

|                | €       |
|----------------|---------|
| Sales          | 213,000 |
| Purchases      | 97,000  |
| Opening stock  | 48,000  |
| Closing stock  | 54,000  |
| Carriage in    | 17,000  |

# Profit and loss account

# Dealing with expenses

The profit and loss account is used to find the net profit or net loss of the business. In a full question the profit and loss account continues on from where the trading account finishes. Therefore, the starting point is the gross profit.

## Question

From the following information prepare a profit and loss account for the year ended 31 December.

|  | € |
|---|---|
| Gross profit | 103,000 |
| Wages | 63,000 |
| Carriage out | 4,000 |
| Advertising | 3,000 |
| Electricity | 6,000 |

## Solution

| Profit and Loss Account for the year ended 31 December | | |
|---|---|---|
|  | € | € |
| Gross profit |  | 103,000 |
| *Less expenses* |  |  |
| Wages | 63,000 |  |
| Carriage out | 4,000 |  |
| Advertising | 3,000 |  |
| Electricity | 6,000 | 76,000 |
| **NET PROFIT** |  | **27,000** |

## Record book 2

Use record book two to prepare the profit and loss account. Start with the gross profit. List the expenses, total them and subtract from the gross profit as shown in the example on the left.

## Net profit or net loss

When the expenses are smaller than the gross profit you get a net profit. If, however, the expenses are greater than the gross profit you get a net loss. The net profit belongs to the shareholders (owners) of the company. Usually they are given a dividend as a reward for the risk they are taking by investing in a business.

## Carriage out

Carriage out is the cost of delivering goods to your customers. It is listed in the profit and loss as an expense and should not be confused with carriage in, which is entered in the trading account.

# Sample question and solution

## Question

From the following information prepare a trading and profit and loss account for the year ended 31 December.

|  | € |
|---|---|
| Cash sales | 360,000 |
| Opening stock | 34,000 |
| Cash purchases | 170,000 |
| Carriage in | 2,000 |
| Closing stock | 30,000 |
| Wages | 84,000 |
| Heating and lighting | 12,000 |
| Advertising | 6,000 |
| Carriage out | 4,000 |
| Dividend paid | 20,000 |

### Dividend

The dividend is the share of the profit given to the investors. In our example, subtract the €20,000 dividend from the net profit to get the reserve. This reserve (€58,000) is the retained profit which can be ploughed back into the firm.

## Solution

### Trading, Profit and Loss Account for the year ended 31 December

|  |  | € | € |
|---|---|---|---|
| Sales |  |  | 360,000 |
| *Less cost of sales* |  |  |  |
| Opening stock |  | 34,000 |  |
| + Purchases |  | 170,000 |  |
| + Carriage in |  | 2,000 |  |
|  |  | 206,000 |  |
| - Closing stock |  | 30,000 |  |
| Cost of sales |  |  | 176,000 |
| **GROSS PROFIT** |  |  | **184,000** |
| *Less expenses* |  |  |  |
| Wages |  | 84,000 |  |
| Heating and lighting |  | 12,000 |  |
| Advertising |  | 6,000 |  |
| Carriage out |  | 4,000 | 106,000 |
| **NET PROFIT** |  |  | **78,000** |
| Dividend paid |  |  | 20,000 |
| **Reserve** |  |  | **58,000** |

## GP% and NP%

The gross profit percentage (GP%) and the net profit percentage (NP%) are ratios that are used to show how profitable a firm is. They are calculated as follows:

$$GP\% = \frac{\text{gross profit}}{\text{sales}} \times 100$$

$$NP\% = \frac{\text{net profit}}{\text{sales}} \times 100$$

## Question

In the question above the GP% and the NP% are as follows:

$$GP\% = \frac{\text{gross profit}}{\text{sales}} \times 100$$

$$= \frac{184,000}{360,000} \times 100$$

$$= 51.11\%$$

$$NP\% = \frac{\text{net profit}}{\text{sales}} \times 100$$

$$= \frac{78,000}{360,000} \times 100$$

$$= 21.66\%$$

*Open for Business*

1. From the following information prepare a profit and loss account for the year ended 31 December.

|                  | €       |
|------------------|---------|
| Gross profit     | 190,000 |
| Wages            | 84,000  |
| Carriage out     | 11,000  |
| Light and heat   | 12,000  |
| Motor expenses   | 30,000  |

2. From the following information prepare a profit and loss account for the year ended 31 December.

|                  | €       |
|------------------|---------|
| Gross profit     | 220,000 |
| Wages            | 120,000 |
| Insurance        | 16,000  |
| Stationery       | 12,000  |
| Discount allowed | 9,000   |

3. From the following information prepare a profit and loss account for the year ended 31 December.

|                  | €       |
|------------------|---------|
| Gross profit     | 157,000 |
| Advertising      | 14,000  |
| Carriage out     | 6,000   |
| Discount allowed | 8,000   |
| Rent and rates   | 12,000  |
| Salaries         | 90,000  |

4. From the following information prepare a profit and loss account for the year ended 31 December.

|                       | €      |
|-----------------------|--------|
| Gross profit          | 89,000 |
| Salaries              | 48,000 |
| Interest on overdraft | 2,000  |
| Advertising           | 3,000  |
| Telephone             | 8,000  |
| Cleaning and repairs  | 1,000  |

5. From the following information prepare a profit and loss account for the year ended 31 December.

|                       | €       |
|-----------------------|---------|
| Gross profit          | 126,000 |
| Petrol and car service| 18,000  |
| Carriage out          | 3,000   |
| Advertising           | 7,000   |
| Heating and lighting  | 12,000  |
| Salaries              | 72,000  |
| Insurance             | 1,000   |

eTest.ie
Try a test on this topic

## Activity 36.2 Preparing a trading and profit and loss account

For each of these questions:
(a) prepare a trading and profit and loss account for the year ended 31 December
(b) calculate the gross profit percentage
(c) calculate the net profit percentage.

**1**

| | € |
|---|---|
| Sales | 250,000 |
| Opening stock | 14,000 |
| Purchases | 100,000 |
| Carriage in | 1,000 |
| Closing stock | 11,000 |
| Petrol and car service | 15,000 |
| Carriage out | 2,000 |
| Advertising | 3,000 |
| Heating and lighting | 14,000 |
| Salaries | 90,000 |
| Dividend paid | 12,000 |

**2**

| | € |
|---|---|
| Sales | 185,000 |
| Opening stock | 18,000 |
| Purchases | 75,000 |
| Carriage in | 3,000 |
| Closing stock | 14,000 |
| Insurance | 4,000 |
| Wages | 55,000 |
| Petrol and car repairs | 6,000 |
| Stationery | 2,000 |
| Rent and rates | 1,000 |
| Dividend paid | 14,000 |

**3**

| | € |
|---|---|
| Sales | 400,000 |
| Opening stock | 25,000 |
| Purchases | 170,000 |
| Carriage in | 16,000 |
| Closing stock | 35,000 |
| Carriage out | 15,000 |
| Interest on overdraft | 3,000 |
| Advertising | 12,000 |
| Wages | 96,000 |
| Dividend paid | 25,000 |

**4**

| | € |
|---|---|
| Sales | 340,000 |
| Opening stock | 11,000 |
| Purchases | 142,000 |
| Carriage in | 4,000 |
| Closing stock | 13,000 |
| Telephone bills | 7,000 |
| Wages | 112,000 |
| Insurance | 5,000 |
| Postage | 2,000 |
| Interest on overdraft | 1,000 |
| Dividend paid | 8,000 |

**5**

| | € |
|---|---|
| Sales | 194,000 |
| Opening stock | 16,000 |
| Purchases | 70,000 |
| Carriage in | 2,000 |
| Closing stock | 17,000 |
| Advertising | 3,000 |
| Heating and lighting | 6,000 |
| Rent | 12,000 |
| Salaries | 65,000 |
| Interest on overdraft | 4,000 |
| Dividend paid | 9,000 |

**6**

| | € |
|---|---|
| Sales | 580,000 |
| Opening stock | 34,000 |
| Purchases | 270,000 |
| Carriage in | 21,000 |
| Closing stock | 38,000 |
| Salaries | 220,000 |
| Rent and rates | 24,000 |
| Light and heat | 18,000 |
| Carriage out | 8,000 |
| Dividend paid | 4,000 |

# Chapter 37

# Profit and loss appropriation account

## Dividing the profit

The profit and loss appropriation account shows how the profit earned by the firm is divided. In a full question the profit and loss appropriation account continues on from where the profit and loss account finishes. Therefore, the starting point is the net profit.

### Question

Foley Ltd has 80,000 ordinary shares issued. Draft the appropriation account for the year ended 31 December given the following information.
● Net profit is €27,000.
● Last year's reserve (profit and loss balance) was €9,000.
● Dividends declared are 10%.

### Solution

Dividends = 10% of 80,000 = €8,000

| Profit and Loss Appropriation Account for the year ended 31 December | | | € | € |
|---|---|---|---|---|
| Net profit | | | | 27,000 |
| + last year's reserve | | | | 9,000 |
| | | | | 36,000 |
| – dividend | | | | 8,000 |
| **Reserve** | | | | **28,000** |

### Record book 2

Use record book two to prepare the profit and loss appropriation account. Start with the net profit. Add the reserve from last year. Then subtract the dividend as shown in the example on the left.

### Dividend

The dividend is the part of the profit given to the shareholders. The dividend is calculated by taking a percentage of the ordinary shares, e.g. a 10% dividend means you must get 10% of the 80,000 ordinary shares. Thus, shareholders receive a dividend of €8,000.

### Reserve

The reserve is that part of the profit left after the dividend has been paid. In the example on the left, a €9,000 reserve was carried forward from last year to this year. This is added to the profit and the dividend is taken away to give a new reserve, €28,000.

## Activity 37.1 Calculating dividends

**1** A company has 250,000 ordinary shares of €1 each issued. Calculate the dividend if a 15% dividend is declared.

**2** A company has 120,000 ordinary shares of €1 each issued. Calculate the dividend if a 20% dividend is declared.

**3** A company has 150,000 ordinary shares of €1 each issued. Calculate the dividend if a 10% dividend is declared.

**4** A company has 220,000 ordinary shares of €1 each issued. Calculate the dividend if a 5% dividend is declared.

**5** A company has 90,000 ordinary shares of €1 each issued. Calculate the dividend if a 15% dividend is declared.

## Activity 37.2 Prepare the appropriation account

**1** Duggan Ltd has 180,000 ordinary shares issued. Draft the appropriation account for the year ended 31 December given the following information.
- Net profit is €87,000.
- Last year's reserve (profit and loss balance) was €7,000.
- Dividends declared are 15%.

**2** Hayes Ltd has 75,000 ordinary shares issued. Draft the appropriation account for the year ended 31 December given the following information.
- Net profit is €43,000.
- Last year's reserve (profit and loss balance) was €11,000.
- Dividends declared are 10%.

**3** Egan Ltd has 230,000 ordinary shares issued. Draft the appropriation account for the year ended 31 December given the following information.
- Net profit is €93,000.
- Last year's reserve (profit and loss balance) was €14,000.
- Dividends declared are 5%.

**4** Coogan Ltd has 140,000 ordinary shares issued. Draft the appropriation account for the year ended 31 December given the following information.
- Net profit is €87,000.
- Last year's reserve (profit and loss balance) was €24,000.
- Dividends declared are 20%.

eTest.ie
Try a test on this topic

# Chapter 38

# Balance sheet

# Assets and liabilities

## Question

From the following information prepare a balance sheet as at 31 December.

|  | € |
|---|---|
| Motor vans | 110,000 |
| Buildings | 120,000 |
| Closing stock | 70,000 |
| Cash on hand | 3,000 |
| Bank overdraft | 50,000 |
| Issued share capital | 240,000 |
| Reserve (profit and loss balance) | 13,000 |

## Solution

| Balance sheet as at 31 December | | | |
|---|---|---|---|
|  |  | € | € |
| **Fixed assets** | | | |
| Motor vans | | | 110,000 |
| Buildings | | | 120,000 |
| | | | 230,000 |
| **Current assets** | | | |
| Closing stock | | 70,000 | |
| Cash on hand | | 3,000 | |
| | | 73,000 | |
| **Current liabilities** | | | |
| Bank overdraft | | 50,000 | 23,000 |
| | | | 253,000 |
| **Financed by** | | | |
| Issued share capital | | | 240,000 |
| Reserve | | | 13,000 |
| | | | 253,000 |

The balance sheet lists the assets and liabilities of the firm. The **assets** are the things the firm *owns* and the **liabilities** are the things the firm *owes.* Fixed assets like vans and buildings will be in the firm for a long time. Current items like stock change value frequently as goods are bought and sold.

## Record book 2

Use record book two to prepare the balance sheet. There are four sections: fixed assets; current assets; current liabilities; and financed by, as shown in the example on the left.

## Working capital

The difference between the current assets and current liabilities is called the working capital. In a healthy company the current assets will be greater than the current liabilities. In the example on the left the working capital is €23,000.

## Capital employed

The fixed assets plus the working capital gives the capital employed. In the example on the left the capital employed is €253,000.

# Sample question and solution

## Question

From the following information prepare a trading and profit and loss account for the year ended 31 December, and a balance sheet as at that date.

| Trial balance as on 31 December | | |
|---|---|---|
| | € | € |
| Cash sales | | 230,000 |
| Opening stock | 30,000 | |
| Cash purchases | 180,000 | |
| Carriage in | 8,000 | |
| Wages | 24,000 | |
| Heating and lighting | 4,000 | |
| Advertising | 5,000 | |
| Carriage out | 3,000 | |
| Dividend paid | 15,000 | |
| Motor vans | 60,000 | |
| Buildings | 90,000 | |
| Cash on hand | 7,000 | |
| Bank overdraft | | 16,000 |
| Issued share capital | | 180,000 |
| | 426,000 | 426,000 |

Closing stock at 31 December is €45,000.

## Closing stock

Notice that in the question above the closing stock is given outside the main trial balance list. The closing stock is entered in the trading account and again in the balance sheet as you can see in the solution on the right.

## Reserve

Notice the reserve of €6,000 is the final figure in the trading and profit and loss account. This is used again in the balance sheet. Look at the solution on the right and you will see the €6,000 as a reserve in the *financed by* section.

## Solution

### Trading, Profit and Loss Account for the year ended 31 December

| | | € | € |
|---|---|---|---|
| Sales | | | 230,000 |
| *Less cost of sales* | | | |
| Opening stock | | 30,000 | |
| + Purchases | | 180,000 | |
| + Carriage in | | 8,000 | |
| | | 218,000 | |
| – Closing stock | | 45,000 | |
| Cost of sales | | | 173,000 |
| **GROSS PROFIT** | | | **57,000** |
| *Less expenses* | | | |
| Wages | | 24,000 | |
| Heating and lighting | | 4,000 | |
| Advertising | | 5,000 | |
| Carriage out | | 3,000 | 36,000 |
| **NET PROFIT** | | | **21,000** |
| Dividend paid | | | 15,000 |
| **Reserve** | | | **6,000** |

### Balance sheet as at 31 December

| | | € | € |
|---|---|---|---|
| **Fixed assets** | | | |
| Motor vans | | | 60,000 |
| Buildings | | | 90,000 |
| | | | 150,000 |
| **Current assets** | | | |
| Closing stock | | 45,000 | |
| Cash on hand | | 7,000 | |
| | | 52,000 | |
| **Current liabilities** | | | |
| Bank overdraft | | 16,000 | 36,000 |
| | | | 186,000 |
| **Financed by** | | | |
| Issued share capital | | | 180,000 |
| Reserve | | | 6,000 |
| | | | 186,000 |

1. From the following information prepare a balance sheet as at 31 December.

|  | € |
|---|---|
| Machinery | 110,000 |
| Buildings | 240,000 |
| Closing stock | 20,000 |
| Cash on hand | 2,000 |
| Bank overdraft | 10,000 |
| Issued share capital | 300,000 |
| Reserve (profit and loss balance) | 62,000 |

2. From the following information prepare a balance sheet as at 31 December.

|  | € |
|---|---|
| Equipment | 80,000 |
| Premises | 200,000 |
| Closing stock | 50,000 |
| Cash on hand | 4,000 |
| Bank overdraft | 30,000 |
| Issued share capital | 240,000 |
| Reserve (profit and loss balance) | 64,000 |

3. From the following information prepare a balance sheet as at 31 December.

|  | € |
|---|---|
| Premises | 340,000 |
| Furniture and fittings | 30,000 |
| Closing stock | 60,000 |
| Cash on hand | 5,000 |
| Bank overdraft | 50,000 |
| Issued share capital | 350,000 |
| Reserve (profit and loss balance) | 35,000 |

4. From the following information prepare a balance sheet as at 31 December.

|  | € |
|---|---|
| Motor vans | 90,000 |
| Furniture and fittings | 70,000 |
| Closing stock | 30,000 |
| Cash on hand | 2,000 |
| Bank overdraft | 12,000 |
| Issued share capital | 100,000 |
| Reserve (profit and loss balance) | 80,000 |

**1** From the following information prepare a trading and profit and loss account for the year ended 31 December, and a balance sheet as at that date.

| Trial balance as on 31 December | | |
|---|---|---|
| | € | € |
| Cash sales | | 750,000 |
| Cash purchases | 542,000 | |
| Carriage inwards | 6,000 | |
| Opening stock | 96,000 | |
| Wages | 47,900 | |
| Telephone | 3,260 | |
| Heating and lighting | 15,590 | |
| Interest on overdraft | 7,800 | |
| Insurance | 37,650 | |
| Dividend paid | 30,000 | |
| Bank overdraft | | 92,200 |
| Cash on hand | 14,000 | |
| Issued share capital | | 300,000 |
| Premises | 250,000 | |
| Delivery vans | 92,000 | |
| | 1,142,200 | 1,142,200 |

Closing stock at 31 December is €119,000.

**2** From the following information prepare a trading and profit and loss account for the year ended 31 December, and a balance sheet as at that date.

| Trial balance as on 31 December | | |
|---|---|---|
| | € | € |
| Cash sales | | 520,300 |
| Cash purchases | 376,000 | |
| Carriage inwards | 4,000 | |
| Opening stock | 102,000 | |
| Rent and rates | 3,300 | |
| Telephone | 4,060 | |
| Wages | 48,990 | |
| Lighting and heating | 12,000 | |
| Advertising | 15,600 | |
| Dividend paid | 37,500 | |
| Bank overdraft | | 10,000 |
| Cash on hand | 8,850 | |
| Issued share capital | | 350,000 |
| Machinery | 148,000 | |
| Motor vehicles | 120,000 | |
| | 880,300 | 880,300 |

Closing stock at 31 December is €105,000.

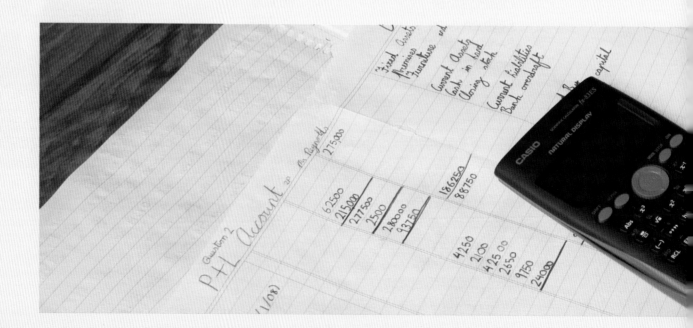

**3** From the following information prepare a trading and profit and loss account for the year ended 31 December, and a balance sheet as at that date.

| Trial balance as on 31 December | | |
|---|---:|---:|
| | € | € |
| Cash sales | | 380,000 |
| Carriage inwards | 2,600 | |
| Cash purchases | 237,000 | |
| Opening stock | 57,000 | |
| Wages | 78,000 | |
| Heating and lighting | 15,000 | |
| Telephone | 4,950 | |
| Insurance | 12,650 | |
| Interest on overdraft | 2,900 | |
| Dividend paid | 23,000 | |
| Bank overdraft | | 50,000 |
| Cash on hand | 3,000 | |
| Issued share capital | | 250,000 |
| Buildings | 125,000 | |
| Motor vans | 118,900 | |
| | 680,000 | 680,000 |

Closing stock at 31 December is €72,000.

**4** From the following information prepare a trading and profit and loss account for the year ended 31 December, and a balance sheet as at that date.

| Trial balance as on 31 December | | |
|---|---:|---:|
| | € | € |
| Cash sales | | 863,000 |
| Cash purchases | 442,000 | |
| Carriage inwards | 46,000 | |
| Opening stock | 66,000 | |
| Interest on overdraft | 5,800 | |
| Insurance | 37,450 | |
| Wages | 47,900 | |
| Telephone | 4,260 | |
| Heating and lighting | 15,590 | |
| Dividend paid | 30,000 | |
| Bank overdraft | | 40,000 |
| Cash on hand | 124,000 | |
| Premises | 250,000 | |
| Delivery vans | 94,000 | |
| Issued share capital | | 260,000 |
| | 1,163,000 | 1,163,000 |

Closing stock at 31 December is €78,000.

**1** From the following information prepare a trading and profit and loss account for the year ended 31 December, and a balance sheet as at that date.

| Trial balance as on 31 December | | |
|---|---|---|
| | € | € |
| Cash sales | | 170,000 |
| Cash purchases | 114,550 | |
| Carriage inwards | 1,800 | |
| Opening stock | 23,750 | |
| Insurance | 7,450 | |
| Wages | 33,250 | |
| Heating and lighting | 9,800 | |
| Rent | 12,150 | |
| Advertising | 1,250 | |
| Dividend paid | 2,200 | |
| Bank overdraft | | 21,750 |
| Cash on hand | 3,550 | |
| Issued share capital | | 200,000 |
| Furniture and fittings | 30,000 | |
| Motor vehicles | 152,000 | |
| | 391,750 | 391,750 |

Closing stock at 31 December is €42,500.

**2** From the following information prepare a trading and profit and loss account for the year ended 31 December, and a balance sheet as at that date.

| Trial balance as on 31 December | | |
|---|---|---|
| | € | € |
| Cash sales | | 413,000 |
| Cash purchases | 246,000 | |
| Carriage inwards | 4,500 | |
| Opening stock | 68,000 | |
| Insurance | 15,400 | |
| Wages | 42,150 | |
| Rent and rates | 23,950 | |
| Advertising | 11,750 | |
| Heating and lighting | 22,450 | |
| Dividend paid | 19,700 | |
| Bank overdraft | | 58,000 |
| Cash on hand | 9,600 | |
| Issued share capital | | 230,000 |
| Equipment | 77,500 | |
| Motor vehicles | 160,000 | |
| | 701,000 | 701,000 |

Closing stock at 31 December is €62,500.

eTest.ie
Try a test on this topic

► Learn how to account for
amounts due and prepaid

► Study how to process the
depreciation of assets

# Chapter 39

# Final *adjustments*

The final accounts are prepared from information contained in
the trial balance. However, the trial balance may not be up to
date. It is therefore necessary to adjust some of the trial
balance figures.

# Expenses due

Most expenses will be paid during the year but in some cases there will be
an amount of money outstanding. This amount due will be paid next year
but in the meantime it must be added to the expenses.

| Dr | | | | Advertising Account | | | Cr |
|---|---|---|---|---|---|---|---|
| Date | Details | F | € | Date | Details | F | € |
| May 1 | Bank | | 5,000 | Dec 31 | Profit and loss | | 6,000 |
| Dec 31 | Balance | c/d | 1,000 | | | | |
| | | | 6,000 | | | | 6,000 |
| | | | | Jan 1 | Balance | b/d | 1,000 |

### Advertising account
The advertising account shows that:
● on 1 May, we paid advertising by
cheque, €5,000
● on 31 December, we owed €1,000
in advertising
● on 31 December, we transferred
€6,000 as an expense to the profit
and loss account.

| Profit and Loss Account for the year ended 31 December (extract) | | € | € |
|---|---|---|---|
| *Less expenses* | | | |
| Advertising | | 6,000 | |

### Profit and loss
The profit and loss account shows the
advertising plus advertising due
(€5,000 + €1,000) = €6,000.

| Balance sheet as at 31 December (extract) | | € | € |
|---|---|---|---|
| **Current liabilities** | | | |
| Advertising due | | 1,000 | |

### Balance sheet
The advertising due is shown as a
current liability in the balance sheet.

# Expenses prepaid

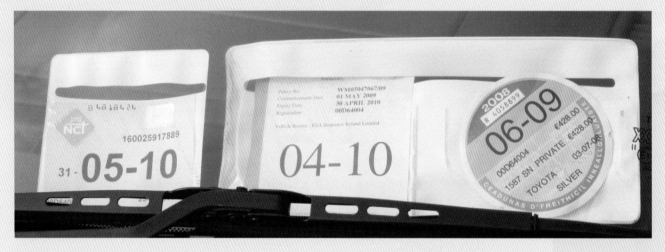

Some expenses, like insurance, are paid once a year and when it comes to 31 December there is an amount of money prepaid into next year. The amount of the insurance prepaid is subtracted from the insurance expense.

| Dr | | | | Insurance Account | | | Cr |
|---|---|---|---|---|---|---|---|
| Date | Details | F | € | Date | Details | F | € |
| Apr 1 | Bank | | 12,000 | Dec 31 | Profit and loss | | 9,000 |
| | | | | 31 | Balance | c/d | 3,000 |
| | | | 12,000 | | | | 12,000 |
| Jan 1 | Balance | b/d | 3,000 | | | | |

## Insurance account

The insurance account shows that:
- on 1 April, we paid insurance by cheque, €12,000
- on 31 December, we had €3,000 insurance prepaid into next year
- on 31 December, we transferred €9,000 as an expense to the profit and loss account.

| Profit and Loss Account for the year ended 31 December (extract) | | | |
|---|---|---|---|
| | | € | € |
| *Less expenses* | | | |
| Insurance | | 9,000 | |

## Profit and loss

The profit and loss account shows the insurance less the insurance prepaid (€12,000 − €3,000) = €9,000.

| Balance sheet as at 31 December (extract) | | | |
|---|---|---|---|
| | | € | € |
| **Current assets** | | | |
| Closing stock | | 3,000 | |

## Balance sheet

The insurance prepaid is shown as a current asset in the balance sheet.

# Gains prepaid

Gains are the opposite of expenses. Rent receivable is a gain for a business. This is money received from subletting part of the factory. The amount of the rent receivable prepaid is subtracted from the gain.

| Dr | | | | Rent Receivable Account | | | Cr |
|---|---|---|---|---|---|---|---|
| Date | Details | F | € | Date | Details | F | € |
| Dec 31 | Profit and loss | | 2,500 | May 1 | Bank | | 6,000 |
| Dec 31 | Balance | c/d | 3,500 | | | | |
| | | | 6,000 | | | | 6,000 |
| | | | | Jan 1 | Balance | b/d | 3,500 |

| Profit and Loss Account for the year ended 31 December (extract) | | | |
|---|---|---|---|
| | | € | € |
| *Plus gains* | | | |
| Rent receivable | | | 2,500 |

| Balance sheet as at 31 December (extract) | | | |
|---|---|---|---|
| | | € | € |
| **Current liabilities** | | | |
| Rent receivable prepaid | | 3,500 | |

## Rent receivable account

This account shows that:

- on 1 May, we received rent by cheque, €6,000
- on 31 December, €3,500 of this rent was carried into next year
- on 31 December, we transferred €2,500 as a gain to the profit and loss account.

## Profit and loss

The profit and loss account shows the rent receivable less the amount prepaid (€6,000 − €3,500) = €2,500.

## Balance sheet

The rent receivable prepaid is shown as a current liability in the balance sheet.

# Depreciation

Depreciation is the reduction in value of an asset due to wear and tear or to age. Straight-line depreciation reduces the value of the asset by an equal amount each year.

Depreciation affects the final accounts in two ways:
- it is entered as an expense in the profit and loss account
- it reduces the value of the asset in the fixed assets of the balance sheet.

## Question

A company bought a van for €15,000. Depreciation is 20% per annum.
Show the entry in the profit and loss account and the balance sheet.

## Solution

| Profit and Loss Account for the year ended 31 December (extract) | | |
|---|---|---|
| | € | € |
| *Less expenses* | | |
| Depreciation of van | 3,000 | |

**Profit and loss**

The depreciation is 20% of €15,000 which is €3,000 per annum. This is written as an expense in the profit and loss account.

| Balance sheet as at 31 December (extract) | | | |
|---|---|---|---|
| | € | € | € |
| **Fixed assets** | Cost | Depr | NBV |
| Van | 15,000 | 3,000 | 12,000 |

**Balance sheet**

The depreciation reduces the value of the van in the fixed assets of the balance sheet as shown on the left. The cost of the van is €15,000. The depreciation (depr) is €3,000. The net book value (NBV) is
€15,000 − €3,000 = €12,000.

**1**

| Dr | | | | Light and Heat Account | | | Cr |
|---|---|---|---|---|---|---|---|
| Date | Details | F | € | Date | Details | F | € |
| Oct 1 | Bank | | 2,000 | Dec 31 | Profit and loss | | 5,000 |
| Dec 31 | Balance | c/d | 3,000 | | | | |
| | | | 5,000 | | | | 5,000 |
| | | | | Jan 1 | Balance | b/d | 3,000 |

(a) What does the balance in this account mean?
(b) Explain the entry on 1 October.

**2**

| Dr | | | | Telephone Account | | | Cr |
|---|---|---|---|---|---|---|---|
| Date | Details | F | € | Date | Details | F | € |
| Nov 1 | Bank | | 7,000 | Dec 31 | Profit and loss | | 9,000 |
| Dec 31 | Balance | c/d | 2,000 | | | | |
| | | | 9,000 | | | | 9,000 |
| | | | | Jan 1 | Balance | b/d | 2,000 |

(a) What does the balance in this account mean?
(b) Explain the entry on 1 November.

**3**

| Dr | | | | Advertising Account | | | Cr |
|---|---|---|---|---|---|---|---|
| Date | Details | F | € | Date | Details | F | € |
| Apr 1 | Bank | | 16,000 | Dec 31 | Profit and loss | | 12,000 |
| | | | | 31 | Balance | c/d | 4,000 |
| | | | 16,000 | | | | 16,000 |
| Jan 1 | Balance | b/d | 4,000 | | | | |

(a) What does the balance in this account mean?
(b) Explain the entry on 1 April.

**4**

| Dr | | | | Insurance Account | | | Cr |
|---|---|---|---|---|---|---|---|
| Date | Details | F | € | Date | Details | F | € |
| Jul 1 | Bank | | 5,000 | Dec 31 | Profit and loss | | 2,500 |
| | | | | 31 | Balance | c/d | 2,500 |
| | | | 5,000 | | | | 5,000 |
| Jan 1 | Balance | b/d | 2,500 | | | | |

(a) What does the balance in this account mean?
(b) Explain the entry on 1 July.

# Activity 39.2 Gains

**1**

| Dr | | | | Rent Receivable Account | | | Cr |
|---|---|---|---|---|---|---|---|
| Date | Details | F | € | Date | Details | F | € |
| Dec 31 | Profit and loss | | 3,000 | Apr 1 | Bank | | 4,000 |
| Dec 31 | Balance | c/d | 1,000 | | | | |
| | | | 4,000 | | | | 4,000 |
| | | | | Jan 1 | Balance | b/d | 1,000 |

(a) What does the balance in this account mean?

(b) Explain the entry on 1 April.

**2**

| Dr | | | | Commission Receivable Account | | | Cr |
|---|---|---|---|---|---|---|---|
| Date | Details | F | € | Date | Details | F | € |
| Dec 31 | Profit and loss | | 6,000 | Sep 1 | Bank | | 9,000 |
| Dec 31 | Balance | c/d | 3,000 | | | | |
| | | | 9,000 | | | | 9,000 |
| | | | | Jan 1 | Balance | b/d | 3,000 |

(a) What does the balance in this account mean?

(b) Explain the entry on 1 September.

eTest.ie
Try a test on this topic

# Activity 39.3 Depreciation

**1** A company bought a van for €25,000. Depreciation is 20% per annum. Show the entry in the profit and loss account and the balance sheet.

**2** A company bought machinery for €20,000. Depreciation is 25% per annum. Show the entry in the profit and loss account and the balance sheet.

**3** A company bought a van for €12,000. Depreciation is 20% per annum. Show the entry in the profit and loss account and the balance sheet.

**4** A company bought buildings for €250,000. Depreciation is 10% per annum. Show the entry in the profit and loss account and the balance sheet.

**5** A company bought furniture for €36,000. Depreciation is 20% per annum. Show the entry in the profit and loss account and the balance sheet.

due
paid

profit

profit

▶ Review the different types of adjustment in final accounts

▶ Learn how to prepare a final accounts question

# Chapter 40

*Worked example*

# Adjustments

The examination question is presented as a trial balance with additional information below it.

| Trial balance as on 31 December | | |
|---|---|---|
| | € | € |
| Purchases and sales | 80,000 | 300,000 |
| Purchases returns | | 4,000 |
| Sales returns | 5,000 | |
| Opening stock | 10,000 | |
| Carriage in | 3,000 | |
| Wages | 116,000 | |
| Insurance | 16,000 | |
| Advertising | 18,000 | |
| Carriage out | 2,000 | |
| Rent receivable | | 15,000 |
| Motor vans | 40,000 | |
| Buildings | 300,000 | |
| Debtors and creditors | 30,000 | 14,000 |
| Bank overdraft | | 7,000 |
| 15-year loan | | 100,000 |
| Reserves (profit and loss) | | 20,000 |
| Issued share capital | | 160,000 |
| | 620,000 | 620,000 |

You are given the following information:

    (i)  Closing stock     €19,000
    (ii)  Rent receivable prepaid  €1,000
    (iii)  Advertising due     €7,000
    (iv)  Insurance prepaid     €6,000
    (v)  Dividends declared, 10%
    (vi)  Depreciation of vans, 20%

**Purchases and sales** The figures follow the words. Thus, the purchases are €80,000 and the sales are €300,000.

**Debtors and creditors** Once again the figures follow the words. Thus, the debtors are €30,000 and the creditors are €14,000.

**Expenses due** The rule is plus due minus prepaid. So advertising plus advertising due is:
$$€18,000 + €7,000 = €25,000$$

**Expenses prepaid** The rule is plus due minus prepaid. So insurance minus insurance prepaid is:
$$€16,000 - €6,000 = €10,000$$

**Gains prepaid** The rule is plus due minus prepaid. So rent receivable minus rent receivable prepaid is:
$$€15,000 - €1,000 = €14,000$$

**Dividends** The dividend is a percentage of the issued share capital. Thus:
$$10\% \text{ of } €160,000 = €16,000$$

**Depreciation** The depreciation is a percentage of the asset. Thus:
$$20\% \text{ of } €40,000 = €8,000$$

# Sample question and solution

## Question

The following trial balance was extracted from the books of Garden Supplies Ltd on 31 December. The authorised share capital is 300,000 €1 ordinary shares.

### Trial balance as on 31 December

| | € | € |
|---|---|---|
| Purchases and sales | 80,000 | 300,000 |
| Purchases returns | | 4,000 |
| Sales returns | 5,000 | |
| Opening stock | 10,000 | |
| Carriage in | 3,000 | |
| Wages | 116,000 | |
| Insurance | 16,000 | |
| Advertising | 18,000 | |
| Carriage out | 2,000 | |
| Rent receivable | | 15,000 |
| Motor vans | 40,000 | |
| Buildings | 300,000 | |
| Debtors and creditors | 30,000 | 14,000 |
| Bank overdraft | | 7,000 |
| 15-year loan | | 100,000 |
| Reserves (profit and loss) | | 20,000 |
| Issued share capital | | 160,000 |
| | 620,000 | 620,000 |

You are required to prepare the company's trading, profit and loss and appropriation accounts for the year ending 31 December and a balance sheet as on that date.

You are given the following information:
- (i) Closing stock — 19,000
- (ii) Rent receivable prepaid — 1,000
- (iii) Advertising due — 7,000
- (iv) Insurance prepaid — 6,000
- (v) Dividends declared, 10%
- (vi) Depreciation of vans, 20%

## Solution

### Trading, Profit and Loss Account for the year ended 31 December

| | | € | € |
|---|---|---|---|
| Sales | | | 300,000 |
| Less sales returns | | | 5,000 |
| | | | 295,000 |
| Less cost of sales | | | |
| Opening stock | | 10,000 | |
| + Purchases | 80,000 | | |
| less purchases returns | 4,000 | 76,000 | |
| + Carriage in | | 3,000 | |
| | | 89,000 | |
| - Closing stock | | 19,000 | |
| Cost of sales | | | 70,000 |
| **GROSS PROFIT** | | | **225,000** |
| *Plus gains* | | | |
| Rent receivable | | | 14,000 |
| | | | 239,000 |
| *Less expenses* | | | |
| Wages | | 116,000 | |
| Insurance | | 10,000 | |
| Advertising | | 25,000 | |
| Carriage out | | 2,000 | |
| Depreciation of vans | | 8,000 | 161,000 |
| **NET PROFIT** | | | **78,000** |
| Plus reserve | | | 20,000 |
| | | | 98,000 |
| Less dividend | | | 16,000 |
| **Reserve** | | | **82,000** |

| Balance sheet as at 31 December | | | |
|---|---|---|---|
| | | € | € |
| **Fixed assets** | Cost | Depr | NBV |
| Motor vans | 40,000 | 8,000 | 32,000 |
| Buildings | 300,000 | - | 300,000 |
| | 340,000 | 8,000 | 332,000 |
| **Current assets** | | | |
| Closing stock | | 19,000 | |
| Debtors | | 30,000 | |
| Insurance prepaid | | 6,000 | |
| | | 55,000 | |
| **Current liabilities** | | | |
| Bank overdraft | 7,000 | | |
| Creditors | 14,000 | | |
| Rent receivable prepaid | 1,000 | | |
| Advertising due | 7,000 | | |
| Dividends due | 16,000 | 45,000 | 10,000 |
| | | | 342,000 |
| **Financed by** | | | |
| Authorised share capital | | | 300,000 |
| Issued share capital | | | 160,000 |
| Reserve | | | 82,000 |
| 15-year loan | | | 100,000 |
| | | | 342,000 |

## Record book 2

Use record book two to prepare the trading, profit and loss and appropriation account, and the balance sheet. Your full solution will not fit on one page so you may as well start the balance sheet on a second page to make it look neater.

## Adjustments

Notice that the figures in the adjustments (the additional information) all appear on the balance sheet page.

- Closing stock, €19,000, is a current asset.
- Rent receivable prepaid, €1,000, is a current liability.
- Advertising due, €7,000, is a current liability.
- Insurance prepaid, €6,000, is a current asset.
- Dividends, €16,000, is a current liability.
- Depreciation of vans, €8,000, is shown in the fixed assets.

## Reserve

Notice the reserve of €82,000 is the final figure on the first page. This is used again in the balance sheet. Look at the solution on the left and you will see the €82,000 as a reserve in the *financed by* section.

## Authorised share capital

The information for the capital employed is given at the very start of the question. In this case the authorised share capital is €300,000. This is shown in the *financed by* section. Double lines are drawn under the figure as it is not added to anything else; it is just there for information.

## Activity 40.1 Prepare the final accounts

**1** The following trial balance was extracted from the books of Mooney Ltd on 31 March. The authorised share capital is 500,000 €1 ordinary shares.

| Trial balance as on 31 March | € | € |
|---|---|---|
| Opening stock | 22,000 | |
| Debtors and creditors | 50,000 | 35,000 |
| Purchases and sales | 120,000 | 300,000 |
| Sales returns | 17,000 | |
| Carriage inwards | 20,000 | |
| Land | 400,000 | |
| Rent | 13,000 | |
| Motor vehicles | 72,000 | |
| Commission receivable | | 15,000 |
| 30-year loan | | 60,000 |
| Cash | 2,200 | |
| Telephone | 5,000 | |
| Bank overdraft | | 5,000 |
| Wages | 60,000 | |
| Reserves | | 30,000 |
| Issued share capital | | 350,000 |
| Advertising | 13,800 | |
| | 795,000 | 795,000 |

You are required to prepare the company's trading, profit and loss and appropriation accounts for the year ending 31 March and a balance sheet as on that date.

You are given the following information:
(i) Closing stock €18,500
(ii) Carriage inwards due €3,000
(iii) Rent prepaid €4,000
(iv) Dividends declared 10%
(v) Commission receivable due €5,000
(vi) Depreciation: motor vehicles 15%

> **Note**
> • Land is a fixed asset.
> • Commission receivable is a gain.

**2** The following trial balance was extracted from the books of Hamill Ltd on 30 April. The authorised share capital is 400,000 €1 ordinary shares.

| Trial balance as on 30 April | € | € |
|---|---|---|
| Purchases and sales | 100,000 | 320,000 |
| Sales returns | 14,000 | |
| Opening stock | 9,000 | |
| Carriage inwards | 4,000 | |
| Debtors and creditors | 28,000 | 13,000 |
| Advertising | 5,000 | |
| Rent receivable | | 12,000 |
| Bank overdraft | | 15,000 |
| Wages | 90,000 | |
| Buildings | 435,000 | |
| Motor vehicles | 84,000 | |
| Bad debts | 3,000 | |
| Machinery | 120,000 | |
| Reserves | | 50,000 |
| Issued share capital | | 442,000 |
| 20-year loan | | 40,000 |
| | 892,000 | 892,000 |

You are required to prepare the company's trading, profit and loss and appropriation accounts for the year ending 30 April and a balance sheet as on that date.

You are given the following information:
(i) Closing stock €16,000
(ii) Advertising due €4,000
(iii) Rent receivable due €5,000
(iv) Dividends declared 4%
(v) Depreciation: motor vehicles 20%; machinery 12%.

> **Note**
> • Bad debts is an expense.
> • Sales returns is taken from sales.

**3** The following trial balance was extracted from the books of Coady Ltd on 31 December. The authorised share capital is 300,000 €1 ordinary shares.

| Trial balance as on 31 December | | |
|---|---|---|
| | € | € |
| Purchases and sales | 120,000 | 260,000 |
| Purchases returns | | 5,000 |
| Opening stock | 14,000 | |
| Import duty | 2,000 | |
| Debtors and creditors | 17,000 | 11,000 |
| Insurance | 5,000 | |
| Wages | 50,000 | |
| Delivery vans | 78,000 | |
| Machinery | 80,000 | |
| Cash | 2,000 | |
| Commission receivable | | 4,000 |
| Reserves | | 15,000 |
| Bank overdraft | | 5,000 |
| Bad debts | 2,000 | |
| Buildings | 180,000 | |
| Issued share capital | | 250,000 |
| | 550,000 | 550,000 |

You are required to prepare the company's trading, profit and loss and appropriation accounts for the year ending 31 December and a balance sheet as on that date.

You are given the following information:
  (i)  Closing stock  €13,000
  (ii)  Commission receivable due  €600
  (iii)  Wages due  €2,000
  (iv)  Dividends declared 5%
  (v)  Depreciation: machinery 10%;
       delivery vans 15%.

▸▸ **Note**
• Purchases returns reduces purchases.
• Import duty is treated the same as carriage in.

**4** The following trial balance was extracted from the books of Curtis Ltd on 31 December. The authorised share capital is 500,000 €1 ordinary shares.

| Trial balance as on 31 December | | |
|---|---|---|
| | € | € |
| Purchases and sales | 130,000 | 290,000 |
| Purchases returns | | 15,000 |
| Opening stock | 36,500 | |
| Import duty | 4,500 | |
| Debtors and creditors | 58,000 | 29,000 |
| Carriage outwards | 16,000 | |
| Insurance | 9,000 | |
| Light and heat | 13,800 | |
| Machinery | 140,000 | |
| Premises | 300,000 | |
| Interest receivable | | 6,500 |
| Cash | 2,700 | |
| Reserves | | 40,000 |
| Issued share capital | | 350,000 |
| 15-year loan | | 50,000 |
| Motor vehicles | 70,000 | |
| | 780,500 | 780,500 |

You are required to prepare the company's trading, profit and loss and appropriation accounts for the year ending 31 December and a balance sheet as on that date.

You are given the following information:
  (i)  Closing stock  €14,500
  (ii)  Light and heat due  €3,200
  (iii)  Interest receivable due  €2,000
  (iv)  Dividends declared 8%
  (v)  Depreciation: machinery 15%;
       motor vehicles 20%

▸▸ **Note**
• Carriage outwards is an expense.
• Interest receivable is a gain.

**1** The following trial balance was extracted from the books of Scott Ltd on 31 May 2008. The authorised share capital is 550,000 €1 ordinary shares.

| Trial balance as on 31 May 2008 | € | € |
| --- | --- | --- |
| Purchases and sales | 175,000 | 273,500 |
| Opening stock | 12,000 | |
| Import duty | 6,700 | |
| Carriage outwards | 4,000 | |
| Debtors and creditors | 60,000 | 30,000 |
| Insurance | 2,900 | |
| Interest receivable | | 6,500 |
| Wages | 44,000 | |
| Machinery | 120,000 | |
| Buildings | 300,000 | |
| Bank | 5,000 | |
| 25-year loan | | 140,000 |
| Cash | 1,400 | |
| Land | 230,000 | |
| Reserves | | 111,000 |
| Issued share capital | | 400,000 |
| | 961,000 | 961,000 |

You are required to prepare the company's trading, profit and loss and appropriation accounts for the year ending 31 May 2008 and a balance sheet as on that date.

You are given the following information:
   (i)  Closing stock       €17,500
  (ii)  Import duty due    €1,300
 (iii)  Interest receivable due   €600
 (iv)  Insurance prepaid    €700
  (v)  Depreciation: machinery 15%
 (vi)  Dividends declared 5%

> ▶▶ **Note**
> • Carriage out is an expense.
> • Interest receivable is a gain.
> • Bank is a current asset.

**2** The following trial balance was extracted from the books of Kelly Ltd on 31 May 2009. The authorised share capital is 350,000 €1 ordinary shares.

| Trial balance as on 31 May 2009 | € | € |
| --- | --- | --- |
| Purchases and sales | 130,000 | 350,000 |
| Sales returns | 10,000 | |
| Opening stock | 18,000 | |
| Carriage inwards | 3,000 | |
| Debtors and creditors | 15,000 | 18,000 |
| Advertising | 2,000 | |
| Wages | 52,000 | |
| Delivery van | 78,000 | |
| Equipment | 110,000 | |
| Rent receivable | | 8,000 |
| Cash | 4,000 | |
| Reserves | | 26,000 |
| 10-year loan | | 20,000 |
| Bad debts | 5,000 | |
| Buildings | 245,000 | |
| Issued share capital | | 250,000 |
| | 672,000 | 672,000 |

You are required to prepare the company's trading, profit and loss and appropriation accounts for the year ending 31 May 2009 and a balance sheet as on that date.

You are given the following information:
   (i)  Closing stock       €21,000
  (ii)  Rent receivable prepaid   €2,000
 (iii)  Wages due       €5,000
 (iv)  Dividends declared 20%
  (v)  Depreciation: equipment 15%;
        delivery vans 12%.

> ▶▶ **Note**
> • Sales returns is taken from sales.
> • Bad debts is an expense.

Try a test on this topic

# Chapter 41

# Assessing the *business*

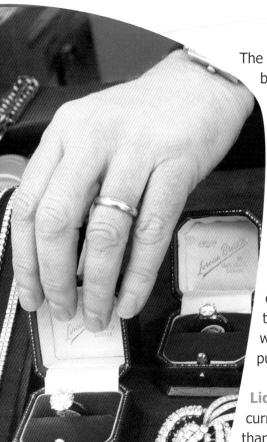

The final accounts of a business are used to assess the firm's performance. The aim is to find out:
(1) Is the business profitable?
(2) Is the business liquid?

**Profitability** Profitability is measured by the return on capital employed. The owners will want a return that is higher than that which they could get if they put their money in a bank.

**Liquidity** A firm is liquid if current assets are greater than current liabilities. The **current ratio** is used to measure a firm's liquidity. In a healthy firm the current ratio will be 2:1. The current ratio is also known as the working capital ratio.

Another measure of liquidity is the **quick ratio**. This compares the quick assets with the current liabilities. The quick assets are current assets less the closing stock. In a healthy firm the quick ratio will be 1:1. Another name for the quick ratio is the **acid test ratio**.

Current (working capital) ratio

$$= \frac{\text{current assets}}{\text{current liabilities}}$$

Acid test (quick) ratio

$$= \frac{\text{current assets - closing stock}}{\text{current liabilities}}$$

Return on capital employed

$$= \frac{\text{net profit}}{\text{capital employed}} \times 100$$

Stock turnover

$$= \frac{\text{cost of sales}}{\text{average stock}}$$

Rate of dividend

$$= \frac{\text{dividend}}{\text{ordinary share capital}} \times 100$$

## TRADING PERFORMANCE

The **rate of stock turnover** is used to find out how much business the firm had. Turnover is the same as sales and profitable firms usually have a high turnover. However, turnover will vary between different kinds of businesses. Goods that do not last long (like newspapers) have high turnovers, whereas luxury goods (like jewellery) have low turnovers. A turnover of 52 means that on average goods were stocked for one week.

# Assessing the trading, profit and loss account

## Question

Study the following account and calculate the following ratios:

(a)  Rate of stock turnover.
(b)  Gross profit percentage.
(c)  Net profit percentage.
(d)  Total expenses as a percentage of sales.
(e)  If the issued share capital is €400,000, what is the rate of dividend?

### Trading, Profit and Loss Account for the year ended 31 December

|  |  | € | € |
|---|---|---|---|
| Sales |  |  | 750,000 |
| *Less cost of sales* |  |  |  |
| Opening stock |  | 40,000 |  |
| + Purchases |  | 320,000 |  |
|  |  | 360,000 |  |
| - Closing stock |  | 60,000 |  |
| Cost of sales |  |  | 300,000 |
| **GROSS PROFIT** |  |  | **450,000** |
| Total expenses |  |  | 200,000 |
| **NET PROFIT** |  |  | **250,000** |
| Less dividend |  |  | **50,000** |
| **Reserve** |  |  | **200,000** |

## Solution

**(a) Rate of stock turnover**

$$= \frac{\text{cost of sales}}{\text{average stock}}$$

$$= \frac{300,000}{(40,000+60,000) \div 2}$$

$$= 6 \text{ times}$$

**(b) Gross profit percentage**

$$= \frac{\text{gross profit}}{\text{sales}} \times 100$$

$$= \frac{450,000}{750,000} \times 100$$

$$= 60\%$$

**(c) Net profit percentage**

$$= \frac{\text{net profit}}{\text{sales}} \times 100$$

$$= \frac{250,000}{750,000} \times 100$$

$$= 33.33\%$$

**(d) Total expenses as a percentage of sales**

$$= \frac{\text{total expenses}}{\text{sales}} \times 100$$

$$= \frac{200,000}{750,000} \times 100$$

$$= 26.67\%$$

**(e) Rate of dividend**

$$= \frac{\text{dividend}}{\text{ordinary share capital}} \times 100$$

$$= \frac{50,000}{400,000} \times 100$$

$$= 12.50\%$$

# Assessing the balance sheet

## Question

Study the following balance sheet, then calculate the following ratios.

(a) Current (working capital) ratio.
(b) Acid test (quick) ratio.
(c) Return on capital employed if the net profit is €250,000.

| Balance sheet as at 31 December | | | | |
|---|---|---|---|---|
| | | | € | € |
| Fixed assets | | | | 650,000 |
| Current assets (including closing stock, €100,000) | | 400,000 | | |
| Current liabilities | | 200,000 | | 200,000 |
| | | | | 850,000 |
| **Financed by** | | | | |
| Issued share capital | | | | 400,000 |
| Reserve | | | | 200,000 |
| Term loan | | | | 250,000 |
| | | | | 850,000 |

## Solution

**(a) Current ratio**

$$= \frac{\text{current assets}}{\text{current liabilities}}$$

$$= \frac{400{,}000}{200{,}000}$$

$$= 2 : 1$$

**(b) Acid test (quick) ratio**

$$= \frac{\text{Current assets - closing stock}}{\text{current liabilities}}$$

$$= \frac{400{,}000 - 100{,}000}{200{,}000}$$

$$= 1.5 : 1$$

**(c) Return on capital employed**

$$= \frac{\text{net profit}}{\text{capital employed}} \times 100$$

$$= \frac{250{,}000}{850{,}000} \times 100$$

$$= 29.41\%$$

## Overtrading

Some firms do too much of the wrong type of business. For example, they may get too much credit without being able to sell the goods, i.e. creditors are much higher than debtors. When this happens the firm is said to be overtrading.

## Solvency

A firm is solvent if total assets are greater than outside liabilities. Examples of outside liabilities are creditors, bank overdraft and long-term loans. If a firm is not solvent there is a great danger it will become bankrupt.

## Limitations of accounts

The final accounts give an incomplete picture of the firm's performance because:

- the accounts do not measure staff morale, motivation or expertise
- it can be difficult to get an accurate value for some of the firm's assets, e.g. premises.

**1** Study the following account and calculate the following ratios:

(a) rate of stock turnover

(b) gross profit percentage

(c) net profit percentage

(d) total expenses as a percentage of sales.

(e) If the issued share capital is €500,000, what is the rate of dividend?

**Trading, Profit and Loss Account for the year ended 31 December**

| | | € | € |
|---|---|---:|---:|
| Sales | | | 600,000 |
| *Less cost of sales* | | | |
| Opening stock | | 30,000 | |
| + Purchases | | 270,000 | |
| | | 300,000 | |
| - Closing stock | | 50,000 | |
| Cost of sales | | | 250,000 |
| **GROSS PROFIT** | | | **350,000** |
| Total expenses | | | 180,000 |
| **NET PROFIT** | | | **170,000** |
| Less dividend | | | **40,000** |
| **Reserve** | | | **130,000** |

**2** The directors of O'Brien Ltd supplied the following information:

| | € |
|---|---:|
| Sales | 550,000 |
| Cost of sales | 210,000 |
| Average stock | 16,800 |
| Total expenses | 75,000 |
| Dividend paid | 50,000 |
| Issued share capital | 350,000 |

Using this information, calculate the following ratios:

(a) rate of stock turnover

(b) gross profit percentage

(c) net profit percentage

(d) total expenses as a percentage of sales

(e) rate of dividend.

## Activity 41.2 Assessing the balance sheet

**1** Study the following balance sheet, then calculate the following ratios:
(a) working capital ratio
(b) acid test (quick) ratio
(c) return on capital employed if the net profit is €150,000.

| Balance sheet as at 31 December | € | € |
|---|---|---|
| Fixed assets | | 740,000 |
| Current assets (including closing stock, €120,000) | 300,000 | |
| Current liabilities | 140,000 | 160,000 |
| | | 900,000 |
| **Financed by** | | |
| Issued share capital | | 650,000 |
| Reserve | | 150,000 |
| Term loan | | 100,000 |
| | | 900,000 |

**2** The directors of Carey Ltd supplied the following information:

| | € |
|---|---|
| Average stock | 21,500 |
| Net profit | 80,000 |
| Cost of sales | 60,000 |
| Dividend paid | 25,000 |
| Current liabilities | 42,000 |
| Current assets | 87,000 |
| Issued share capital | 200,000 |
| Capital employed | 300,000 |

Using this information, calculate the following ratios:
(a) rate of stock turnover
(b) rate of dividend
(c) return on capital employed
(d) current ratio.

(a) The following four ratios are used by Jack Ltd, Tralee Road, Limerick to assess the performance of its business:
   (i) rate of stock turnover
  (ii) rate of dividend
 (iii) return on capital employed
 (iv) current ratio.

The directors of Jack Ltd supplied the following information for the year 2009.

|  | € |
| --- | --- |
| Average stock | 17,500 |
| Net profit | 60,000 |
| Cost of sales | 70,000 |
| Dividend paid | 30,000 |
| Current liabilities | 30,000 |
| Current assets | 45,000 |
| Issued share capital | 300,000 |
| Capital employed | 400,000 |

Using this information, calculate the four ratios for the year 2009.

(b) The relevant figures for 2008 were:

| Rate of stock turnover | 3 times |
| --- | --- |
| Rate of dividend | 20% |
| Return on capital employed | 15% |
| Current ratio | 2 : 1 |

Assume you are Michael Moran, Financial Adviser, Golf View, Limerick. Prepare a report, on today's date, for the directors of Jack Ltd comparing and commenting on the performance of the company for 2008 and 2009.

(JCHL, adapted)

▸▸**Note**
● To revise the layout of a report see Chapter 19, page 118.

Try a test on this topic

# Club accounts

# Club meetings

The members of a club will usually elect a committee to run the club. The committee will have a chairperson, secretary and treasurer.

**Chairperson** The chairperson is the highest position in the club. He or she is responsible for leading the members and developing the club. At club meetings the chairperson:
- takes charge of the meeting
- ensures that the items on the agenda are followed.

**Secretary** The secretary carries out the administrative duties of the club, e.g. writing letters, making phone calls and filing club

documents. At club meetings the secretary:
- sets out the agenda for the meeting
- keeps the minutes of the meeting.

**Treasurer** The treasurer is responsible for the financial matters of the club and must do the following:
- collect the subscriptions from members
- lodge receipts in the bank
- issue cheques or pay cash when necessary
- present the treasurer's report at the annual general meeting (AGM) of the club.

## TREASURER'S REPORT

This is prepared by the treasurer to keep the members informed on the finances and to show that the funds are being used correctly. The treasurer's report contains:
- the receipts and payments account
- the income and expenditure account
- the balance sheet
- recommendations for an increase in the subscription if necessary.

# Receipts and payments

All the money coming into and going out of a club is recorded in the receipts and payments account. Receipts are shown on the debit side and payments on the credit side. Some clubs use suitable analysis columns to get a clearer picture of where the money is coming from and where it is being spent.

## Question

The following transactions took place in the Shannon Golf Club during July. (All dealings are in cash.)

| July | 1 | Cash on hand since last month, €400 |
| --- | --- | --- |
| | 7 | Received annual subscriptions from members, €80 |
| | 8 | Paid competition prizes, €50 (cheque no. 400) |
| | 9 | Received competition entry fees, €120 |
| | 11 | Disco night: received €350 at the door |
| | 14 | Paid DJ €150 for running the disco (cheque no. 401) |
| | 17 | Received annual subscriptions from members, €80 |
| | 21 | Paid caretaker's wages, €300 (cheque no. 402) |
| | 23 | Bought prizes for next competition, €70 (cheque no. 403) |
| | 25 | Received competition entry fees, €5 each from 50 members |
| | 28 | Disco night: received €450 at the door |
| | 29 | Paid caretaker's wages, €300 (cheque no. 404) |
| | 31 | Paid DJ €150 for running the disco (cheque no. 405) |

Write up and balance the analysed receipts and payments account of the club for the month of July. Use the following headings for the receipts and payments and total each column:

**Debit (Receipts) side:** Total; Subscriptions; Competitions; Disco.
**Credit (Payments) side:** Total; Wages; Competitions; Disco.

## Solution

| Dr | | | | | | | Analysed Receipts and Payments Account | | | | | | Cr |
| --- | --- | --- | --- | --- | --- | --- | --- | --- | --- | --- | --- | --- | --- |
| Date | Details | F | Total | Subs | Competitions | Disco | Date | Details | F | Total | Wages | Competitions | Disco |
| Jul | | | € | € | € | € | Jul | | | € | € | € | € |
| 1 | Balance | b/d | 400 | | | | 8 | Prizes | 400 | 50 | | 50 | |
| 7 | Subs | | 80 | 80 | | | 14 | DJ | 401 | 150 | | | 150 |
| 9 | Entry fees | | 120 | | 120 | | 21 | Caretaker | 402 | 300 | 300 | | |
| 11 | Disco | | 350 | | | 350 | 23 | Prizes | 403 | 70 | | 70 | |
| 17 | Subs | | 80 | 80 | | | 29 | Caretaker | 404 | 300 | 300 | | |
| 25 | Entry fees | | 250 | | 250 | | 31 | DJ | 405 | 150 | | | 150 |
| 28 | Disco | | 450 | | | 450 | 31 | Balance | c/d | 710 | | | |
| | | | 1,730 | 160 | 370 | 800 | | | | 1,730 | 600 | 120 | 300 |
| Aug 1 | Balance | | 710 | | | | | | | | | | |

# Summary receipts and payments

Using the information from the total columns in the receipts and payments account on the previous page it is possible to prepare a summary receipts and payments account as shown below.

| Summary Receipts and Payments Account | | | | | | | |
|---|---|---|---|---|---|---|---|
| Jul 1 | Balance | b/d | 400 | | Wages | | 600 |
| | Subscriptions | | 160 | | Competitions | | 120 |
| | Competitions | | 370 | | Disco | | 300 |
| | Disco | | 800 | Jul 31 | Balance | c/d | 710 |
| | | | 1,730 | | | | 1,730 |
| Aug 1 | Balance | b/d | 710 | | | | |

**Summary receipts and payments**
The summary receipts and payments account shows the receipts on the debit and the payments on the credit. The balance is the difference between the receipts and the payments. The balance is brought down to the next month.

# Accumulated fund

The accumulated fund is the main source of finance for a club. It is similar to capital in a company. To calculate the accumulated fund you must find the difference between the assets and the liabilities.

### Question
Find the accumulated fund for the Moatefield Rugby Club given the following assets and liabilities:

Clubhouse €240,000; Equipment €170,000;
Term Loan €30,000; Cash €4,000.

### Solution

| Accumulated Fund | | | | € |
|---|---|---|---|---|
| | Clubhouse | | | 240,000 |
| | Equipment | | | 170,000 |
| | Cash | | | 4,000 |
| | | | | 414,000 |
| | – Term Loan | | | 30,000 |
| | **ACCUMULATED FUND** | | | **384,000** |

**Accumulated fund**
The clubhouse, equipment and cash are all assets. The term loan is a liability. The total assets are €414,000 and the liabilities are €30,000. The difference of €384,000 is the accumulated fund for the club.

The **income and expenditure** account is used to record the expenses for the year, whether paid or not, and the income, whether received or not. It is similar to the profit and loss account. The difference between the income and the expenditure is either a **surplus** (income exceeds expenditure) or a **deficit** (expenditure exceeds income). The income and expenditure does not show the purchase and sale of fixed assets. These are shown in the balance sheet. There are three types of question that you need to prepare for:
- income and expenditure with an accumulated fund and summary receipts and payments account
- income and expenditure with balance sheet
- income and expenditure with bar trading account.

# Income and expenditure
## with accumulated fund

**Question**

On 1 June 2009, Gracefield Tennis Club had the following assets and liabilities:

Clubhouse €140,000; Equipment €217,000; Term Loan €40,000; Cash €3,000.

The following is a summary of the club's financial transactions for the year ended 31 May 2010:

| Receipts: | € |
|---|---|
| Competition fees | 42,300 |
| Subscriptions | 76,460 |
| Annual sponsorship | 15,000 |

| Payments: | € |
|---|---|
| Repairs | 2,340 |
| Stationery | 1,270 |
| Wages | 24,600 |
| Competition expenses | 7,100 |
| Insurance | 3,870 |
| Purchase of land | 17,900 |

**Additional information at 31 May 2010:**
   (i)  Subscriptions prepaid €2,160.
  (ii)  Stationery on hand €370.
 (iii)  Wages due €900.
 (iv)  Depreciation:
       Equipment 15% of €217,000.

**Prepare:**
   (i)  A statement calculating the club's accumulated fund.
  (ii)  Receipts and payments account.
 (iii)  Income and expenditure account.

**Hints**

There are a few things to remember when answering this type of question:
- **Purchase of land**
  This is entered in the receipts and payments but it is NOT shown in the income and expenditure.
- **Amounts prepaid and due**
  The rule is plus due, minus prepaid.
- **Stationery on hand**
  This is treated like an expense prepaid. So it is subtracted from the expense.

*Open for Business*

## Solution

**Accumulated Fund**

| | | | € |
|---|---|---|---:|
| Clubhouse | | | 140,000 |
| Equipment | | | 217,000 |
| Cash | | | 3,000 |
| | | | 360,000 |
| – Term Loan | | | 40,000 |
| **ACCUMULATED FUND** | | | **320,000** |

### Accumulated fund
The clubhouse, equipment and cash are all assets. The term loan is a liability. The total assets are €414,000 and the liabilities are €30,000. The difference of €384,000 is the accumulated fund for the club.

**Receipts and Payments Account**

| | | | | | | | |
|---|---|---|---:|---|---|---|---:|
| Jun 1 | Balance | b/d | 3,000 | | Repairs | | 2,340 |
| | Competition fees | | 42,300 | | Stationery | | 1,270 |
| | Subscriptions | | 76,460 | | Wages | | 24,600 |
| | Sponsorship | | 15,000 | | Competition expenses | | 7,100 |
| | | | | | Insurance | | 3,870 |
| | | | | | Land | | 17,900 |
| | | | | Jun 30 | Balance | c/d | 79,680 |
| | | | 136,760 | | | | 136,760 |
| Jul 1 | Balance | b/d | 79,680 | | | | |

### Summary receipts and payments
The summary receipts and payments account shows the receipts on the debit and the payments on the credit. The balance is the difference between the rec eipts and the payments. The balance is brought down to next year.

**Income and Expenditure Account**

| | | € | € |
|---|---|---:|---:|
| *Income* | | | |
| Competition profit | | 35,200 | |
| Subscriptions | | 74,300 | |
| Annual Sponsorship | | 15,000 | 124,500 |
| *Expenditure* | | | |
| Repairs | | 2,340 | |
| Stationery | | 900 | |
| Wages | | 25,500 | |
| Insurance | | 3,870 | |
| Depreciation of equipment | | 32,550 | 65,160 |
| **SURPLUS** | | | **59,340** |

### Income and expenditure
The additional information has the following effect on the income and expenditure account.

- **Competition**
  Competition profit:
  $$42,300 - 7,100 = 35,200$$

- **Subscriptions**
  $$76,460 - 2,160 = 74,300$$

- **Stationery**
  Stationery on hand is like having stationery prepaid:
  $$1,270 - 370 = 900$$

- **Wages**
  $$24,600 + 900 = 25,500$$

- **Depreciation**
  Equipment: 15% of 217,000 = 32,550

# Income and expenditure
## with balance sheet

The balance sheet of a club shows the club's assets and liabilities in the usual way, except that the capital is referred to as the accumulated fund.

## Question

On 1 June 2009, Roundwell Golf Club had an accumulated fund of €322,760.
The following is a summary of the club's financial transactions for the year ended 31 May 2010:

| Receipts: | € |
|---|---|
| Competition fees | 38,000 |
| Subscriptions | 80,000 |
| Annual sponsorship | 10,000 |
| **Payments:** | **€** |
| Repairs | 2,500 |
| Stationery | 4,000 |
| Wages | 36,000 |
| Competition expenses | 9,000 |
| Insurance | 5,000 |

**Additional information at 31 May 2010:**

(i) Subscriptions prepaid €3,000
(ii) Stationery on hand €500
(iii) Wages due €1,000
(iv) Cash at bank €14,260
(v) Depreciation:
   Clubhouse 2% of €160,000
   Equipment 15% of €220,000.

**Prepare:**

(i) Income and expenditure account
(ii) Balance sheet.

## Solution

### Income and Expenditure Account

| | € | € |
|---|---|---|
| *Income* | | |
| Competition profit | 29,000 | |
| Subscriptions | 77,000 | |
| Annual Sponsorship | 10,000 | 116,000 |
| *Expenditure* | | |
| Repairs | 2,500 | |
| Stationery | 3,500 | |
| Wages | 37,000 | |
| Insurance | 5,000 | |
| Depreciation of clubhouse | 3,200 | |
| Depreciation of equipment | 33,000 | 84,200 |
| **SURPLUS** | | **31,800** |

### Income and expenditure

The additional information has the following effect on the income and expenditure account.

### Competition

Competition profit:
$$38,000 - 9,000 = 29,000$$

### Subscriptions

$$80,000 - 3,000 = 77,000$$

### Stationery

Stationery on hand is like having stationery prepaid:
$$4,000 - 500 = 3,500$$

### Wages

$$36,000 + 1,000 = 37,000$$

### Depreciation

Clubhouse: 2% of 160,000 = 3,200
Equipment: 15% of 220,000 = 33,000

| Balance sheet as at 31 December | | | |
|---|---|---|---|
| | | € | € |
| **Fixed assets** | Cost | Depr | NBV |
| Clubhouse | 160,000 | 3,200 | 156,800 |
| Equipment | 220,000 | 33,000 | 187,000 |
| | 380,000 | 36,200 | 343,800 |
| | | | |
| **Current assets** | | | |
| Stationery on hand | 500 | | |
| Cash at Bank | 14,260 | 14,760 | |
| | | | |
| **Current liabilities** | | | |
| Subs prepaid | 3,000 | | |
| Wages due | 1,000 | 4,000 | 10,760 |
| | | | 354,560 |
| **Financed by** | | | |
| Accumulated Fund | | | 322,760 |
| Surplus | | | 31,800 |
| | | | 354,560 |

## Balance sheet

The additional information has the following effect on the balance sheet.

- Subs prepaid is a current liability.
- Stationery on hand is a current asset.
- Wages due is a current liability.
- Cash at bank is a current asset.
- The depreciation reduces the cost of the asset in the fixed asset section.

### Differences between company accounts and club accounts

There are a number of differences between the accounts of a club and the accounts of a company. Club accounts are different because they are prepared by nonprofit-making organisations. In a club:

- the cash account is called the receipts and payments account
- the profit and loss account is called the income and expenditure account
- the difference in the income and expenditure account is not called a net profit, it is called a surplus. A loss is called a deficit
- the capital is called the accumulated fund.

# Income and expenditure

The bar trading is similar to a company trading account.

## Question

The treasurer of the Roundwood Sports Club has prepared the following receipts and payments account:

**Receipts and Payments Account**

| | | | | | | |
|---|---|---|---|---|---|---|
| Jan 1 | Balance | b/d | 13,000 | Caretaker's wages | | 5,000 |
| | Subscriptions | | 4,000 | Insurance | | 2,200 |
| | Bar sales | | 35,000 | Coach hire | | 3,900 |
| | Gate receipts | | 5,000 | Bar purchases | | 24,000 |
| | | | | Purchase of equipment | | 8,000 |
| | | | | Dec 31 Balance | c/d | 13,900 |
| | | | 57,000 | | | 57,000 |
| Jan 1 | Balance | b/d | 13,900 | | | |

The following information should also be taken into consideration:

(i) Subs due are €1,200
(ii) Insurance prepaid is €300
(iii) Depreciation of equipment is 10% per annum
(iv) Bar stock on 1 January is €4,000
(v) Bar stock on 31 December is €7,000.

**Prepare:**

(i) Bar trading account
(ii) Income and expenditure account.

## Solution

**Bar Trading Account**

| | | € | € |
|---|---|---|---|
| Sales | | | 35,000 |
| Opening stock | | 4,000 | |
| + Purchases | | 24,000 | |
| | | 28,000 | |
| - Closing stock | | 7,000 | 21,000 |
| **BAR PROFIT** | | | **14,000** |

### Bar trading account

Use record book 2 to prepare the bar trading account. The final bar profit figure of €14,000 is shown as income in the income and expenditure account below.

**Income and Expenditure Account**

| | € | € |
|---|---|---|
| *Income* | | |
| Bar profit | 14,000 | |
| Subscriptions plus subs due | 5,200 | |
| Gate receipts | 5,000 | 24,200 |
| *Expenditure* | | |
| Caretaker's wages | 5,000 | |
| Insurance less prepaid | 1,900 | |
| Coach hire | 3,900 | |
| Depreciation of equipment | 800 | 11,600 |
| **SURPLUS** | | **12,600** |

### Income and expenditure

The additional information has the following effect on the income and expenditure account.

- **Subscriptions**
  4,000 + 1,200 = 5,200

- **Insurance**
  2,200 − 300 = 1,900

- **Depreciation**
  10% of 8,000 = 800

# Activity 42.1 Prepare the receipts and payments

**1** The following transactions took place in the Erne Football Club during August. (All dealings are in cash.)

| | |
|---|---|
| Aug 1 | Cash on hand since last month, €600 |
| 6 | Paid competition prizes, €140 (cheque no. 520) |
| 8 | Received annual subscriptions from members, €220 |
| 11 | Paid caretaker's wages, €500 (cheque no. 521) |
| 13 | Received competition entry fees, €340 |
| 15 | Disco night: received €420 at the door |
| 16 | Paid DJ €180 for running the disco (cheque no. 522) |
| 19 | Received annual subscriptions from members, €140 |
| 21 | Bought prizes for next competition, €150 (cheque no. 523) |
| 23 | Disco night: received €560 at the door |
| 26 | Paid DJ €180 for running the disco (cheque no. 524) |
| 27 | Paid caretaker's wages, €500 (cheque no. 525) |
| 28 | Received competition entry fees, €5 each from 60 members |

Write up and balance the analysed receipts and payments account of the club for the month of August. Use the following headings for the receipts and payments and total each column:
**Debit (Receipts) side:** Total; Subscriptions; Competitions; Disco.
**Credit (Payments) side:** Total; Wages; Competitions; Disco.

**2** The following transactions took place in the Sheelin Golf Club during September. (All dealings are in cash.)

| | |
|---|---|
| Sep 1 | Balance of €610 in the bank. |
| 5 | Paid for trophies for competition €210 (cheque no. 630) |
| 6 | Received annual membership fee, €80 each from 30 members |
| 8 | Paid for posters to advertise the club lotto €200 (cheque no. 631) |
| 10 | Received competition entry fees €675 |
| 12 | Received money from sale of club lotto tickets €1,790 |
| 14 | Paid wages to ground staff €640 (cheque no. 632) |
| 16 | Received annual membership fee, €80 each from 25 members |
| 17 | Received money from sale of club lotto tickets €3,460 |
| 19 | Bought prizes for competition €600 (cheque no. 633) |
| 22 | Paid the winner of club lotto draw €2,500 (cheque no. 634) |
| 25 | Paid for repairs to greens mower €710 (cheque no. 635) |
| 26 | Received competition entry fees €380 |
| 29 | Paid wages to ground staff €700 (cheque no. 636) |

Write up the analysed receipts and payments account using the following headings:
**Debit (Receipts) Side:** Bank; Competitions; Lotto; Membership Fees.
**Credit (Payments) Side:** Bank; Competitions; Lotto; Wages; Other.

## Activity 42.2 Prepare the income and expenditure

**1** Hilltop Golf Club, Blarney, Co. Cork, had the following assets and liabilities on 1 January 2009:

Clubhouse €180,000; Land €300,000; Term Loan €150,000; Cash €4,000.

The following is a summary of the club's financial transactions for the year ending 31 December 2009:

| Receipts: | € |
|---|---|
| Competition fees | 12,200 |
| Subscriptions | 23,400 |
| Annual sponsorship | 5,000 |

| Payments: | € |
|---|---|
| Insurance | 9,000 |
| Competition expenses | 3,000 |
| Secretary's expenses | 4,000 |
| Purchase of equipment | 12,900 |
| Light and heat | 6,100 |

Additional information on 31 December 2009:
 (i) Insurance prepaid €3,000.
 (ii) Subscriptions due €600.
 (iii) Clubhouse to be depreciated by 5%.
 (iv) Light and heat due €200.

(a) Prepare a statement calculating the club's accumulated fund on 1 January 2009.

(b) Prepare a receipts and payments account for the year ending 31 December 2009.

(c) Prepare an income and expenditure account for the year ending 31 December 2009.

---

**Hints**

When dealing with the additional information the general rule to remember is:
**plus due minus prepaid.**

Therefore, when preparing the income and expenditure:
- subs due is added to subs
- insurance prepaid is subtracted from insurance
- light and heat due is added to light and heat.

---

**2** The treasurer of the Deele Sports Club has prepared the following receipts and payments account:

| Receipts and Payments Account | | | | | |
|---|---|---|---|---|---|
| Jan 1 Balance | b/d | 11,000 | Caretaker's wages | | 7,500 |
| Subscriptions | | 9,000 | Insurance | | 3,500 |
| Bar sales | | 42,000 | Coach hire | | 4,600 |
| Gate receipts | | 6,000 | Bar purchases | | 18,700 |
| | | | Purchase of equipment | | 9,000 |

The following information should also be taken into consideration:
  (i) Subs due are €3,600.
  (ii) Insurance prepaid is €500.
  (iii) Depreciation of equipment is 10% per annum.
  (iv) Bar stock on 1 January is €3,800.
  (v) Bar stock on 31 December is €4,100.

(a) Prepare a bar trading account.
(b) Prepare an income and expenditure account.

**3** The treasurer of the Bradan Sports Club has prepared the following receipts and payments account:

| Receipts and Payments Account | | | | | |
|---|---|---|---|---|---|
| Jan 1 Balance | b/d | 15,800 | Caretaker's wages | | 19,400 |
| Subscriptions | | 5,900 | Insurance | | 4,800 |
| Bar sales | | 48,000 | Light and heat | | 6,100 |
| Gate receipts | | 6,000 | Bar purchases | | 19,700 |
| | | | Purchase of lawnmower | | 3,800 |

The following information should also be taken into consideration:
  (i) Bar stock on 1 January is €8,200.
  (ii) Bar stock on 31 December is €9,600.
  (iii) Light and heat due €174.
  (iv) Subscriptions prepaid €1,800.
  (v) Insurance prepaid €1,600.
  (vi) Lawnmower to be depreciated by 20%.

(a) Prepare a bar trading account.
(b) Prepare an income and expenditure account.

**4** On 1 June 2009, Greenfield Golf Club had an accumulated fund of €332,000.
The following is a summary of the club's financial transactions for the year ended 31 May 2010:

| Receipts: | € |
|---|---|
| Competition fees | 30,000 |
| Subscriptions | 90,000 |
| Annual sponsorship | 20,000 |

| Payments: | € |
|---|---|
| Repairs | 1,500 |
| Stationery | 2,500 |
| Wages | 32,000 |
| Competition expenses | 4,000 |
| Insurance | 2,000 |
| General expenses | 30,000 |

Additional information at 31 May 2010:
- (i) Subscriptions prepaid €3,000.
- (ii) Stationery on hand €500.
- (iii) Wages due €6,000.
- (iv) Cash at bank €15,000.
- (v) Depreciation:
    - Clubhouse 2% of €300,000
    - Equipment 15% of €100,000.

(a) Prepare an income and expenditure account for the year ended 31 May 2010.

(b) Prepare a balance sheet as at 31 May 2010.

**Hints**

When preparing the income and expenditure the additional information has this effect:
- subs prepaid is subtracted from subs
- stationery on hand is subtracted from stationery
- wages due is added to wages.

When preparing the balance sheet the additional information has this effect:
- subs prepaid is a current liability
- stationery on hand is a current asset
- wages due is a current liability.

**1** The Tiger Pitch and Putt Club had the following transactions during March 2007.

Mar 1    Balance of €455 in the bank
   2    Paid for trophies for competition €360 (cheque no. 421)
   4    Received competition entry fees €545
   6    Received annual membership fee, €75 each from 20 members
   7    Paid for posters to advertise the club lotto €180 (cheque no. 422)
   9    Paid wages to ground staff €850 (cheque no. 423)
  12    Received money from sale of club lotto tickets €2,350
  13    Received annual membership fee, €75 each from 25 members
  15    Received money from sale of club lotto tickets €1,650
  16    Bought prizes for competition €400. (cheque no. 424)
  17    Received competition entry fees €450
  22    Paid for repairs to greens mower €540 (cheque no. 425)
  23    Paid wages to ground staff €900 (cheque no. 426)
  29    Paid the winner of club lotto draw €3,000 (cheque no. 427)

Write up the analysed receipts and payments account using the following headings:

**Debit (Receipts) Side:** Bank; Competitions; Lotto; Membership Fees.

**Credit (Payments) Side:** Bank; Competitions; Lotto; Wages; Other.

**2** The members of the Downtown Swimming Club pay an annual subscription to the club. The club runs regular swimming competitions for its members and pays wages to the lifeguards. It also organises raffles to raise funds. Here is what happened at the club during May 2008. (All dealings are in cash.)

May 1    Cash on hand since last month €564
   2    Paid for posters to advertise the raffle €100 (cheque no. 152)
   3    Paid for trophies for swimming competition €125 (cheque no. 153)
   4    Received competition entry fees €185
   9    Paid wages to lifeguards €300 (cheque no. 154)
  12    Received money from sale of raffle tickets €850
  14    Received annual subscriptions from members €530
  15    Paid for prizes for the raffle €295 (cheque no. 155)
  16    Received money from sale of raffle tickets €750
  17    Bought prizes for swimming competition €240 (cheque no. 156)
  18    Received competition entry fees €5 each from 60 members
  23    Paid wages to lifeguards €300 (cheque no. 157)
  29    Received annual subscriptions from members €740

Write up the analysed receipts and payments account using the following headings:

**Debit (Receipts) Side:** Total, Subscriptions, Competitions and Raffle.

**Credit (Payments) Side:** Total, Wages, Competitions and Raffle.

**3** Lee Valley Angling Club, Macroom, Co. Cork, had the following assets and liabilities on 1 January 2009:

Clubhouse €100,000; Boats €30,000;Term Loan €40,000; Cash €2,500.

The following is a summary of the club's financial transactions for the year ending 31 December 2009:

| **Receipts:** | **€** |
|---|---|
| Competition fees | 1,370 |
| Subscriptions | 562 |
| Angling fees | 2,004 |
| Annual sponsorship | 300 |

| **Payments:** | **€** |
|---|---|
| Insurance | 880 |
| Competition expenses | 878 |
| Secretary's expenses | 163 |
| Purchase of equipment | 1,200 |
| Light and heat | 850 |

Additional information on 31 December 2009:
- (i) Insurance prepaid €130.
- (ii) Subscriptions due €90.
- (iii) Boats to be depreciated by 5%.
- (iv) Light and heat due €45.

(a) Prepare a statement calculating the club's accumulated fund on 1 January 2009.

(b) Prepare:
- (i) A receipts and payments account for the year ending 31 December 2009.
- (ii) An income and expenditure account for the year ending 31 December 2009.

(c) (i) Explain the role of the club treasurer.
- (ii) What is the purpose of his/her report?

**4** On 1 June 2009, Greenfield Golf Club had an accumulated fund of €305,770.
The following is a summary of the club's financial transactions for the year ended 31 May 2010:

| Receipts: | € |
|---|---|
| Competition fees | 34,400 |
| Subscriptions | 89,550 |
| Annual sponsorship | 17,650 |

| Payments: | € |
|---|---|
| Repairs | 1,850 |
| Stationery | 2,460 |
| Wages | 27,800 |
| Competition expenses | 6,200 |
| Insurance | 1,440 |
| General expenses | 25,000 |

Additional information at 31 May 2010:
   (i) Subscriptions prepaid €1,450.
   (ii) Stationery on hand €240.
   (iii) Wages due €2,400.
   (iv) Cash at bank €15,620.
   (v) Depreciation:
           Clubhouse 2% of €252,000
           Equipment 15% of €115,000.

(a) Prepare:
   (i) An income and expenditure account for the year ended 31 May 2010.
   (ii) A balance sheet as at 31 May 2010.

(b) Explain three functions of a club treasurer.

**5** City Football Club had an opening stock of €12,000 in the bar on 1 May 2009. The following is a summary of the club's financial transactions for the year ending 30 April 2010:

| Receipts: | € |
|---|---|
| Club lotto | 24,400 |
| Bar sales | 47,600 |
| Subscriptions | 52,000 |

| Payments: | € |
|---|---|
| Groundsman's wages | 22,100 |
| Light and heat | 5,960 |
| Purchase of tractor | 25,000 |
| Bar purchases | 30,960 |
| Insurance | 11,200 |
| Club lotto prizes | 8,140 |
| Telephone | 1,655 |
| Repairs and maintenance | 17,895 |

Additional information on 30 April 2010:
  (i) Bar stock €14,400.
 (ii) Light and heat due €345.
(iii) Subscriptions prepaid €2,500.
(iv) Insurance prepaid €2,800.
 (v) Tractor to be depreciated by 20%.

(a) Prepare:
  (i) A bar trading account for the year ending 30 April 2010.
 (ii) An income and expenditure account for the year ending 30 April 2010.

(b) At the AGM, Mary Casey, the club officer who prepares the accounts, stated in her annual report that the bar's gross profit percentage (gross margin) had improved this year.
  (i) Identify the officer who prepares the accounts in a club.
 (ii) Calculate the bar's gross profit percentage.
(iii) Explain two other reasons why Mary Casey would prepare an annual report.

▸▸**Note**
• To revise the calculation of the gross profit percentage see page 216.

eTest.ie
Try a test on this topic

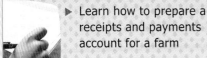

# Chapter 43

# Farm *accounts*

There are many reasons why a farmer should keep accounts:

- to keep track of receipts and payments
- to determine the profit or loss for the year
- to estimate the value of the farm
- to have a set of figures for presentation to the bank or government on application for a loan or grant
- to determine the extent and timing of expansion.

## RECEIPTS AND PAYMENTS

The receipts and payments account for a farm will be very similar to that for a club. Use record book one to prepare the account. Receipts like the sale of cattle and EU grants will be recorded on the debit of the account. Payments like the purchase of calves, purchase of diesel and vet fees will be recorded on the credit of the account.

Kate Sullivan is a farmer who keeps an analysed receipts and payments book. All money received is lodged in her bank current account on the same day and all payments are made by cheque. She had the following transactions during May 2009:

May 1    Balance in bank €3,500
5    Sold cattle for €9,500 (receipt no. 401)
8    Sold cattle at the mart for €8,500 (receipt no. 402)
9    Purchased cattle feed for €925 (cheque no. 811)
11    Purchased cattle (calves) for €3,000 (cheque no. 812)
12    Paid for repairs to tractor €850 (cheque no. 813)
14    Purchased diesel oil for machinery €550 (cheque no. 814)
17    Paid fees to vet €475 (cheque no. 815)
18    Sold cattle at the mart for €7,500 (receipt no. 403)
19    Purchased cattle feed for €2,400 (cheque no. 816)
20    Received a state grant of €1,000 (receipt no. 404)
25    Purchased cattle (calves) for €4,800 (cheque no. 817)
28    Purchased diesel oil for machinery €700 (cheque no. 818)

(a) Write up the analysed receipts and payments book of Kate Sullivan for the month of May 2009, using the following money column headings:

**Receipts Side:** Total, Cattle, Grants, Other.
**Payments Side:** Total, Cattle, Feed, Diesel, Other.

Total each analysis column and balance the total columns at the end of May.

(b) State three reasons why farmers should keep accounts.

eTest.ie
Try a test on this topic

| Business | Domestic |
|---|---|
| € | € |
| 3,300 | |
| | 600 |

| | € |
|---|---|
| 40,000 | |
| 25,000 | |
| 48,000 | |
| 75,000 | 188,000 |
| 20,000 | |
| 5,000 | |
| 4,000 | |

> Learn how to prepare a receipts and payments account for a service firm

> Find out how to prepare an operating statement

# Chapter 44

## Service *firms*

Service firms usually keep an analysed receipts and payments book and classify their income and expenditure under suitable headings. This helps the owners identify where money is being earned and spent. There are many types of service firms but one thing they all have in common is that they have no trading stock. Examples of service firms are taxi driver, delivery company, travel agency, accountant, doctor, dentist and so on.

## WHY KEEP RECORDS?

There are many reasons why a service firm should keep accounts.

- To keep track of receipts and payments.
- To determine the profit or loss for the year.
- To estimate the value of the firm.
- To have a set of figures for presentation to the bank on application for a loan.
- To determine the extent and timing of expansion.

# Receipts and payments

## Question

Ella Doolin owns a delivery company called Vanella Ltd. She keeps an analysed receipts and payments book. Her customers are either businesses (with Ltd in their name) or private individuals (domestic). All money received is lodged in her bank current account on the same day and all payments are made by cheque. She had the following transactions during July:

Jul 1   Balance in bank, €2,000
   3   Received €3,300 from Kelly Ltd (receipt no. 601)
   7   Paid van driver's wages, €2,000 (cheque no. 911)
   9   Received €500 from M. Lyle (receipt no. 602)
  10   Paid for diesel, €300 (cheque no. 912)
  13   Paid for repairs to van, €800 (cheque no. 913)
  14   Paid van driver's wages, €2,000 (cheque no. 914)
  18   Received €600 from A. Carthy (receipt no. 603)
  21   Paid van driver's wages, €2,000 (cheque no. 915)
  24   Received €2,600 from Walsh Ltd (receipt no. 604)
  26   Paid for office cleaning, €200 (cheque no. 916)
  27   Received €900 from B. Brady (receipt no. 605)
  28   Paid van driver's wages, €2,000 (cheque no. 917)
  29   Received €3,500 from Smyth Ltd (receipt no. 606)

Write up and balance the analysed receipts and payments account of the firm for the month of July. Use the following headings for the receipts and payments and total each column:

**Debit (Receipts) side:** Total; Business; Domestic.
**Credit (Payments) side:** Total; Wages; Motor; Other.

## Solution

| Dr | | | | | | | Analysed Receipts and Payments Account | | | | | | Cr |
|---|---|---|---|---|---|---|---|---|---|---|---|---|---|
| Date | Details | F | Total | Business | Domestic | | Date | Details | F | Total | Wages | Motor | Other |
| Jul | | | € | € | € | | Jul | | | € | € | € | € |
| 1 | Balance | b/d | 2,000 | | | | 7 | Wages | 911 | 2,000 | 2,000 | | |
| 3 | Kelly Ltd | | 3,300 | 3,300 | | | 10 | Diesel | 912 | 300 | | 300 | |
| 18 | A. Carthy | | 600 | | 600 | | 13 | Repairs | 913 | 800 | | 800 | |
| 24 | Walsh Ltd | | 2,600 | 2,600 | | | 14 | Wages | 914 | 2,000 | 2,000 | | |
| 27 | B. Brady | | 900 | | 900 | | 21 | Wages | 915 | 2,000 | 2,000 | | |
| 29 | Smyth Ltd | | 3,500 | 3,500 | | | 26 | Cleaning | 916 | 200 | | | 200 |
| | | | | | | | 28 | Wages | 917 | 2,000 | 2,000 | | |
| | | | | | | | 31 | Balance | c/d | 3,600 | | | |
| | | | 12,900 | 9,400 | 1,500 | | | | | 12,900 | 8,000 | 1,100 | 200 |
| Aug 1 | Balance | b/d | 3,600 | | | | | | | | | | |

# Operating statement

## Question

From the following information prepare an operating statement for the year ended 31 December, and a balance sheet as at that date.

| Trial balance as on 31 December | | |
|---|---:|---:|
| | € | € |
| Income from tours | | 40,000 |
| Income from weddings | | 25,000 |
| Income from daytime | | 46,000 |
| Income from nighttime | | 75,000 |
| Secretary's wages | 20,000 | |
| Heating and lighting | 5,000 | |
| Advertising | 4,000 | |
| Petrol | 30,000 | |
| Insurance | 15,000 | |
| Vehicles | 80,000 | |
| Premises | 180,000 | |
| Cash on hand | 6,000 | |
| Bank overdraft | | 4,000 |
| Issued share capital | | 150,000 |
| | 340,000 | 340,000 |

## Operating statement

The operating statement is like the trading and profit and loss account you may have studied already. The difference is there is no need to show opening or closing stock, and there are no purchases of goods for resale. The statement is simply two lists showing income and expenditure. The difference is the operating profit or loss.

## Solution

| Operating Statement | | | | |
|---|---|---|---:|---:|
| | | | € | € |
| *Income* | | | | |
| Tours | | | 40,000 | |
| Weddings | | | 25,000 | |
| Daytime | | | 46,000 | |
| Nighttime | | | 75,000 | 186,000 |
| *Expenditure* | | | | |
| Secretary's wages | | | 20,000 | |
| Heating and lighting | | | 5,000 | |
| Advertising | | | 4,000 | |
| Petrol | | | 30,000 | |
| Insurance | | | 15,000 | 74,000 |
| **OPERATING PROFIT** | | | | **112,000** |

| Balance sheet as at 31 December | | | | |
|---|---|---|---:|---:|
| | | | € | € |
| **Fixed assets** | | | | |
| Vehicles | | | | 80,000 |
| Premises | | | | 180,000 |
| | | | | 260,000 |
| **Current assets** | | | | |
| Cash on hand | | | 6,000 | |
| **Current liabilities** | | | | |
| Bank overdraft | | | 4,000 | 2,000 |
| | | | | 262,000 |
| **Financed by** | | | | |
| Issued share capital | | | | 150,000 |
| Operating profit | | | | 112,000 |
| | | | | 262,000 |

## Activity 44.1 Prepare the receipts and payments

**1** Jim Toomey is a solicitor, and he keeps an analysed receipts and payments book. All money received is lodged in his bank current account on the same day and all payments are made by cheque. He had the following transactions during September:

Sep 1    Balance in bank, €3,600
     4    Receipts from clients – Wills, €1,700 (receipt no. 701)
     7    Paid rent of office, €900 (cheque no. 611)
     8    Receipts from clients – House, €4,500 (receipt no. 702)
   11    Paid for stationery, €300 (cheque no. 612)
   13    Paid cleaner's wages, €750 (cheque no. 613)
   15    Paid electricity bill, €340 (cheque no. 614)
   18    Receipts from clients – House, €7,300 (receipt no. 703)
   23    Paid secretary's wages, €2,200 (cheque no. 615)
   24    Receipts from clients – Wills, €1,400 (receipt no. 704)
   27    Paid for heating oil, €900 (cheque no. 616)
   29    Receipts from clients – House, €5,900 (receipt no. 705)

Write up and balance the analysed receipts and payments account of the firm for the month of September. Use the following headings for the receipts and payments and total each column:
**Debit (Receipts) side:** Total; Wills; House.
**Credit (Payments) side:** Total; Wages; Light and heat; Other.

**2** Paula Byrne is an accountant and she keeps an analysed receipts and payments book. All money received is lodged in her bank current account on the same day and all payments are made by cheque. She had the following transactions during October:

Oct 1    Balance in bank, €2,870
     3    Received €2,800 from Curtis Ltd (receipt no. 601)
     7    Paid secretary's wages, €1,200 (cheque no. 911)
     9    Received €1,500 from N. Tormey (receipt no. 602)
   10    Paid for heating oil, €950 (cheque no. 912)
   13    Paid for repairs to computer, €140 (cheque no. 913)
   14    Paid cleaner's wages, €680 (cheque no. 914)
   18    Received €3,200 from A. Fagan (receipt no. 603)
   21    Paid secretary's wages, €1,200 (cheque no. 915)
   24    Received €3,100 from Donoghue Ltd (receipt no. 604)
   26    Paid for electricity, €860 (cheque no. 916)
   27    Received €1,700 from B. Benett (receipt no. 605)

Write up and balance the analysed receipts and payments account of the firm for the month of October. Use the following headings for the receipts and payments and total each column:
**Debit (Receipts) side:** Total; Business; Domestic.
**Credit (Payments) side:** Total; Wages; Light and heat; Other.

# Activity 44.2 Prepare the operating statement

**1** From the following information prepare an operating statement for the year ended 31 December, and a balance sheet as at that date.

### Trial balance as on 31 December

| | € | € |
|---|---|---|
| Income from guards | | 30,000 |
| Income from couriers | | 15,000 |
| Income from detectives | | 26,000 |
| Income from key-holding | | 56,000 |
| Wages | 40,000 | |
| Heating and lighting | 3,000 | |
| Petrol | 6,000 | |
| Stationery | 30,000 | |
| Insurance | 17,000 | |
| Vehicles | 40,000 | |
| Premises | 100,000 | |
| Cash on hand | 4,000 | |
| Bank overdraft | | 3,000 |
| Issued share capital | | 110,000 |
| | 240,000 | 240,000 |

**2** From the following information prepare an operating statement for the year ended 31 December, and a balance sheet as at that date.

### Trial balance as on 31 December

| | € | € |
|---|---|---|
| Income from Irish holidays | | 40,000 |
| Income from European holidays | | 43,000 |
| Income from American holidays | | 36,000 |
| Postage | 6,000 | |
| Wages | 81,000 | |
| Advertising | 8,000 | |
| Heating and lighting | 3,000 | |
| Insurance | 9,000 | |
| Repairs to computers | 4,000 | |
| Equipment | 36,000 | |
| Premises | 200,000 | |
| Cash on hand | 3,000 | |
| Bank overdraft | | 1,000 |
| Issued share capital | | 230,000 |
| | 350,000 | 350,000 |

Blue Cabs Ltd is a firm that provides a taxi service in three different towns. The firm prepares an operating statement (profit and loss account) and balance sheet at the end of each year. The following trial balance was taken from the books on 31 December 2009, the end of its financial year:

| Trial balance as on 31 December | | |
|---|---|---|
| | € | € |
| Income from Naas | | 130,000 |
| Income from Navan | | 125,700 |
| Income from Mullingar | | 103,500 |
| Insurance | 35,920 | |
| Light and heat | 3,900 | |
| Telephone | 14,750 | |
| Drivers' wages | 47,300 | |
| Petrol and car service | 28,180 | |
| Road tax | 6,450 | |
| Advertising | 5,300 | |
| Bank overdraft | | 4,950 |
| Cash on hand | 6,350 | |
| Ordinary share capital | | 80,000 |
| Premises and equipment | 70,000 | |
| Motor vehicles | 226,000 | |
| | 444,150 | 444,150 |

Prepare an operating statement for Blue Cabs Ltd for the year ended 31 December 2009 and a balance sheet as at that date.

eTest.ie
Try a test on this topic

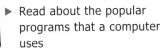
## Information *technology*

# Buying a computer

Jana and Eric Scanlon own an electrical shop and are thinking of buying a new computer and payroll software on credit for €2,500 from DataTech Ltd.

### How will a computer help them?

With the new computer and payroll software they will be able to prepare the wages more quickly. They will be able to get summary reports, print out payslips and find the total due for PAYE and PRSI. The new computer system will:

- increase productivity
- improve working conditions
- improve the company image.

### What is the full cost of the system?

There are several costs connected with owning and running a computer. Besides the machine itself and the software, Jana and Eric will need a printer, paper and disks, and they may need training.

### Record book 2

Assets purchased on credit are recorded in the general journal as shown on the left.

### Record book 3

Use record book three to show the ledger accounts for the double-entry. The computer account is debited with €2,500 and the DataTech account is credited with the €2,500.

| General Journal | | | Dr | Cr |
|---|---|---|---|---|
| | | | € | € |
| Mar | | | | |
| 5 | Computer | | 2,500 | |
| | DataTech Ltd | | | 2,500 |
| | (purchase of computer) | | | |

| Dr | Computer Account | | | | | | | Cr |
|---|---|---|---|---|---|---|---|---|
| Date | Details | F | € | Date | Details | F | € | |
| Mar 5 | DataTech Ltd | | 2,500 | | | | | |

| Dr | DataTech Ltd Account | | | | | | | Cr |
|---|---|---|---|---|---|---|---|---|
| Date | Details | F | € | Date | Details | F | € | |
| | | | | Mar 5 | Computer | | 2,500 | |

A computer system is made up of many pieces of equipment known as the computer hardware. There are three parts to understand: output devices, input devices and the CPU.

# HARDWARE

**Output devices** Output devices let you get information out of the computer, e.g. monitor and printer.

### Monitor
The monitor is similar to a television screen. It displays the program you are working on. It is also called a visual display unit (VDU).

### Printer
This enables the computer to give you information on paper, called a printout or hard copy. The version on the screen is known as a soft copy.

### Keyboard
It is called a QWERTY keyboard after the first six letters on the top left line.

### Mouse
This enables you to launch and use programs without using the keyboard.

**Input devices** Input devices let you put information into the computer, e.g. keyboard and mouse.

# CENTRAL PROCESSING UNIT (CPU)

The CPU is at the heart of the computer. It consists of small microchips about the size of your little finger and has three main parts.

### The arithmetic unit
This carries out calculations on data.

### The control unit
This controls the operation of the computer.

### The main storage or memory
The computer has two types of storage: read-only memory (**ROM**) and random access memory (**RAM**). The RAM is used for short-term memory whereas the ROM has information kept permanently. The information in the RAM is lost when the computer is switched off.

# MEMORY

A computer stores information on disk drives. The drives are the memory of the computer. The memory is measured in kilobytes (Kb), megabytes (Mb) and gigabytes (Gb). For example, you might have a machine with a 250Gb hard drive. The type of disk drive are:
- hard drive
- flash drive.

**Hard drive**
A computer will come with a hard drive fixed permanently inside the computer. You can now buy external hard drives for additional storage.

**Flash drive**
A flash drive or memory stick is used to transfer data from one machine to another.

## SOFTWARE

The programs (note the spelling) that a computer uses are called software, e.g. word processor, spreadsheet, database, payroll, computer-aided design (CAD).

### Word processing
Word processing is a computerised way of typing letters and other documents. The letter can then be saved and used again. The main advantages are:
- more time is freed up for new work
- multiple copies can easily be made
- work can be saved and returned to later.

### Spreadsheet
The spreadsheet is used to perform mathematical and financial calculations. You can use a spreadsheet to prepare a household budget, cash flow, trading, profit and loss, and balance sheet. Here are some ways a business will use a spreadsheet.
- To analyse income and expenditure.
- To create a budget.
- To estimate profit at various sales levels.

## DATABASE

A database is a computerised filing system. It allows you to store, edit and list data in various formats. For example, if you have a database with the names and addresses of your customers you could extract all the customers who live in the Galway region, or those who order over €3,000 a month. The types of data stored by a firm are:
- customer lists
- stock records
- wages files
- mailing lists.

### Mail merge
This is a way of linking names and addresses stored in the database with a letter prepared using a word processor. For example, suppose you want to send a letter to your customers about a new product. First you would type the letter, then you would use the mail merge facility to link the letter with the customer list. Each letter will look identical except each letter will have a different customer name and address on it.

## Activity 45.1 Chapter Review

**1** List three benefits to a business of using a computer.

**2** Besides the cost of the computer itself, name three expenses related to owning a computer.

**3** Explain the difference between hardware and software.

**4** Name two output devices and two input devices.

**5** Why is the keyboard called a querty keyboard?

**6** What do these letters stand for?
- CPU
- RAM
- ROM
- Kb
- Mb
- Gb
- CAD
- VDU

**7** Explain the difference between a hard drive and a flash (USB) drive.

**8** What is word processing and what are the main advantages of word processing?

**9** What is a spreadsheet and when would a business use a spreadsheet?

**10** What is a database and what types of data are stored in a database?

**11** Briefly describe how mail merge works.

eTest.ie
Try a test on this topic

## Activity 45.2 State Exam Practice

**1** Joe Byrne contacted the Computer Store Ltd, Main Street, Castlebar, and spoke to the manager, Fiona Twomey. 'I know nothing about computers or information technology,' said Joe, 'but my friends tell me I should buy a computer. Please send me some information. My address is The Cottage, Balla, Co Mayo.'

Fiona wrote a letter to Joe, thanking him for his telephone enquiry. In the letter, dated 7 June 2009, she listed three examples of information technology which could be found in the home and which Joe could be using every day without realising it. She also stated three advantages for Joe of using a computer. She concluded by inviting Joe to visit the shop someday so that she could show him the latest computer models.

(a) Write the letter that Fiona Twomey sent to Joe Byrne on 7 June 2009.
(b) State three examples of information technology used in banking.
(c) Hardware and software are well-known computer terms. Explain clearly each of these terms (one sentence in each case).

**2** Una Rogan, who lives at Meadowlands, Trim, Co. Meath, is a farmer's wife. She has taken classes in information technology and now wishes to buy a computer.

On 14 May 2009, Una writes a letter to Joan Hills, Editor, Consumer Advice Magazine Ltd, Green Street, Dublin 1. She informs Joan that she wishes to buy a computer which would be suitable for home and farm use. She wants to keep records of all farm stock and feedstuffs on computer, as well as all the farm's financial accounts. She would also like to be able to check the farm's bank account on the Internet. Finally, she would need a word-processing package and some good computer games for the family. She asks Joan to advise her on a computer and printer that would be suitable for all this work.

(a) Write the letter that Una Rogan sent to Joan Hills, Editor, Consumer Advice Magazine Ltd on 14 May 2009.
(b) State three reasons why farmers should keep accounts.

Joan Hills replied to Una the next day with this advice:
You should buy a computer and printer with the following features:
**Computer**
        1 GHz Processor; 512 MB <u>RAM;</u> 250GB <u>Hard Drive</u>;
        DVD Drive
        <u>Modem</u>; Digital Sound with Speakers; 19 inch <u>VDU</u>;
        Mouse.
**Software**
        Windows XP and Microsoft Office including <u>database</u>,
        <u>spreadsheet</u> and <u>word processing.</u>
**Printer**
        <u>Inkjet</u> or <u>laser.</u>

Try a test on this topic

(c) Explain three of the underlined words.

# Index